Funny Thing
About the Civil War

Funny Thing About the Civil War

The Humor of an American Tragedy

THOMAS F. CURRAN

McFarland & Company, Inc., Publishers
Jefferson, North Carolina

LIBRARY OF CONGRESS CATALOGUING-IN-PUBLICATION DATA

Names: Curran, Thomas F., author.
Title: Funny thing about the Civil War : the humor of an American tragedy / Thomas F. Curran.
Description: Jefferson, North Carolina : McFarland & Company, Inc., Publishers, 2023. | Includes bibliographical references and index.
Identifiers: LCCN 2023025203 | ISBN 9781476692357 (paperback : acid free paper) ∞
ISBN 9781476650296 (ebook)
Subjects: LCSH: United States—History—Civil War, 1861–1865—Literature and the war. | United States—History—Civil War, 1861–1865—Humor. | American wit and humor—History and criticism. | Literature and society—United States—History—19th century.
Classification: LCC PS217.C58 C87 2023 | DDC 810.9/358—dc23/eng/20230605
LC record available at https://lccn.loc.gov/2023025203

BRITISH LIBRARY CATALOGUING DATA ARE AVAILABLE

ISBN (print) 978-1-4766-9235-7
ISBN (ebook) 978-1-4766-5029-6

© 2023 Thomas F. Curran. All rights reserved

No part of this book may be reproduced or transmitted in any form or by any means, electronic or mechanical, including photocopying or recording, or by any information storage and retrieval system, without permission in writing from the publisher.

On the cover: "The voluntary manner in which some of the Southern volunteers enlist," New York: Currier & Ives, 1861 (Library of Congress); eagle and flags from a map showing the battle field at Harrisburg, Miss., July 13–15, 1864 (Library of Congress); frame © Shutterstock

Printed in the United States of America

McFarland & Company, Inc., Publishers
Box 611, Jefferson, North Carolina 28640
www.mcfarlandpub.com

To the people with whom I've laughed more than anyone else:
my siblings JOHN, SUE, and GARY CURRAN.

Contents

Preface: What's So Funny About the Civil War?   1

Part I. "Crude partisan versifying on both sides": The Wartime Writers   5
   The Crackerbox Philosophers   5
   "Where are the women among … the 'literary comedians' of the 1860s?"   16
   The Biblical Satirists   19
   The Scarlet Copperhead   22
   "A period which produced so many good war songs, and so much bad war verse"   29
   Two Fremantles, a Mule, and the Civil Wargasm   43
   This Book Is Brought to You by the Committee to Elect George McClellan   51
   Appendix (or Is That Appendage?)   57
   "A delightful denunciation of Federal commanders"   59
   Are "Two Federal Pens" Mightier Than Two Swords?   65

Part II. "The war was a draw game, and … both sides were whipped": The Post-War Writers   71
   How I Put Down the Rebellion   73
   My Real Story Will Never Get into the Century's Battles and Leaders Books   77
   After a While They All Sound the Same…   81
   … But This One Looks Like a Comic Book   94
   The Pen Is Mightier Than the Sword (or Is That the Pin?)   98
   The Many Lives of the Jordan Anderson Letter   104
   Grant vs. Lee   109

A Tale of Two Kleggs	113
Uncle Remus Was White!	118
And Ambrose Bierce Was "an Equal-Opportunity Hater"	122
An Unrenowned Warrior	125
Postmodernism? We Haven't Even Done Modernism Yet!	128
Girls Will Be Boys and Boys Will Be Girls	134
Part III. "Those who still fight the last romantic war": The Next Generations	**139**
The Blue and Gray in Black and White, Then in Technicolor	140
What If Lincoln's Doctor's Dog Wrote a Biography?	145
Frankly, I Do Give a Damn	149
Happy Birthday, Gray and Blue	157
States' Rights of the Living Dead	167
Everything Old Is New Again	175
Conclusion	185
Chapter Notes	187
Works Cited	199
Index	213

Preface: What's So Funny About the Civil War?

Writing about the Civil War in 1882, poet Walt Whitman predicted, "The real war will never get in the books,"[1] thus assuring that Walt Whitman and this quotation—"The real war will never get in the books"—would appear in practically every study of books about the Civil War and many others not about Civil War literature or not about the Civil War at all. The quotation even made its way into a book on the Nazis' use of methamphetamines to fuel their World War II blitzkrieg strategy that was published first in German.[2] Whitman's lament, of course, referred to the experience of war, the results of which he saw firsthand as a volunteer nurse in Washington. He probably did not have in mind the debate that ensued over why there was a war and what it meant. One thing is certain: since the American Civil War broke out in 1861, a vast sea of literature has been published depicting some version of the war. All but a small percentage of these works convey a grave tone, and rightly so. Consider the major themes on which authors often focus: the rending of the nation by secession; the fratricidal nature of the war, which cost over seven hundred thousand lives; slavery and emancipation; the redefining of racial and gender relations, just to name a few. It should come as little surprise that over the past years, when I told people about this project, I often got responses something like this: "What? The Civil War was funny?"

Perhaps the issue is not just the Civil War as subject matter, but rather the whole historical discipline. Not long ago, Dane Kennedy, the Elmer Louis Kayser Professor of History at George Washington University, asked, "Where's the humor in history?" He bemoaned the lack of humor historical scholarship exhibits, even when dealing with subjects that are on the lighter side. "We are prisoners to our professional pretensions," he averred. "How can we persuade one another that our work is important if we don't insist on its seriousness? How can we stay in good standing in that exclusive club of academic historians if we intentionally elicit laughter?"[3]

Interesting questions, but I have no intention of letting the elicitation of laughter trouble me when discussing this fratricidal humor.

As I began this study, the sesquicentennial of the Civil War was just underway. Already the flow of new books on the war—arguably the most popular topic in American history publishing—had turned into a deluge. During this hallmark anniversary, a variety of books on the subject of Civil War literature appeared. One notable book on the subject of humor and the war made its way into print: Cameron C. Nickels' *Civil War Humor*.[4] I was a bit relieved that there weren't more but not surprised. With the exception of a few books on some of the more notable wartime humorists and a number on Abraham Lincoln's sense of humor, not much has been written on the subject. Academic studies of Civil War literature almost always ignore works of humor and satire, with Edmund Wilson's seminal work *Patriotic Gore* leading the way, Wilson mentioning not once anything that might evoke a titter or two in his eight-hundred-page tome.[5] This study looks at some of the more interesting specimens of Civil War literature reflecting a humorous take on the war (whether intentionally or not) that appeared between the start of war and the early twenty-first century.

No other undertaking like this exists, so it comes as little surprise that Cameron Nickels wrote a very different book from the one I offer. We do share one thing in common. According to one reviewer of *Civil War Humor,* Nickels covers "a wide range of types or genres of humor," including "satire, caricature, sarcasm, mockery, derision, wit, parody, lampoon, slapstick, visual and verbal, burlesque, the ludicrous, irony, the ridiculous, the whimsical, the wry, farce, jest, and spoof." I'm sure I, too, cover a wide range of types or genres of humor in the array of works I include. There are at least a couple of pastiches, to boot. This reviewer then went on to criticize Nickels for not defining these types of humor.[6] I'm afraid that I am guilty of that, as well. In fact, I define humor broadly, ranging from the laugh-out-loud, gut-busting funny to the chuckle-inducing lightly humorous. There's humor that has stood the test of time, and some that has not. Much of what I look at was meant to evoke laughs, but some was not, and yet it now has that effect. Trying to pigeon-hole a particular work into a specific type of humor for the sake of doing it takes away from appreciating the work for what it has to tell us.

Some of what I include was written by well-known literary figures of their day, such as Petroleum Nasby, Artemus Ward, and Bill Arp, the usual gang of idiots that gets attention when addressing humor produced during the war. I also involve postwar authors like Mark Twain, Ambrose Bierce, and Joel Chandler Harris, along with several veteran memoirists from both sides of the conflict. And twentieth-century authors are represented by the likes of James Thurber, Edith Wharton, and Ishmael Reed.

Preface: What's So Funny About the Civil War? 3

There are a number of not-so-well-known contributors, too. I give attention to African Americans, women, bad poets, and Civil War zombies. And Walt Whitman makes his way into the book. What follows is a review of literature—in print and on the big and small screens—that discusses, explains, or depicts the Civil War using humor or that just pokes fun at the war. I bring in fact-based narratives and works of fiction, and often the line between fact and fiction is rather blurry.

I include works that have historical significance and have left a lasting impact of some type. I also have resurrected certain items from obscurity simply because I find them funny. In the end, that proved to be my most important measuring stick for what I included: did it make me laugh or did it make me laugh at it? Or did it make me wonder who laughed at it and why? Readers may disagree with what they find contained in this volume, and so I encourage those unsatisfied with my study to write their own.

Along the way I share my thoughts on the works included in the book, although the reader should not expect any new, ground-breaking theoretical framework complete with deep, jargon-laden analysis, parsing, and deconstruction. I leave that for others who are far more clever than I about things literary. As E.B. White once commented, "Humor can be dissected, as a frog can, but the thing dies in the process and the innards are discouraging to any but the pure scientific mind." Or, to paraphrase the multi-talented Steve Martin, once you start analyzing humor, it stops being funny.[7] Rather, I'm interested in what people laughed at, whom they laughed with, what they found funny, and what they made fun of, which relates something about their mindsets and their views of the world and events transpiring around them. I'm also interested in the stories behind the stories. Who produced narratives and why? What impact did they have in the short-term and the long?

In *Civil War Humor*, Nickels argues, "The most fundamental purpose of humor during any war is to define the enemy, to put him in his comic, satiric place and thus make him and the cause he stands for laughable." Humor served as a form of rhetorical propaganda, this is true, but it was not always aimed at the enemy, and it certainly was not always used to "justify killing people," as Nickels further suggests.[8] Humor during the war was often designed to cope with the disagreeable and nastier side of the war, caused by a variety of sources. After the war, many authors and movie and television producers employed humor to shape the way we remember the war, to perpetuate myths about the war and related stereotypes that became ingrained in the American memory of our past. On the other hand, some used humor to counteract the myths and stereotypes. To be sure, as is true that sometimes a cigar is just a cigar, sometimes humor was just meant to be funny. Nevertheless, both during the war and after, Civil War humor often reflected serious issues, whether intentionally or not. Despite my admittedly tongue-in-cheek approach, I address these issues in a serious way.

To maintain the authentic voices of those who produced the works addressed here, quotations are reproduced as they appear in their original texts. That means that some rather offensive words will appear in the quotations, words often used in insulting, caustic, and even violent ways. They are also often used casually. It would be easy to dismiss these pejoratives as the common terminology of a work's era, used in a banal sort of way, but that would not account for the works that use them with vicious intent. I do take up this language issue in a number of places.[9]

Also, a warning to grammarians. There's some pretty unpleasant grammar in the quotations. When necessary or appropriate, I use [sic] to try to clarify, but even that doesn't cure some of the unpleasantness.

Many of the works included here have their biases, and so do I, but when it comes to the cause of the war, I'm a scholar, despite my unorthodox approach here. The legitimate scholarship on what started the war is pretty convincing: slavery sits solidly as the root cause of the Civil War. Any and every issue that divided North and South in the decades leading up to the war did so because of slavery. The war was fought over issues related to slavery, issues that could not be resolved through political compromise. It does not matter why someone's great-great-grandpappy personally went off to fight on one side or the other. Unless the great-great-grandpappy personally started the war, why he fought, and good scholarship has shown that soldiers fought for a variety of reasons, is irrelevant.[10] Without the clash over slavery, he would not have had a war to go off to fight. Yes, I'm a Yankee. While I do not know exactly why my great-great-grandfather and his brothers joined the Union army in 1862, I suspect it had nothing to do with slavery. On the other hand, I know that the evidence shows that the war they went off to fight had everything to do with slavery. More of my biases will become apparent as this narrative progresses. Some of them are quite critical of the North and certain Yankee leaders, too.

Part I focuses on the war years and how humor was used to combat the war, criticize the conflict, and cope with the event's fouler side. Part II looks at how postwar authors recorded the war, how through memoir and fiction they sought to shape the remembrance of the conflict, and how some desired to refight the rebellion while others strove to achieve reconciliation and reunion. Part III continues the theme of memory while exploring how modern technologies and new platforms combined with print methods to present both traditional depictions and postmodern interpretations of the war. Along the way, connections will be made from one period to the next, and certain themes will reoccur, particularly sectionalism, race, and gender. Beyond that, you'll have to read for yourself. I hope you enjoy it.

PART I

"Crude partisan versifying on both sides"
The Wartime Writers

Civil War-related writings began to appear shortly after the smoke cleared over Fort Sumter and continued with a fury throughout the war. According to Civil War literature specialist Will Kaufman, much of this "wartime literary output" amounted to "crude partisan versifying on both sides." Humorists added to the partisan rhetoric. Cameron C. Nickels observed in his book on Civil War humor, "The ultimate purpose of the rhetoric of any war generally is to justify killing people, a principle all the more troublesome in this conflict because those 'people' were in so many cases and so immediately, and often literally, 'family.' The most fundamental purpose of humor in any war is to define the enemy, to put him in his comic, satiric place and thus make him and the cause he stands for laughable." This certainly holds true for the Civil War, but humor also was used as a tool to help cope with the war, the deaths, and the devastation it caused and to reassure fellow partisans that not all was gloom and doom.[1] Writers did not always plunge their satirical sword at the enemy, often aiming their wit, as well as their criticism, at their own leaders and armies to express frustrations concerning military setbacks, controversial wartime policies, and other sufferings generated by the conflict. Whatever their style of writing, the humorists of the Civil War years intended to do much more than just make people laugh.

The Crackerbox Philosophers

In the 1990s, comedian Jeff Foxworthy became a celebrity with the six words "You might be a redneck if...." Foxworthy did not invent a new genre of comedy. Rather, he tapped into a strain of humor that has a long and successful tradition, personified by the nineteenth-century literary character known as the crackerbox philosopher, a term coined by literary scholar Jennette Tandy to describe an archetype character found in American literature. Tandy gave many names to these characters: "the homely Americans"; "rural sage people"; "rustic types"; and "the comic countryman," to name a few. But she shared the term "crackerbox philosophers" as the title of her book. The crackerbox philosopher "represents a viewpoint of the man of the people," according to Tandy. "With wise saws and rustic anecdotes and deliberately cruel innuendo he interprets the provincial eccentricities of American life and the petty corruptions of American political life," Tandy explained, such literary characters, indeed caricatures, "had by right the ear of many who were deaf to the ordinary appeals of editor or orator," the American plain folk.[2] These literary figures often speak, or their words are often presented, in what George P. Krapp identified as "Eye Dialect," described as a form of spelling in which "the convention violated is one of the eyes, not of the ear. Thus, spellings ... indicate that those represented as using them are uneducated, youthful, rustic, or otherwise unlike the readership," who can feel superior to, yet not threatened by, the humble speaker.[3] Both Tandy and Krapp wrote about these literary figures in 1925. Evidently the crackerbox philosopher must have been one of that year's trending topics.

Several authors sought to explain the Civil War as it was occurring using this style of homespun, hokey humor. In the North two rather popular crackerbox philosopher authors were Charles Farrar Browne, who published as Artemus Ward, and David Ross Locke, better known as Petroleum V. Nasby. Browne gained a reputation for his humorous writings on public affairs, eventually leading to employment with the Cleveland *Plain Dealer*. From there his reputation grew nationally, and Browne took on the pen name Artemus Ward. Using a Midwestern rural dialect, Browne's writings discussed and poked fun at a long list of things.[4]

As the secession crisis developed, Browne's Ward added his two cents. In a presentation called "The Crisis," Ward first blames the slaves for the hostilities: "It's a pity he cooden't go orf sumwhares quietly by hisself ... without havin eternal fuss kickt up about him." In this way Browne placed slavery at the heart of the division between North and South. Like many other Northerners, Browne underestimated the seriousness of the Southern threats. "In my travels threw the Sonny South," Ward notes in an essay written shortly after the war commenced, "I heared a heap of talk about Seceshon and bustin up the Union, but I didn't think it mounted to nothin." Nevertheless, Ward insists, "Under no circumstances whatsomever will I secesh.... The country may go to the devil, bit I won't!" In a mock conversation between Ward and Jefferson Davis, president of the "Southern Conthieveracy," the narrator asserts a strong sense of patriotism in defense of the Union: "Many of us was your sincere frends, and thought certin parties amung us was fussin about you and meddlin with your consarns intirely too much. But J. Davis, the minit you fire a gun at the piece of dry-goods called the Star-Spangled Banner, the North gits up and rises en massy, in defence of that banner."⁵

Browne also criticized what he saw as lack of support for the war at home. In "A War Meeting," which takes place in Artemus Ward's fictional "Baldinsville" hometown, Browne took to task men who "air willin' to talk and urge others to go to wars, but … don't go to the wars [themselves]." He also confronted those who evaded conscription in "The Draft in Baldinsville." "There was a evident desine to evade the Draft, as [Ward] observed." The narrator describes sixteen men who bought shares of the local stagecoach line, despite the fact that it received little business, because "stagedrivers is exempt" from service. Against this, Browne asserted the need to be willing to sacrifice to defeat the Confederacy. "We do want *men*, and we must have them," his hero exclaims. "We must carry a whirlwind of fire among our foe. We must crush the ungrateful rebels who are poundin' the Goddess of Liberty over the head with slung-shots, and stabbin' her with stolen knives! We must lick 'em quick." Noticeably, Browne's editorializing uses minimal dialect in his serious messages, like the one above.⁶ In Artemus Ward, Browne fabricated a loyal spokesman who defended the Union war effort against the rebels in the South and their disloyal allies in the North.

To mock Northern war opponents, editor David Ross Locke created the character Petroleum V. Nasby, a "Copperhead," or Northern antiwar Democrat also known as a Peace Democrat. In the form of letters to the editor, a common vehicle used by the crackerbox philosophers, Locke's Nasby exposed the racist attitudes of local Democrats and the way that the Democratic political opposition manipulated that sentiment. For instance, in a letter dated "Joon the 1st," 1862, Locke crafted a fictitious conversation between Nasby and outspoken Peace Democrat and Ohio Senator Clement Vallandigham concerning the approaching congressional elections. Vallandigham claims that the "nigger is our trump card—we must lead off with it." Therefore, the strategy for electoral success must include several tactics: letting "no niggers vote in Ohio"; prohibiting "the immense emygrashen uv niggers" into the state as well as the "alarmin amalgamashun uv the races"; squelching "the idee uv allowin the nigger to stand on a equality with the whites"; and letting "no nigger to hev [political] offis in Ohio." When Nasby points out to Vallandigham that these were not really problems, the senator replies, "A man uv straw is the eeziest knockt down, especially ef yoo hev set him up yerself fer the purpus uv knockin uv him down."⁷

Spreading lies concerning the mass migration of freed slaves to the North and racial amalgamation represented just part of the Peace Democrats' agenda, according to Locke. In a later letter discussing his run for Ohio governor, Vallandigham tells Nasby, "Elect me and therd be no more trouble about drafts, unless we shood git involved in a war with the United States. The Confedracy wood be recognised, Ohio wood go with the South, and slavery wood be interdoost, and as we woodent hev eny further use er em, poor men awoodent be allowed to vote, making me perpetooal Guvernor."[8] The Copperhead politician lost the election, both in the Nasby letters and in the state of Ohio.

Petroleum Nasby represented a critic of disloyalty both in the South and in the North. In the character known as Major Jack Downing, readers found a manifestation of pro–Copperhead sentiment. Created in 1830 by Seba Smith, the publisher of a small newspaper in Portland, Maine, Major Jack Downing introduced what became known as Down East humor into the written word. Through letters to the editor, Smith's Jack Downing commented on state and national politics in the 1830s and 1840s. The Downing letters became quite popular, and soon editors of papers across the country began reprinting them. Copycats also began mimicking Smith's Down East style, in some cases even using the Jack Downing name in their own fictitious letters.[9]

During the Civil War, a pseudo–Jack Downing figure reemerged in print, appearing in a series of letters published in the New York *Weekly Caucasian*. This new batch of faux–Jack Downing letters started in 1862, and they had many vicious things to say about those enslaved and those who wanted to see slavery's demise. The author advocates a negotiated settlement to keep "the Constitution as it is, and the Union as it was," a catch phrase of Peace Democrats that had grown in popularity by 1862. In a letter dated July 21, 1862, Downing blames Lincoln for prolonging the war because he continues to "stick to them Abolishinists." As long as the president does that, Downing rebukes Lincoln, "the Union will not only stay split, but will grow wider." Ironically, in the real world, on July 21, 1862, the real Abraham Lincoln informed his real advisors in his cabinet that he intended to begin liberating enslaved people through a presidential proclamation of emancipation. The frequency of the wartime Downing letters diminished with the issuance of the Emancipation Proclamation, which the author through Jack Downing calls "the deth warrent of the Union." "The Abolishinists have killed the Union," the author declares in a letter dated November 19, 1863. "The poor nigger is only the means that they used to do it."[10] On that real date in his address given at the dedication of the cemetery at Gettysburg, Lincoln predicted that this war testing whether a nation "conceived in liberty, and dedicated to the proposition that all men are created equal," would cause the nation to experience "a new birth of freedom."

While Northern Copperheads continued their opposition to the war and wartime policies at least through the 1864 presidential election, the wartime Downing letters ended in early 1864. In the last letter, Downing predicts a clash between Lincoln and Secretary of the Treasury Salmon P. Chase for the Republican nomination and promises to continue his reports. He did not.

Another crackerbox philosopher of the antebellum era to reemerge during the Civil War was Hosea Biglow, the creation of poet, abolitionist and *Atlantic Monthly* editor James Russell Lowell. Lowell first created Biglow, an unschooled Yankee (meaning more Down East humor), in 1846 and used the character to comment on national politics, the war with Mexico, and slavery. Hosea Biglow's first incarnation ended in 1848, after which Lowell republished the writings in a volume titled *The Biglow Papers*. Lowell resurrected the characters once the Civil War began, producing another series of papers appearing in the *Atlantic Monthly*, of which he had just stepped down as editor. A year after the war ended, Lowell published the wartime collection of *The Biglow Papers* as a second series. Unlike the first series, which includes by way of an introduction a section called "Note to Title-Page," poking fun at the nineteenth-century publishing convention of including a long list of credentials of the author on the title page, and another whimsical section relating several fabricated review blurbs from fictitious newspapers, Lowell's second series includes a seventy-five page "Introduction" explaining his use of language and specifically the Yankee dialect, and the use of language and dialect in general.[11] What compelled Lowell to do this is beyond me. It is pedantic, dry, and excruciatingly boring, enough so to induce narcolepsy in a crack addict. Frankly, the rest of the second appearance of *The Biglow Papers* is pretty tiresome, too. Perhaps Lowell should have left Biglow in retirement.

Yet another poet and editor to produce a crackerbox philosopher during the war was Robert H. Newell, who fabricated the character Orpheus C. Kerr, a play on the words "office seeker," disparaging the many men who sought presidential appointments from Abraham Lincoln (and every other nineteenth-century president) through the "spoils system." In the form of letters, the Kerr writings first found print in the *New York Mercury* and then in book form as *The Orpheus C. Kerr Papers* in three volumes. The Kerr writings lack the heavy dialect and phonetic spelling found in most other similar writings, making them much easier to read.[12] Newell probably did not anticipate the direction his letters would take. He explains in the third installment, dated March 31, 1861, that he arrived in Washington, D.C., as the "private secretary and speech-scribe to an unscrupulous and, therefore, rising politician" from New York, but that did not satisfy this man on the make. He has his eye on a "certain postmastership," Kerr continues, "but war's alarms indicate that I may do better as an amateur hero."[13] Thus, Kerr joins the fictional Mackerel Brigade and begins his new career as a Union soldier.

Through Kerr, Newell criticized the glorification of war, the overblown patriotism he witnessed, and the sentimentalism that many used to characterize the war in the face of mounting casualties and deaths. Newell crafted his letters using humor worthy of Groucho Marx. In describing an incident in a military hospital, Kerr explains, "The surgeon was formerly a blacksmith, my boy, and got his diploma by inventing some pills with iron in them. He proved that the blood of six healthy men contained enough iron to make six horse-shoes, and then invented the pills to cure hoarseness." One can easily imagine Groucho flicking his cigar and fluttering his painted-on eyebrows while delivering these lines. Hospital scenes like this, Kerr reminds us, "are things to make the spectator remember that we are but dust, and that to return to dust is our dustiny."[14] One could also insert the lines, "One morning I shot a rebel in my pajamas. How he got into my pajamas I'll never know" into any number of Kerr's letters.

Unfortunately, the Marx Brothers never did a film set during the Civil War, but in their classic *Duck Soup*, the four brothers did don Civil War uniforms briefly during the final battle scene in defense of the fictitious nation of Fredonia. The Three Stooges, on the other hand, took on the Civil War in two of their short films. In the 1935 release *Uncivil Warriors*, the boys are Union spies sent behind Confederate lines on a mission to gather information. More than a decade later, they appeared in the similarly named short *Uncivil War Birds*. Stylized after the 1939 blockbuster *Gone with the Wind*, *Birds* depicts the Stooges belonging to a Southern family divided by the war, struggling to stay together while North and South fight it out. While *Warriors* shows clear partisanship toward the North, *Birds*, filmed in the wake of the World War II unity felt by the nation, takes no side except that of Curly, Larry, and Moe. But I digress from Orpheus Kerr.[15]

Newell took the war very seriously, and he did so as a supporter of Lincoln and the Union. Nevertheless, he disparaged the way in which the Lincoln administration placated the loyal border states and what Newell depicted as the Union army's unwillingness to do anything that might offend Southern civilians and jeopardize future reconciliation and reconstruction. This, of course, was a slam against the conservatism of Union Major General George McClellan, who commanded the Army of the Potomac until being fired in late 1862. McClellan, whom Newell's Kerr refers to as the General of the Mackerel Brigade, opposed any actions that would lead to the freeing of enslaved people. Despite the criticism, or perhaps because of it, Abraham Lincoln became a big fan of Newell's creation, although he also enjoyed Artemus Ward and Petroleum Nasby. Upon learning that the Union army's Commissary General Montgomery Meigs was unfamiliar with the Kerr papers, Lincoln commented, "Anyone who has not read them is a heathen," giving fans of Orpheus C. Kerr a quote to crow about for a century and a half to come.[16]

In Orpheus Kerr, Newell created a soldier who put a satirical spin on the war. Irish immigrant and journalist Charles Graham Halpine was a real soldier who did the same. After the attack on Fort Sumter, Halpine volunteered to put down the rebellion. He received a commission as a second lieutenant and then became *aide-de-camp* to Colonel, and then Brigadier General, David Hunter. Halpine also continued to write for the papers back in New York, sending items on conditions in the army and signed with pseudonyms of his initials "H.G.P." or just "H."[17]

A supporter of the Democratic Party, Halpine nonetheless strongly backed the war against the Confederacy and the policies of Abraham Lincoln and used his pen to promote them, especially among his fellow Irish immigrants. That does not mean that he shied away from controversy or criticism when he felt compelled. In September of 1863, Halpine anonymously published a letter in the New York *Herald*, supposedly written by a correspondent stationed with the army off the coast of South Carolina. In the letter, Halpine came to the defense of Admiral Samuel DuPont, who had taken blame and was removed from command when his naval forces failed to dislodge the Confederates from their control of Fort Sumter in the mouth of Charleston Harbor. The next letter from Halpine, written in very serious tones, begins with the tale of "an odd character named Miles O'Reilly, who has frequently relieved the monotony of camp life by scribbling songs of all sorts of subjects" while a private in one of the New York regiments. One such song got O'Reilly in hot water and led to his incarceration by the provost-marshal-general of his command, the correspondent told readers. The song defended Admiral DuPont while lambasting DuPont's successor, Admiral John Dahlgren. Halpine had actually invented the O'Reilly character and inserted one of his "songs" into an April 1863 letter he wrote to President Lincoln's secretary John Nicolay, this time using the Irish private's voice to criticize Secretary of the Navy Gideon Wells. That letter, too, graced the pages of the New York *Herald*, but the second appearance of O'Reilly gained the nonexistent lyricist a new level of notoriety. The public came to accept the tale of woe Halpine spun about the private, and Halpine ran with it.[18] Thus, Halpine as the nameless newspaper correspondent became the straight man to Halpine's fictitious funny man, Miles O'Reilly.

Halpine's next contribution to the *Herald* continued the story of O'Reilly and his attempt to convince Secretary of War Edwin Stanton to secure for him a presidential pardon. In short time, public concern for the fictional O'Reilly grew. One in the twenty-first century can imagine that if such a story evoked similar sympathy, it would be depicted and promoted through multiple websites, blogs, dedicated Facebook pages, tweets from celebrities, and at least two tribute songs from overly famous musical acts or combinations thereof. Finally, the *Herald* was "gratified to be able to announce" through a dispatch dated from Washington "that the President, always attentive to the cry of suffering and deserving soldiers, has granted a free pardon to private Miles O'Reilly."[19] The public felt great relief to learn of the presidential pardon that released O'Reilly. The president, on the other hand, must have been a bit confused. According to Charles Halpine, the president, like many other readers, believed the yarn. Whether or not Lincoln came to believe that he had actually pardoned a private named Miles O'Reilly is a different story.

According to Halpine's narrative, the president decided to release O'Reilly in part because he saw the private's offensive poem as an attempt at harmless humor by the Irishman. Also influencing the fictional Lincoln was another verse written by O'Reilly that allegedly had come to the president's attention defending the use of African American soldiers in the Union army. In real life, the poem had been written by Halpine and circulated among the troops under General Hunter's command in early 1863 to promote the general's controversial experiment with Black soldiers, now sanctioned as formal policy through the Emancipation Proclamation. The rhyme, appearing in the same correspondence that announced O'Reilly's pardon, was titled "Sambo's Right to Be Kilt." In introducing the poem in the *Herald*, Halpine noted that the "verses ... had been of the utmost value in reconciling the minds of the soldiery of the old 10th Army Corps [Hunter's command] to the experiment of the 1st South Carolina Volunteers [the unit of African American soldiers raised by Hunter]." The lyrics quickly circulated through the North in other newspapers and in sheet music form, and made the use of Black soldiers called for in Lincoln's proclamation much more palatable to those who had opposed it, especially Irish immigrants. As historian Randall Jimerson noted of the poem, "Its humor was cruel and cold-blooded, but it could persuade whites to accept black enlistment without disturbing their deep-seated racial prejudices."[20] Considering that by the end of the war about one tenth of the soldiers who wore Union blue were African American, Halpine's racist ditty may have done more than make people laugh; it may have helped to win the war in a tangible way. Using the O'Reilly pseudonym, Halpine continued to write essays for the New York press during the war, many of which were published in a volume called *Baked Meats of the Funeral*, memorable if only for its title.

Another journalist-turned-soldier and satirist was Alfred C. Hills, albeit a much more obscure one. Hills wrote for the *New York Evening Post*, but at some point, probably after New Orleans fell to Union forces, he moved to the Crescent City and became an officer in the Fourth Louisiana Native Guards, a Union militia group made up of African American soldiers with white officers. At the same time, he fabricated the character "James B. MacPherson," his crackerbox *nom de plume*. Hills' MacPherson was a Confederate soldier home on furlough from the army and residing in the small town of Madisonville, north of New Orleans. Hills' writings, in the usual form of letters, probably appeared first in one or more of the New Orleans newspapers with which he was affiliated. In 1864 he published the letters in book form under the elongated title *MacPherson, the Great Confederate Philosopher and Southern Blower. A Record of His Philosophy, His Career as a Warrior, Traveller* [sic]*, Clergyman, Poet, and Newspaper Publisher. His Death, Resuscitation, and Subsequent Election to the Office of Governor of Louisiana*. While there are a few funny bits in the letters, they mainly refer to events specific to New Orleans that no doubt would have been understood by readers from that city but little appreciated by others.[21]

The North did not have a monopoly on the crackerbox philosophers. The leading crackerbox voice of the wartime South belonged to Charles Henry Smith. A native Georgian, Smith served as a staff officer under several Confederate generals in the Army of Northern Virginia through the first two years of the war. That did not stop him from submitting to his hometown newspaper in Rome, Georgia, the first of a series of humorous critiques of Lincoln, the North, and Federal policy using the pen name Bill Arp. Smith's Bill Arp pieces appeared sporadically throughout the war.[22] Early in the conflict, Arp mocked Lincoln's call for volunteers after the attack of Ft. Sumter, the performance of Union troops at the Battle of Bull Run, the impending issuance of the Emancipation Proclamation, and Lincoln's propensity for issuing presidential proclamations in general. As the war progressed, Smith's criticism as expressed through Bill Arp focused more and more on the Confederacy's faults. Arp castigates the "*skulkers* and *shirkers* and *dodgers*" who stayed at home while "the good ones are gittin killed up." He condemns the "Konfederit cavilry," which in the last year of the war foraged liberally in Georgia, "pirootin aroun" and "steelin from our side," but was nowhere to be found when the enemy arrived. The horsemen cannot be beaten, Arp asserts, and "the reeson they can't be whipped" is because every time the Yankees come, "they have always *jest left*."[23]

Smith found fault higher up the Confederate echelon, as well. In "A MESSIG TO ALL FOAKS," Arp proclaims:

> The War, and the Yankees, and old Linkhorn, and his threats of subgugation, xterminashun, amalgamashun, desloashun … is a big thing, turrible and horrible. But old Habeus Korpus *hung up* [suspended], and sekret sessions [of the Confederate congress], and the Kurrency Bill, and konskription, are far more bigger and orfuller in the xtreme. Or soljers ort to let the Yankees alone, and cum home, and fite these savage beesteses, and you, my feller-sitizens, art to arm yourselves with stiks, and roks, and thrashpoles, and hot water, and pikes, and make a vierlent assalt upon these 'most mosterous paradoxes.'[24]

In this "messig," Arp criticizes the Confederate government for abusing power; he also explains the "KAUSE OF THE WAR":

> Sum foaks say it was the Abolishunists that got up thiss fuss. *Sum say they didn't.* Sum say it was the politishuns, and sum say it wer a supernatral thing called *manifest destiny.* Sum are of the opinyon that the *nigger* was at the bottom of it, and that ever since the Romans karried the war into Afriky, Afriky have karried it everywhere else. But, my feller sitizens, it wer kaused xklusively by Gen. States Rights goin to sleep one day, and old Kolonel Federlist cum along and tride to kut his ham-string.

In other words, Smith perceived the Federal government's assault on states' rights as the source of the conflict that led to the war. Yet Arp also criticizes politicians like C.S.A. vice president Alexander Stephens and especially Georgia governor Joseph Brown for clinging too rigidly to states' rights. "While General [Joseph] Johnston and his gallant boys are fitin Sherman at the front, Joseph and his friends are kikin up a dust in the rear, and exhibitin on the pole the awful pikter of a Bear named *Habeus Corpus*," a shield Brown used to keep Georgia men enrolled in the Georgia militia from being sent to fight with the Confederate army in other states. If the protection of states' rights proved to be the cause of the war, then Arp, or Smith, may have agreed, at least in part, with historian Frank Lawrence Owsley's famous assertion that the Confederacy "DIED OF STATE RIGHTS."[25]

In his introduction to a 2009 republication of Bill Arp's newspaper articles from the Civil War and Reconstruction era, historian David B. Parker identified Charles Henry Smith as "the Confederacy's most popular humorist." The competition, however, was pretty slim. One contender, Rensalear Reed Gilbert, a Vermont-born physician by training and volunteer in the Sixth Texas Infantry, published letters that appeared in the *Houston Tri-Weekly Telegraph* under the name "High Private." While Gilbert became quite popular in Texas, his fame did not extend much further than that. Perhaps the "High Private" was a victim of geography, separated from having his pieces reprinted in the larger newspapers of the East first by distance and later by the Federal control of the Mississippi River.[26]

While Gilbert avoided use of eye dialect, he addressed many of the issues soldiers could appreciate. His letters poked fun at life in camp, tackling such issues as the lack of uniforms and shoes, the long wait for pay, the monotony of military drills, and the ongoing battle waged against a persistent foe, fleas. His regiment, the 6th Texas Infantry, "was attacked by a force greatly superior to our own in numbers." He reports: "The individuals composing this force first attacked our right and left *flanks*. Not being supplied with ammunition at that time, we showered curses upon them, and being short of lead, we resorted to *nails*. Yet they gained upon us. We next tried 'fire and swords,' but with like results. We then demanded a cessation of hostilities, but they turned a deaf ear to all demands. We entreated; we expostulated; we stormed; we did everything but flea [sic]; yet the attack on their part continued." After five months of this onslaught, the regiment "resolved to send for a great gross of 'flea powder.' Upon its rival it was duly administered, and for a few hours there was more hopping and kicking and sneezing than was ever heard or seen before outside the walls of Jericho! Then for the first time all was quiet, for not a live enemy was left to tell the tale!"[27]

A few other Southern authors produced scattered pieces during the war. A young Joel Chandler Harris, future author of the Uncle Remus tales, penned a crackerbox letter to Abraham Lincoln signed by a character named Obadiah Skinflint and published in a small-time Georgia newspaper to which he had been apprenticed. And George Washington Harris as Sut Lovingood also produced letters to Lincoln with advice in March 1861, but then he went silent until after the war.[28]

The style of crackerbox philosopher lived on into the twentieth century. It could be found in the funny pages, with comic strips such as "Li'l Abner," "Snuffy Smith," and "Pogo." Then in the 1960s, a variety of it populated television in the form of the "southern rural comedy." ABC innovated the genre with the show *The Real McCoys* in 1957, but CBS came to dominate it with programs like *The Andy Griffith Show*; its spin-off *Gomer Pyle, U.S.M.C.*; *The Beverly Hillbillies*; *Petticoat Junction*; *Green Acres*; and *Hee Haw*. These productions found appeal among many viewers because they showed an America that was untroubled by social unrest, free of Cold War anxiety (despite one being set on a Marine base), and very white in complexion, especially in light of the Civil Rights movement.[29] The shows had a strong Southern influence and occasionally tied the Civil War into their story lines. For example, the nouveau riche Clampetts of *The Beverly Hillbillies* hail from the Ozark region of Missouri, and the family matriarch Granny occasionally dons her rebel gray uniform and pulls out her musket to defend her heritage from the Yankees. In a three-episode arc broadcast first in 1967, Granny mistakes a movie about the Civil War being filmed nearby (why in Beverly Hills I can't explain) as a resumption of the fratricidal conflict, and the whole family, including neighbor and family banker Mr. Drysdale, mobilizes to join in. In the process, Granny captures the actor playing Ulysses S. Grant, who, stereotypical of Grant, is drunk. *The Andy Griffith Show*, set in North Carolina, makes numerous references to the war, although without the intention of continuing it. And who can forget Gomer Pyle, in Washington, D.C., to sing at a special concert attended by the president but suffering from laryngitis, only to regain his voice at the Lincoln Memorial reading the Gettysburg Address?

Still, not everyone was fond of the crackerbox precursors to the Southern rural comedies. At the same time that these sitcoms ruled the television ratings, some literary scholars expressed their disdain for the writers who inspired them. For instance, E.B. White, of Strunk and White's *Elements of Style* fame, characterized the crackerbox philosophers as "rather dreary," while Kenneth S. Lynn found "Petroleum Nasby, Josh Billings and many another 'phunny phellow' ... dull." Russell Baker posited that "dialect humor ... is nearly impenetrable to the modern reader." And Henry C. Carlisle, Jr. identified the crackerbox "notorious fashion for phonetic spelling" as "a blight on the prime Civil War crop of humor."[30] Civil War–era readers disagreed.

"Where are the women among ... the 'literary comedians' of the 1860s?"

A noticeable shortage among Civil War humorists is the voice of women. It's not that there were not any nineteenth-century women who wrote from a humorous perspective. There were. And it's not that women didn't write about the war during the war. They did. It's just that they didn't seem to do both at the same time, which prompted Alfred Habegger to ask, "Where are the women among ... the 'literary comedians' of the 1860's?" Not surprisingly, when nineteenth-century author Kate Sanborn put together a volume titled *The Wit of Women*, an overview of the subject from colonial times to the 1880s, none of the pieces she included related to the Civil War.[31] That's why I became excited when I came across a series of items published in *Harper's Weekly* during the war attributed to "Charity Grimes." Unfortunately, "Charity Grimes" appears to be a pseudonym, and to whom it belongs, male or female, remains a bit of a mystery.

The name may be drawn from the writings of Frances M. Whitcher, a literary humorist who published items in *Neal's Saturday Gazette*, *Godey's*

Lady's Book, and elsewhere. Whitcher's character Grimes, found in a collection of her works under the title *The Widow Bedott Papers*, is very much unlike this Charity Grimes, however. Whitcher describes Grimes, a bitter spinster who had been trying to get married for two decades, as "stiff as a poker, prim as a pea pod," and "a starched up, affected old critter." More significantly, considering that Whitcher died in 1852, her only contribution to the letters appears to be the name.[32] The Charity Grimes items are written in the style of a crackerbox philosopher, complete with eye dialect, and while Whitcher wrote in dialect, her prose lacks any resemblance to that of the Grimes pieces. The style does bear a striking similarity to that of David Ross Locke, also known as Petroleum V. Nasby. In 1879 Locke did adapt Whitcher's *The Widow Bedott Papers* for the stage, but that was a decade and a half after these letters made print. The author simply may have copied Locke's style. Literary scholar Kathleen Diffley suggests that the author may have been the second wife of Whitcher's widower, Martha Letetia Ward Whitcher. The second Mrs. Whitcher did put together *The Widow Bedott Papers* for publication as well as another volume of the first Mrs. Whitcher's writings. She also completed some of her predecessor's unfinished writings and published them. And she was an author in her own right, publishing poetry and later a local history.[33] Of course, the author may not have been Whitcher, but for the sake of argument, let's assume that the author was a woman.

Charity Grimes first writes "To the Edditer of Harper's Weekly" in the fall of 1862 to expose the disloyalty of her friend, Sarah Blue. "I call myself a thorrough administratrix," Charity proclaims. "I go fur the administrashun, thet is, fur the present one. None ov yure sham democrkracys fur me!" The same is not true of Sarah. "Sarah is a good administratrix jest as long as affares go on tu suit her, but jest the eyedentical minit things go against the grain, she's off on the other side like a roket." On top of that, Grimes continues, "Her father was the gratest turn-coat yu ever did see. He was brot up a methodist—then turned dimmycrat." Then she casts aspersions on the father's manhood, even though he, no doubt, would have been too old to serve: "Sense the war broke aout he's jined the Quakers, and every time he hears ov a draft bein' spoken of he quakes like a piece o' crab-apple jelly when yu fust turn it ker slap aout of the mold." Grimes turns her attention back to Sarah and her opposition to Lincoln's plan to issue the Emancipation Proclamation. Says Sarah, "Kill the Saouth with yure bagonets, run 'em thro' with sords, shute 'em with pistuls. and knock 'em over with the cannon's rore, but spare, oh! spare thare pockets! Skin 'em alive, but don't tuch their niggars!"[34]

Into 1863 Charity Grimes continued to contribute items to *Harper's*, usually in the form of poems. A frequent target of her verses was the

Copperheads, or Peace Democrats. "I m a Dimmycrat, dyed in the wool," she writes mockingly. "I go fur free trade, and that sort ov thing; I think it's rite tu let Slavery rule / Sooner'n hev Lincoln I's vote fur a king / And hev the Saouth fur an aristockracy." She also offers a poem in defense of Union general Benjamin Butler. Hated in the South, Butler faced a price of $10,000 on his head placed by South Carolinian Richard Yeadon, "a rank pizen Rebel," accusing the general of murdering a Confederate loyalist in New Orleans. Of course, there were many other reasons why Southerners wanted to get their hands on Butler's head, but Butler reported in his autobiography, Yeadon "did not get my head." Surprisingly, Grimes did get her poem about Butler republished in the *Southern Literary Messenger* just months after it appeared in *Harper's*.[35]

A notable exception to the scarcity of female Civil War humorists is Sarah Jane Lippincott, who published and lectured using the name Grace Greenwood. According to Kate Sanborn, "Grace Greenwood probably made more puns in print than any other woman, and her conversations were full of them." In the 1850s she became a Washington correspondent for a Philadelphia newspaper, the first woman to serve in this capacity according to Sanborn, and later corresponded for the *New-York Tribune* and *New York Times*, as well as occasionally publishing pieces in Washington's *National Era*. Sanborn further noted that Greenwood's "letters were racy, full of wit, sentiment, and discriminating criticism, plenty of fur and a little sarcasm, but not so audaciously personal and aggressive as some letter-writers from the capital." Greenwood also regularly lectured during the war, presenting patriotic speeches and also orating on the "Characteristics of Yankee Humor." During at least one such lecture, she explained her positions on a number of issues. "To prevent any misapprehensions," a newspaper reported, she claimed:

> She was a rabid Unionist, a rabider abolitionist; a woman's rights woman, and a dark complexioned republican. She believed in the Bible and the Declaration of Independence; in the constitution of the United States, and the proclamation of emancipation. She believed in Thomas Jefferson and Wendell Phillips; in George Washington and Abraham Lincoln; in Patrick Henry and Henry Beecher Ward; Alexander Hamilton and Charles Sumner; in John Brown and Benjamin F. Butler."[36]

Speaking of Butler again, Greenwood related an encounter she had with the general at the president's mansion when she had an audience with Lincoln. Also in attendance were "a famous and terrible ogre, and the prince of all the dwarfs,—General Butler, just in from New Orleans, and General Tom Thumb, with his fair young bride," Lavinia. Greenwood noted the comical scene of Abraham Lincoln, all six foot four of him, bending over to shake hands with his diminutive guests, made famous by P.T. Barnum. She then added, "As the bridal pair walked about the drawing-room, or took their wine and cake off a chair, I fancied the little bridegroom glanced apprehensively now and then at General Butler, as though fearing he might be moved to pounce upon and devour that dainty morsel of flesh and blood at his side. But the ogre had evidently dined,—or perhaps didn't consider the fair Lavinia 'contraband of War.'" Or perhaps Tom Thumb was eyeing Butler with the recently offered ten grand reward for the ogre's head in mind.[37]

As for the president, Greenwood declared, "If Abraham Lincoln does not lead like a Tell, or drive like a Cromwell, he stands shoulder to shoulder with the masses of the people,—which is perhaps better for our times."[38] I'm sure that Charity Grimes would have heartily approved of Grace Greenwood as a "thorough administratrix."

The Biblical Satirists

In 1866 Richard Grant White published *Poetry: Lyrical, Narrative and Satirical of the Civil War*, a collection of poems that had been published during the previous five years in various popular magazines and newspapers.[39] White proved to be eminently qualified for such a task. A prolific writer, White had just completed his acclaimed twelve volume edited collection of *The Works of William Shakespeare* (1857–1866). A native of New York City and contributor to many popular magazines and journals of the day, White gained appointment as the chief clerk of the marine revenue bureau of the New York Custom House through the Lincoln administration, a position he held until 1878. He also became secretary of the wartime Metropolitan Sanitary Fair, held to raise money for the benefit of Union soldiers. In addition, unknown to the general public, White had also recently published *The New Gospel of Peace*, a satirical attack on the Peace Democrats and their resistance to the war policies of the Lincoln administration.[40] White wrote *The New Gospel* in a mock-Biblical style known as Biblical satire or Biblical parody. The Bible proved to be a source with which literate eighteenth- and nineteenth-century Americans would be familiar, and White's anonymously published polemic stimulated a spate of responses, also mimicking the Bible or other religiously oriented writings.

On July 27, 1863, White published the first installment of *The New Gospel of Peace*, attacking pro–Confederate Peace Democrats and critiquing New York politics. Sounding like a cross between the Old Testament and Dr. Seuss and using a form of eye dialect, *The New Gospel of Peace* is set during the "days of Abraham" in the "land of Unculpsalm" during a terrible war. The narrative begins before the war in the "country of Mannatton, in the city which is called Gotham," inhabited by many "Pahdees," Irish immigrants, who were "not of the land of Unculpsalm." The Pahdees unite with "certain men of Unculpsalm … who called themselves Dimmichrats" in order to control Gotham and to elect "Phernandiwud," New York Democrat Fernando Wood, "chief ruler of the city."[41]

White then narrates the history of Unculpsalm, describing the division between North and South over slavery and using easily recognizable phrases like "the border of Masunandicson" and "Phiretahs" and names like "Prestenbruux" and "Charles, who was surnamed the Summoner." When one of the offending Northerners, "Abraham the Honest," is elected to "rule in the land of Unculpsalm," the "Phiretahs … gathered together in their provinces, and said, Our provinces shall no longer be a part of the land of Unculpsalm, for we will not have this man Abraham to rule over us." This leads to war between the two sections, the blame for which Richard Grant White placed on the shoulders of the South. As time progresses, "certain men of the Dimmichrats" came to oppose the war and the rule of Abraham. Thus, Phernandiwud begins preaching the new gospel of peace. "Let us make war without ceasing" on those that support the war and emancipation by seeking "every occasion to bring the rulers of our country to scorn and derision in the time of her trial," and by aiding "Jeph the Repudiator," Jefferson Davis, "and his spies, and his emissaries."[42]

The Peace Democrats sought to restore the nation as it was, with slavery intact, even if, Richard Grant White argued, it meant waging war against the government and those who opposed the Confederacy. "Book Second" of *The New Gospel of Peace* appeared in October 1863. Much of it focusses on how Phernandiwud and this new gospel of peace encourages "Robbutleeh, the chief captain of the Tshivulree," to invade the North, and the Pahdees of Gotham to riot against the draft. Rather than being true advocates of peace, the "Kopur-hedds" accepted war and violence as ways to advance their cause. By the way, actual practicing pacifists, who opposed the use of violence in all cases, saw only hypocrisy in the Peace Democrats and remained quite critical of their activities. Ironically, real pacifists also criticized the war against the South and sought an end to it.[43]

Through his anonymously-published *New Gospel of Peace*, Richard Grant White attacked the Peace Democrats and did so without having to worry about retribution. Although some suspected him of its authorship, White continued to deny it well after publication. The pamphlets contained many disclaimers that the individuals and events appearing in the text bore no connection to actual people and events. Nevertheless, *New Gospel* did much to discredit the Peace Democrats.[44]

White strongly supported the Union cause, but he was not averse to making an occasional criticism of Lincoln Administration war measures. Despite this, Richard Grant White probably did not author two pamphlets often attributed to him: *Revelations: A Companion to the "New Gospel of Peace" According to Abraham* and *Book of the Prophet Stephen, Son of Douglas. Wherein Marvellous [sic] Things Are Foretold of the Reign of Abraham*. These works, also biblical parodies, were highly critical of Lincoln and the Union cause and appear to be Peace Democrat responses to White. White's *New Gospel* generated other copycats, mostly in opposition to the original. As historian Forrest G. Wood notes, these pamphlets "had virtually no literary merit." Part of the broader "'collected works' of racism" published "during the Civil War era," they are "a monument to bigotry's dearth of intellect and imagination." Since readers were most likely set in their prejudices, these polemics "probably introduced a little humor into what was ordinarily a serious matter" but won over few new supporters.[45]

On the other hand, two months after the first *New Gospel* pamphlet appeared in print, the *Boston Daily Advertiser* reported, "The little *brochure* continues to sell with wonderful rapidity." This and subsequent installments did well. According to one May 1866 source, nearly one hundred and thirty-five thousand copies of the first three books of *The New Gospel of Peace* had been sold to date. A later source asserted that White made over $10,000 on the *New Gospel*, much more than he made on his Shakespearean opus. Although the impact of *The New Gospel of Peace* is impossible to quantify, many Northern newspapers praised White's pamphlets and agreed that they did much to discredit the Peace Democrats. Of course, not everyone agreed. For instance, *The Index*, a pro–Confederate British publication, commented on the occasion of the republication of *The New Gospel* in England that it would "not pollute [its] columns by describing, much less by quoting from" what it termed an "infamous parody" of the Bible.[46]

After the appearance of the first pamphlet, the term "new gospel of peace" was often used by loyal Unionists to describe the activities of the Democrats, Peace or otherwise, and behaviors or people in general that they deemed disloyal. The phrase continued in usage years after the war. Indeed, evoking the phrase "New Gospel of Peace" appears to have become a method of "waving the bloody shirt." By the end of the century, a new use for the term emerged, this time championed by Theodore Roosevelt. In 1899 the Spanish-American War hero and newly elected governor of New York published several essays and gave several speeches promoting annexation of the Philippines and other former Spanish territories. In a piece appearing in *The Independent* in December 1899, the future president compared the anti-imperialists to the Copperheads of the Civil War. "Peace may come only through war," Roosevelt asserted. "There are men in our country who seemingly forget that at the outbreak of the Civil War the great cry raised by the opponents of the war was the cry for peace." He continued, "One of the most amusing and most biting satires written by the friends of union and liberty during the Civil War was called the 'New Gospel of Peace,' in derision of this attitude." Roosevelt did not mention Richard Grant White by name, but he certainly gave him and his pamphlets credit for contributing to the success of Lincoln and the Union war effort. In the end the North's superiority in manpower, money, and materials overwhelmed the Confederate States. Perhaps to this list of advantages we should add the acerbic wit of Richard Grant White.[47]

One more publication worth mentioning for its use of religious imagery combined with dialect not completely unlike that employed by the crackerbox philosopher authors is *De Histori ov Magnus Mahárba end de Blak Dragun*, attributed to Kristofur Kadmus. Written by Nathan Brown, a nineteenth-century Baptist missionary, the brief book does not appear in the dialect of an uneducated rube but rather it uses an almost unreadable form identified on the copyright page as "rectified Saxon orthography." The narrative of the book tells a story of a struggle of Biblical proportion between Magnus Mahárba, representing Abraham Lincoln, or "Abraham the Great," and the Blak Dragun, standing for Southern slavery. It begins, and I will translate into a recognizable English, "A small planet in one of the starry clusters of the outer margin of the universe was the scene of the transactions recorded in the following pages. They occurred about six thousand years after that orb began to be peopled with rational intelligence."[48] Or perhaps another translation could be "A long time ago in a galaxy far, far away...." For anyone interested in works of fantasy, science fiction, fratricidal war, and nearly indecipherable writing, Nathan Brown's volume is your book.

The Scarlet Copperhead

In 2007, Michael Dunne published a book arguing that a major source of humor in American literature is Calvinism. This "Calvinist humor," he claimed, "consists in the perception of imperfections," especially other people's imperfections. It manifests itself in two strains, Dunne explained. In the first, Calvinist humor is created when we think "that we are the only ones smart enough to figure out something that is actually evident to everyone." The second strain "shows us that other people are fallen from perfection without any necessary recognition that we may be in the same boat ourselves."[49] Dunne traced Calvinist humor in American literature back to the writings of the early Puritans of seventeenth-century New

England, citing several well-known colonists as practitioners, including Plymouth governor William Bradford, one-time captive of Native Americans Mary Rowlandson, and famed eighteenth-century theologian Jonathan Edward, especially his most famous sermon, "Sinners in the Hands of an Angry God." It is hard to imagine Edwards provoking laughter with this or any other sermon, and I doubt that anyone thought his discourses funny. I'm sure, though, that if one guy in the crowd laughed, say when Edwards compared sinners to "loathsome insects," he would have ended up in the stocks. Hey! That's an example of Calvinist humor!

Dunne does not discuss any biblical satirists, Civil War–era or otherwise, in his book, but he does include a section on a prominent author who did make a contribution to the body of humorous Civil War literature: Nathaniel Hawthorne. If any nineteenth-century author has a claim to the Calvinist Puritan legacy, it is Hawthorne. His classic *The Scarlet Letter* has done more to shape people's understanding of Puritans—accurately or not—than the work of any historian living or dead. The book continues to bedevil high school students from one end of the nation to the other.

In the spring of 1862, Hawthorne wrote a piece titled "Chiefly About War Matters" for publication in the prominent literary magazine *The Atlantic*.[50] Rather than signing his own name, he attributed the essay to "A Peaceable Man." At the war's outset, Hawthorne informed several confidants that had he been younger, he would enlist. A year later, it appears, he felt differently, and not because he had discovered a calling for pacifism. A long-time supporter of the Democratic Party, the author sided with the Peace Democrat wing of the party. Instead of using military force to coerce the South back into the Union, he confided to a friend, "Amputation seems to me much the better plan." He continued, "All we ought to fight for is the liberty of selecting the point where our diseased members shall be lop't off."[51]

Hawthorne's Peaceable Man offers a satirical critique, at times subtle and at others not so subtle, of Northern prowar culture, sentiment, and policy. The essay begins with a comment on the pervasiveness of the influence of the war on daily life. "There is no remoteness of life and thought, no hermetically sealed seclusion, except, possibly, that of the grave, into which the disturbing influences of this war do not penetrate," he observes, adding "that there is a kind of treason in insulating one's self from the universal fear and sorrow [generated by the war], and thinking one's idle thoughts in the dread time of civil war." The Peaceable Man's "idle thoughts," one may presume, are not in tune with the prevailing patriotic pro–Union sentiment. "Could a man be so cold and hard-hearted" as to have contradicting opinions, he informs his readers, "he would better deserve to be sent to Fort Warren," a prison on an island in Boston Harbor used to confine captured Confederate officers and civilian political prisoners charged with treasonous activities, "than many who have found their way thither on the score of violent, but misdirected sympathies."[52] Here, no doubt, Hawthorne protested the arrest and confinement of civilians for disloyalty because they opposed or criticized the war.

The Peaceable Man later elaborates on this issue of treason. "It is a strange thing in human life, that the greatest errors both of men and women often spring from their sweetest and most generous qualities," he observes in a humorously Calvinist (or Calvinisticly humorous) way, "and so, undoubtedly, thousands of warm-hearted, sympathetic, and impulsive persons have joined the Rebels, not from any real zeal for the cause, but because, between two conflicting loyalties they chose that which necessarily lay nearest the heart." The fault, however, did not reside in the imperfections of these people but rather in the imperfections of the government. The course of action government should take is clear to the Peaceable Man: "If a man loves his own State ... and is content to be ruined with her, let us shoot him, if we can, but allow him an honorable burial in the soil he fights for."[53]

Most of "Chiefly About War Matters" recounts Hawthorne's observations made during a trip to the nation's capital and northern Virginia completed with a friend in the spring of 1862. Early in the trip, the Peaceable Man and his entourage have the opportunity to meet with Abraham Lincoln. Readers would have to wait until 1871 to read the description Hawthorne offered of the president because *The Atlantic*'s editor found the characterization unacceptable at the time.[54] Had readers seen the section in 1862, they would have been treated to images of a president who had a "tall, loose-fitted figure" and exhibited a "lengthy awkwardness" and an "uncouthness of ... movement." "He was dressed in a rusty black frockcoat and pantaloons, unbrushed, and worn so faithfully that the suit had adapted itself to the curves and angularities of his figure, and had grown to be an outer skin of the man." Plus, he wore "shabby slippers." As for his hair, it "was black, still unmixed with gray, stiff, somewhat bushy, and had apparently been acquainted with neither brush nor comb that morning." In short, Lincoln was "the homeliest man" that the Peaceable Man "ever saw, yet by no means repulsive or disagreeable." Yet Lincoln had "a kindly though serious look out of his eyes, and an expression of homely sagacity" and "a great deal of native sense; no bookish cultivation, no refinement; honest at heart, and thoroughly so, and yet, in some sort, sly." The narrator concludes, "President Lincoln is the essential representative of all Yankees, and the veritable specimen, physically, of what the world seems determined to regard as our characteristic qualities." I'm not sure if that is complimentary of either Lincoln or all Yankees. "It is the strangest and fittingest thing in the jumble of human vicissitudes, that he, out of so many millions, unlooked for, unselected by any intelligible process that could be based upon his genuine qualities, unknown to those who chose him, and unsuspected of what endowments may adapt him for his tremendous responsibility, should have found the way open for him to fling his lank personality into the chair of state."[55] All things considered, Hawthorne's depiction of the president is rather back-handed and his assessment of the people who put him in office rather low.

Getting back to what Hawthorne's essay did include in the 1862 edition, the Peaceable Man describes how just before his arrival in the capital, a large force of Union soldiers that had amassed there pushed out into Virginia. While Hawthorne assumes this would be another foray against the rebels at Manassas, it was actually the outset of Major General George McClellan's Peninsula Campaign. Here Hawthorne took aim at the militaristic buildup and the anticipation for battle Unionists had felt in the many months since the Battle of Bull Run, the first and most recent major encounter between Federal troops and the Confederates in that region, creating the impression that the war was much ado about nothing: "Almost with [the troops'] first step into the Virginia mud, the phantasmagory of a countless host and impregnable ramparts, before which they had so long remained quiescent, dissolved quite away. It was as if General McClellan had thrust his sword into a gigantic enemy, and, beholding him suddenly collapse, had discovered to himself and the world that he had merely punctured an enormous swollen bladder." The Peaceable Man likens the situation to

> instances of a similar character in old romances, where great armies are long kept at bay by the arts of necromancers, who build airy towers and battlements, and muster warriors of terrible aspect, and thus feign a defence [sic] of seeming impregnability, until some bolder champion of the besiegers dashes forward to try an encounter with the foremost foeman, and finds him melt away in the death-grapple. With such heroic adventures let the march upon Manassas be hereafter reckoned.

It is not clear if Hawthorne meant McClellan as the "bolder champion," because McClellan himself had done much to promote the idea that the Union forces on the Potomac faced an opposing army much larger and more formidable than it actually was. Unlike those who criticized McClellan for the delays, most of whom were Republicans, Hawthorne's gripe was with the war itself and its supporters. "The whole business," Man asserts, "though connected with the destinies of the nation, takes inevitably a tinge of the ludicrous. The vast preparation of men and warlike materials,—the majestic patience and docility with which the people waited through those weary and dreary months,—the martial skill, courage, and caution, with which our movement was ultimately made,—and, at last, the tremendous shock with which we were brought suddenly up against nothing at all!" To add insult to injury, Hawthorne cast the army as the butt of a Confederate joke. The Peaceable Man concludes: "The Southerners show little sense of humor nowadays, but I think they must have meant to provoke a laugh at our expense, when they planted those Quaker guns. At all events, no other Rebel artillery has played upon us with such overwhelming effect." According to Quaker gun specialist Thomas F. Curran, "Quaker guns were logs painted black and attached to wheels to resemble cannons." The Confederates used the ruse effectively along their defensive lines in the months before McClellan's advance.[56]

McClellan did not go ignored by Hawthorne, however. "There was, and is, a most fierce and bitter outcry, and detraction loud and low, against General McClellan," the Peaceable Man reports, "accusing him of sloth, imbecility, cowardice, treasonable purposes, and, in short, utterly denying his ability as a soldier, and questioning his integrity as a man." The writer at first appears to agree: "Nor was this to be wondered at; for when before, in all history, do we find a general in command of half a million men, and in presence of an enemy inferior in numbers and no better disciplined than his own troops, leaving it still debatable, after the better part of a year, whether he is a soldier or no? The question would seem to answer itself in the very asking." Being "profoundly ignorant of the art of war," the Peaceable Man jumps at the opportunity to see the general for himself. He catches up with McClellan's slow-moving army and witnesses the general interact with some of his soldiers. The men "received him with loud shouts, by the eager uproar of which—now near, now in the centre, now on the outskirts of the division, and now sweeping back towards us in great volume of sound—we could trace his progress through the ranks." The scene wows the narrator: "If he is a coward, or a traitor, or a humbug, or anything less than a brave, true, and able man, that mass of intelligent soldiers whose lives and honor he had in charge, were utterly deceived, and so was the present writer; for they believed in him, and so did I; and had I stood in the ranks, I should have shouted with the lustiest of them." What he would have shouted is not mentioned, but perhaps it would have been Woodrow Wilson's 1916 reelection campaign slogan, "He Kept Us Out of War." Whatever the case, the Peaceable Man concludes that he "shall not give up [his] faith in General McClellan's soldiership until he is defeated, nor in his courage and integrity even then."[57] With such gushing prose, one might suspect that Hawthorne anticipated that after being fired by President Lincoln, the general would capture the nomination of the Democratic Party for the presidential election of 1864 against Lincoln.

On their judgment of McClellan, Hawthorne put more faith in the soldiers than he did the general's critics. His criticism of the war's effect on the soldiers was much clearer. During his sojourn into Virginia, his alter ego visits a bivouac. "The atmosphere of the camp and the battlefield are morally invigorating," the Peaceable Man testifies. "The hardy virtues flourish in them, the nonsense dies like a wilted weed. The enervating effects of centuries of civilization vanish at once, and leave these young men to enjoy a life of hardship, and the exhilarating sense of danger,—to kill men blamelessly, or to be killed gloriously,—and to be happy in flowing out their native instincts of destruction." Such was the uncivilizing effect of war on men: "Set men face to face, with weapons in their hands, and they are as ready to slaughter one another now, after playing at peace and good-will for so many years, as in the rudest ages, that never heard of peace-societies."[58] Of course, these were the same men whose opinion Hawthorne valued in their assessment of George McClellan.

Still, Hawthorne thought that perhaps the wrong men were in the army. Rather than taking young men, the army should fill the ranks with the old. This would allow young men to enjoy "the many fervent summers of manhood in the spring and prime, with all that they include of possible benefit to mankind," while for an old man, "a bullet offers such a brief and easy way, such a pretty little orifice, through which the weary spirit might seize the opportunity to be exhaled!" His plan, readers are told, has several advantages. First, "the productive part of the population would be undisturbed even by the bloodiest war." Plus, "and, best of all, those thousands of our Northern girls, whose proper mates will perish in camp-hospitals or on Southern battle-fields, would avoid their doom of forlorn old-maidenhood." Unfortunately, he concludes, "the plan will be pooh-poohed down by the War Department."[59]

As for Southern soldiers, Hawthorne presented a sympathetic but demeaning description of the few his Peaceable Man encountered as prisoners of the Union army. "Almost to a man, they were simple, bumpkin-like fellows, dressed in homespun clothes, with faces singularly vacant of meaning, but sufficiently good-humored: a breed of men, in short, such as I did not suppose to exist in this country, although I have seen their like in some other parts of the world. They were peasants, and of a very low order: a class of people with whom our Northern rural population has not a single trait in common." Taking another jab at his Northern neighbors, he adds, the prisoners "were exceedingly respectful,—more so than a rustic New Englander ever dreams of being towards anybody, except perhaps his minister." Nevertheless, he concludes, "It is my belief that not a single bumpkin of them all ... had the remotest comprehension of what they had been fighting for." The Peaceable Man believes that Southerners had much to gain by losing the war, specifically to be elevated from the "thraldom [sic] in which they scarcely begin to be responsible beings." Defeat for the Confederacy could mean for these men

> the removal of a foul scurf [another word for dandruff] that has overgrown their life, and keeps them in a state of disease and decrepitude, one of the chief symptoms of which is, that, the more they suffer and are debased, the more they imagine themselves strong and beautiful.... Therefore, it struck [the Peaceable Man] as an immense absurdity that they should fancy us their enemies; since, whether we intend it so or no, they have a far greater stake on our success than we can possibly have.

So, Union victory could mean freedom from their "thraldom" for these poor white rubes. What neither Hawthorne nor his Peaceable Man mention is anything about freeing the slaves. Slaves and slavery barely earn a few inconsequential mentions in the essay.[60]

Either to lessen the backlash that his essay might generate and to make it more acceptable to the editor of *The Atlantic*, his friend and pro–Union man James T. Fields, or to magnify the dissonant meaning of his prose, Hawthorne included a series of editorial notes written by himself, which take the author to task for some of the more controversial things he wrote and even claimed to delete sections that "might be liable to misconstruction." The fact that Hawthorne published the essay under a pseudonym provided him with little protection as the news quickly spread that he authored the piece.[61]

Nevertheless, it was the author's bromance with fellow Democrat and former president Franklin Pierce that really brought his loyalty under scrutiny. In 1852 Hawthorne wrote Pierce's campaign biography. Pierce then went on to enact the controversial Kansas-Nebraska Act and take other measures that exacerbated the growing rift between North and South. During the war, he argued in Copperhead fashion that the war should be brought to an end with "The Union as It Was." On the Fourth of July in 1863, the day after the Battle of Gettysburg ended, the former president gave an oration in Concord, New Hampshire, in which he deplored the use of force by the Federal government against the South. Sitting on the speakers' platform was Pierce's good pal, Nathaniel Hawthorne, a fact that did not escape the eye of critical observers. Many attacked Pierce as a traitor, and Hawthorne, regardless of whatever he may have done on his own to gain the Northern public's opprobrium, was guilty by association. Hawthorne lived only a short while after this incident, dying in May 1864, but for the rest of his life, he wore the stigma of disloyalty as his own scarlet letter.[62]

"A period which produced so many good war songs, and so much bad war verse"

During the Civil War, poetry flourished, some of it good and some, maybe a lot of it, not so good. A century after the conflict ended, the preeminent scholar of Civil War literature Edmund Wilson commented, "The period of the Civil War was not at all a favorable one for poetry. An immense amount of verse was written in connection with the war itself, but today [1962] it makes barren reading." Literary scholar Jennette Tandy was even harsher. In 1925 she complained that the "period which produced so many good war songs" produced "so much bad war verse." As early as 1865, as the proverbial smoke was still clearing from the battlefield, the war's poetry experienced disparagement from those who believed that the war generated "no real poetry." This sentiment prompted polymath Oliver Wendell Holmes, Sr., to come to the wartime poetry's defense before he launched into a lecture titled "The Poetry of the War." Even then, according to a report on the lecture appearing in the *New York Times*, the esteemed Holmes found Southern poetry sub-standard to that of the victorious North. Some Southerners agreed. "To be perfectly candid," journalist, politician, former Confederate soldier, and future diplomat Anthony M. Keiley acknowledged in 1866, "our poetic literature was contemptible throughout the struggle." And in 1863, editor of the *Southern Literary Messenger* George W. Bagby complained, "We are receiving too much trash in rhyme."[63]

Not all was bad, however. At least not as bad as Vogon poetry (the third worst poetry in the Universe).[64] Since the war's end, some of the poetry produced during that four-year span has been reprinted, anthologized, and analyzed. Receiving much attention have been the works of Walt Whitman, Herman Melville, Emily Dickinson, and, of course, Julia Ward Howe, whose "Battle Hymn of the Republic" became the anthem for the Union cause. Like most Civil War poetry, there is not much humor here or elsewhere in the Civil War poetry that receives notice. To find humor in Civil War poetry, one needs to look deeper than the obvious contributors, to the more obscure, and usually less talented, indeed, often bad, rhymesters.

In late summer of 1863, a slim, anonymously authored volume containing an extended poem titled *This War, a Satire for the Times* appeared, written by an obscure man named John Sullivan Brown, whose only claim to fame appears to be this obscure book.[65] The volume contains an acerbic attack on the slave-owning South, Southern secession, and the war that Southerners started, exposing what many abolitionists and the early Republican Party labeled the "slave-power conspiracy" to force slavery on the entire nation. On a scale of one to ten measuring pro–Union and anti-Confederate bias, Brown's work needs a scale that goes to eleven. That's what I find humorous in it. Just when you might think Brown has peaked in his caustic (and effusive) ramblings, he ratchets it up even more. In fact, some might conclude that the volume, labeled "a Satire," is actually satirizing extreme patriotism and blind support for the Union cause. Instead, I think it is just a bad word choice. Someone should tell him, "I do not think that word means what you think it means."

Brown uses the phrase "Conspiracy of Southern traitors" to describe his antagonists, and he undoubtedly knew the phrase's meaning. He employs other terms of endearment like "treason justifiers," "*evil* croakers" and "a pack of human demons." He describes the Civil War as the outcome of a series of calculated steps and much manipulation on the part of Southern slave owners. After years of trying to force slavery on the entire nation, Brown explains, the South turned to "their cherished scheme, their final hope," secession. Then, Brown reveals, Southerners' "demon would be free to sail their ship of state off to its own Utopia!" After fracturing the nation, Brown continues, Southerners planned to create their own empire from the Atlantic to the Pacific, including Mexico and Cuba. Their nation would have only two classes, the "master" and the "slave," with the "poor white man" finding himself also enslaved by the planters unless he could escape their realm. Then, the poem posits, the Southern planters believed they would control the world through the power of "King Cotton," or the "cottonocracy!"[66]

Brown's heavy-handed explanation of the coming of the Civil War goes on for ten pages of verse. He spends little time discussing specifics of the war itself. Rather he filled the majority of the book's eighty pages with assaults on the institution of slavery and the defense of it; the treason of the South; Northern "Copperheads" and "peace men"; the Southern-sympathetic press; the Democratic Party (although not by name), which Southerners dominated until it splintered in 1860; and anyone who dared question the causes of Union and liberty fought for by the North. Nevertheless, the poet remained confident that the North, the Union, and goodness would prevail, and in the end, the South, the "paragon of greatest wickedness," would suffer "an immortality of infamy," taught to school children "in story and in song."[67]

Brown finds no gray areas in the causes of the war. All is vividly portrayed in black and white, which certainly made some readers see red. Others might be green with envy because of the unrelenting attack on slavery he produced. Of course, Brown probably felt blue about the whole endeavor because it appears that few people read the work, leaving Brown in the red. The only review, or even mention, of the book that I could find noted simply, "The writer has, to avail ourselves of the old joke, commenced each line with a capital, which, unfortunately, does not alleviate its other grammatical and rhetorical shortcomings."[68]

Demonizing the enemy, literally, became commonplace during the war, often in long poetic form. Another pro–Union extended poem in book form written to do that is *The Devil in Dixie: A Tale of the Times. Serio-Comical, Semi-Historical, and Quasi-Diabolical* by George William Lloyd. An immigrant from England and a Presbyterian minister, Lloyd strongly supported the Union cause and used his New Jersey pulpit to express his loyalty, much to the displeasure of those who supported the Southern Confederacy in his divided congregation. In fact, one such sympathizer became so angry that he took a shot at the minister with a pistol, just barely missing him. Undeterred by the incident, Lloyd produced *The Devil in Dixie* to expose the satanic roots of the war.[69]

The poem opens with a scene from Hell, circa "A.D. 1782–3," with Satan lamenting that "Freedom's flag is victorious," referring to the triumph of the Continental Army over the British. For many years old Nick had been trying to determine "how best" to "break up that very annoying nest / Of men who love Liberty, civil and sacred." To this challenge one of the Devil's imps responds with a scheme that centered on slavery, making sure that slavery was written into the new Constitution and continued to spread into new territories. Exposure to slavery would then destroy the morals of the nation and its citizens, and before long the government would be dominated by the "traders in human flesh," who would become "more exacting and arrogant day by day." Within two generations, the imp concludes, freedom would be destroyed, and treason and tyranny would reign in the "land of the 'noble free.'"[70]

Lucifer embraces the idea, rewards the imp who proposed it, and immediately puts the plan into action. The narrative of the poem next flashes forward to "A.D. 1863." The Devil rejoices and calls for a celebration, complete with music (or what passes as music in Hell), gongs, drums, cannons firing, and banners, especially "the Devil's own flag—the 'Stars and Bars'!" And his minions parade. In vivid and comical terms, Lloyd paints a rather cartoonish image of this satanic celebration he envisioned. Next, we see the imp who concocted the fiendish plot—Satan had made him "commander in chief / Of his forces in Dixie"—speak to the rest of the minions and to Satan, boasting of the success of his plan. The imp professes responsibility for every incident that brought the nation closer to civil war, even the 1860 split in the Democratic Party and the election of Abraham Lincoln, which provided the pretext for the South "to knock Freedom over, the Union divide, / And the triumph of Might over Right decide." The imp deserves credit for "each crushing Union disaster"; loyal soldiers killed; "imprisoned martyrs ... in Richmond's loathsome dens"; the Copperheads; the New York City draft riots; even "the generalship of 'Little Mac!'" As for "Abe Lincoln's Proclamation, / Decreeing the slaves' emancipation," the imp scoffs at what he categorizes as "such impotent acts."[71]

But not all was lost. The narrator describes the arrival on this scene of "a Heaven-commissioned seeress"—the goddess Columbia—carrying in her right hand the "Flag of liberty," inscribed with the names of "victories won" and those "that should be yet won." Satan and his minions, now cowering at the threat to their plans, are treated to a vision of the Union victory that was to come, especially with the freeing of the slaves. Through this intervention, goodness prevails, triumphing over Satan's evil plans. Lloyd included a Postscript to his narrative, no doubt written days (or even hours) after the surrender of Robert E. Lee, praising the Union victory and the army that defeated the Confederacy; everyone who sacrificed for and contributed to the war effort; and, of course, "Father Abraham." Finally, "to God," Lloyd gives "high praise for the victory / That *indeed* makes Columbia the 'Land of the Free!'" At some point shortly after writing these words, Lloyd learned of the assassination of Abraham Lincoln. Rather than changing what he had already written, he prepared another postscript mourning the loss of the president.[72]

Unfortunately for Lloyd, *The Devil in Dixie* sold poorly, probably a result of bad timing. By the time it hit the market, the war was already over, deflating the book's propaganda appeal and its ultimate optimistic message. The book's likely audience was more concerned with putting the nation back together rather than explaining what had torn it apart. However, Lloyd's verse could make an interesting basis for an animated treatment of the war. I envision something that looks like a cross between the 1940s Warner Brothers studio style of politically incorrect cartooning and contemporary Japanese anime: "Merry Melodies" meets Manga.

By the way, Warner Brothers did produce three Civil War related cartoons. In 1940 the studio released *Confederate Honey* featuring Porky Pig as Ned Cutler, who despite other suitors was the object of Miss Crimson O'Hairoil's affection. (The cartoon appeared just a year after *Gone with the Wind* hit the silver screen.) O'Hairoil's father owns a Kentucky plantation with many slaves, depicted in a stereotypical Jim Crow style. Before Ned can ask Crimson that all important question, the Civil War breaks out, and our hero goes off to fight with the Confederate army while Crimson awaits his return. In 1953's *Southern Fried Rabbit* Bugs Bunny heads to Alabama for a bumper carrot crop. As soon as he crosses the Mason-Dixon line, he is confronted by Yosemite Sam, dressed as a Confederate officer with orders from General Lee to stop any Yankees from crossing the line. Bugs tells Sam, "Why, the War Between the States ended almost ninety years ago," but that does not matter to Sam, who calls Bugs a "fur-bearing carpetbagger." Bugs impersonates a slave begging not to be whipped (another Jim Crow caricature), Abraham Lincoln, General Brickwall Jackson, and a Southern belle named Scarlett. He also asks, "I wonder why they put the South so far south," a question Tweety Bird also queries in 1961's *Rebel Without Claws*. Tweety plays a Confederate carrier pigeon tasked with getting a message to headquarters. Sylvester the Cat plays a Yankee "messenger destroyer." "I tawt I taw a damn Yankee tat," Tweety announces. Eventually Sylvester captures Tweety, but in the end, the Yankee firing squad ordered to shoot the bird shoots the cat. It's a good thing that Sylvester has nine lives, or it would be "That's All Folks!"[73]

Meanwhile, folks who cannot get enough of these types of extended poems can also read Samuel Silsbee's *D.D.D.: Or Death, the Devil, and the Doctor, on the War*, published in 1862. A doctor from Cincinnati, Silsbee wrote the poem from the perspective of the doctor, presumably him, and used it to critique corruption in the government, especially in war contracts; the inaction of the Army of the Potomac; political ineptitude; rebellious Southerners; disloyal Northerners; and the impact of disease on the soldiers. But Silsbee also used his publication as a delivery system for three love poems he wrote in honor of Union general and the Republican Party's first presidential candidate John C. Frémont. Frémont had come under scrutiny for his management of affairs while in control of Missouri in 1861 and the proclamation he issued unilaterally freeing Missouri's slaves, which prompted the president to relieve the general of his command. In fact, Silsbee dedicated the entire volume to Frémont, describing him as "The man whose timely words, and noble deeds, have struck a genial chord in the hearts of true lovers of Freedom." And of the Pathfinder and his critics, Silsbee remarks, "being himself incapable of the practices of the political Jackals who pursue him, their malice may, for a time, retard his progress and hinder his usefulness, but can not displace him in the love and admiration of all who appreciate the faithful student, ardent explorer, distinguished scholar, glorious leader, and model gentleman."[74] It is unknown if Frémont reciprocated.

Supporters of the Confederacy also had their own extended comical verses. In 1863, Alabama politician, poet, and Confederate congressman William Russell Smith published *The Royal Ape: A Dramatic Poem* in the form of a closet drama, a play meant to be read out loud by a person or group rather than performed on a stage. Daniel Fish, who compiled and published "A Bibliographic Account of Books and Pamphlets relating to Abraham Lincoln" in 1900, further described Smith's effort as "a very unpleasant display of one phase of Confederate sentiment."[75]

The play centers on the hours before, during, and just after the Battle of Bull Run, and its title character, of course, is Abraham Lincoln. What distinguishes this long poetic treatment from its pro–Union counterparts is its bawdiness. The president is portrayed as a bumbling buffoon and despot who may have been insane. Yet particularly receiving Smith's ridicule is Lincoln's son Robert, who was a mere seventeen years old when Bull Run took place. Early in the text, Smith describes Robert's romantic connections with two of the maids, or "inmates of the White House." Robert first makes plans for a romantic tryst with one maid, "Kitty," at midnight, and then the other, "Kate," an hour later. Being the son of the president has its perks. Later, Robert deliberates whether to go watch the battle as it unfolds along Bull Run Creek or to stay with Kitty *and* Kate. He chooses the latter.[76]

Robert is not the only one looking for a little action. The elder Lincoln hits on Kate early in the play, asking her "could you love me" after feeding her a cringe-inducing line worthy of a college sophomore at a fraternity party: "Kate, your eyes are very blue! / And blue eyes always pierce me through and through! / I had a dream of you!" Kate tactfully rebuffs his overture but then regrets at least not stringing the president along for some personal gain:

> Ah! Silly Kate, you've made a sad mistake;
> You should have push'd your bark upon that lake!
> He was in good times to make vows and pledges;
> His watery lips ran over the edges;
> His eyes were lit with torches of desire,
> And he work'd his blood up into fire!
> A little teazing would have saved, perhaps,
> This royal engine from complete collapse.

Watery lips? Torches of desire? Working blood up? A royal engine? A collapsing one at that. I'm surprised there is no train going into a tunnel. After learning of the defeat at Bull Run, the president laments, "I that was sev'n feet high, am suddenly / Shrunk into seven inches." If that is not emasculating enough, Smith has young Robert dressing in Kate's and Kitty's clothes so that he can escape Washington disguised as a woman in the face of a feared rebel invasion.[77]

No wonder the Confederate press responded so harshly to Smith's work. Even Smith's other message, that Lincoln was an evil tyrant, could not improve the South's reaction to the play. To be sure, during the war there was a market for dirty material, available through mail order catalogues. The demand for pornography in image and print form thrived, especially among soldiers, causing great concern among political, military, and civic leaders. Even then, while naughty stories in print sold well during the Civil War, naughty stories in print about the war appear to be nonexistent, with the exception of *The Royal Ape*. Near the end of the war, Congress passed a law making it illegal to ship pornographic material through the U.S. mail, and soon after the war, U.S. Postal Inspector Anthony Comstock launched his famous anti-pornography campaign.[78] While the Gilded Age witnessed an outpouring of Civil War-related publications, both fiction and nonfiction, none appear to be very salacious, despite titles like *Beauty and Booty* and *Rebel Private: Front and Rear*.[79]

A century later, just in time for the centennial of the war, things heated up with the publication of James Kendrick's *She Wouldn't Surrender*, a romance novel billed as the story of "The Wild Days and Nights of Belle Boyd—The Notorious Confederate Spy." In the book's opening scene, the seventeen-year-old main character, naked, sneaks up on a Union sentry guarding a bridge she must cross to get a message to the Confederates. "Yankee man!" she calls out, as she gets close to the soldier: "The soldier turned, bringing his rifle down from his shoulder—how his eyes bulged as he saw her leap naked for him!—and stood a long moment in frozen stupefaction. Too late he saw the rock in her hand. Too late he had stared at the jouncing breasts and quivering thighs." Today, the book would get an R-rating more for its depictions of violence against women than for its sexual content. Kendricks, a pen name for "a well known writer in the paperback field," affirms that Boyd was "as much the American patriot as Abraham Lincoln or Ulysses S. Grant."[80]

While neither Lincoln nor Grant appear in *She Wouldn't Surrender*, both can be found in *I Am Abraham* by acclaimed author of fiction and nonfiction Jerome Charyn. According to Charyn, "The novel is told entirely in Lincoln's voice, that strange mix of the vernacular and the formal tones of a man who only had a few months of learning at a 'blab school' and essentially had to teach himself." Most of the narration is quite articulate and does not evoke "the wordiness of earlier times." Still, vernacular does slip in. (Lincoln uses the word "pantaloons" an awful lot.) What also slips in is the fact that Charyn's title character is a pretty raunchy guy, especially in his young adult years. When our narrator discusses sex, it's not in "formal tones" or even "the vernacular," but rather in the voice of a horny middle-school-aged boy, one who has not had sex education yet. Of his first dance with future wife Mary Todd, our storyteller depicts, ahem, the excitable state in which he found himself. The dance is even more thrilling for Lincoln than when Ann Rutledge let him get to second base. As for his wedding night, Abraham spares no detail, but I'll spare you the details. Once president, our narrator leaves the impression that Lincoln's sexual dalliances were scarcer than a Union victory in the

Eastern Theater prior to Gettysburg. By that point in the book, most readers will be happy for it to be all quiet on the Potomac.[81]

Lincoln is also the focus of an X-rated (NC-17-rated?) short story titled *Abraham Lincoln Spanked Me: Punished by the President*, in which a young twenty-first-century woman unsatisfied by the men she meets goes back in time and, well, you get the picture from the title. Who knew Lincoln was into S and M? Then there is Rayburn Sharp's *From the Case Files of Abraham Lincoln's Penis, Private Eye, Part 1*. The title character is in fact Lincoln's penis, or as he, or it, tells us, Lincoln's "holy poker ... trouser serpent ... glister pipe ... battering piece," sounding an awful lot like an old George Carlin routine. Known as the Colonel, the penis explains that it is "an anatomical anomaly ... an extra-human occurrence existing separately from Mr. Lincoln and yet linked to him inextricably." The penis does the "dirty work" for Lincoln, including the detective work for the law firm, such as the case of marital infidelity depicted in the story. And the penis also has sex for the president. Unlike the explicit sex scene witnessed by the penis in his detective work and described in detail, the Colonel's sexual prowess is left to the reader's imagination, for which I am grateful because I had enough of Lincoln's penis in *Abraham Lincoln Spanked Me!* I was also relieved to learn that the provocatively-titled 1979 mystery novel *The Lincoln Diddle* was not about Lincoln diddling.[82]

Enough naughty bits. *The Royal Ape* was not the only pro–Confederate closet drama to appear during the war. Shortly after the fighting began, Stephen Franks Miller, a journalist and author from Georgia, penned a brief script he called *Ahab Lincoln: A Tragedy of the Potomac*, which may have been better remembered for its uncanny predictions had it not been for the fact that Lincoln never claimed responsibility for causing the war, nor expressed his regret for not letting the Confederacy secede in peace, nor committed suicide in anguish over the above two central plot issues. And the inclusion of a scene in which "Ahab" pursues a behemoth white whale would also have livened up the story, but alas, there is none. There are a few more of these closet dramas produced by pro–Confederate authors, all of which in one way or another attack Abraham Lincoln and predict a Southern victory. Scholars of the theater describe them as "Yankee Goon dramas."[83] Perhaps these long poems, both Northern and Southern, should remain tucked away in a closet somewhere.

Another 1863 publication called *Abram, A Military Poem* came from the pen of a Confederate calling himself "A. Young Rebelle, Esq., of the Army." Thus far I have been unable to identify Mr. Rebelle's true identity, but according to *The Southern Literary Messenger*, he was a Texan and a member of General John Bell Hood's brigade in the Army of Northern Virginia. While not a closet drama, the poem is part Yankee Goon drama, depicting Lincoln as the scheming amalgamationist and a litany of Union generals as inept cowards, and part hymn of praise to the Confederate army and its soldiers, especially to General Thomas "Stonewall" Jackson. Notable for its unmitigated optimism—it was written before the death of Jackson and the rebel defeats at Gettysburg and Vicksburg—the work predicts that the war would soon end in Confederate triumph and that Jefferson Davis would personally hang Abraham Lincoln. What makes the publication somewhat noteworthy is not the poetry, but rather the book's preface, found in the back of the slim edition rather than in the front. Mr. Rebelle explains, "A distinguished author once wrote a book, and either to save labor, or for some other cause, upon which history is silent, omitted all punctuations. To make up for this deficiency, however, he submitted an *addenda*, made of commas, colons, semi-colons, dashes, apostrophes, asterisks, &c., &c., and left it to his readers to spice their literary dish to the taste." Here, Mr. Rebelle refers to an 1802 book put forth by Timothy Dexter and titled *A Pickle for the Knowing Ones, or Plain Truth in a Homespun Dress*, in which the eccentric Massachusetts merchant Dexter vented his criticism toward politicians, the clergy, and his "nagging" wife. Rather brashly, Mr. Rebelle continues, "I submit that with this distinguished precedent before me, I have the same right to affix my Preface here without further explanation or impertinent inquiry."[84] Different, but not quite as *avant-garde* as Dexter's punctuationless prose.

Mr. Rebelle provides a description of himself, especially for the "female portion" of his readers. He pictures his early life: "The author was ... first born, owing to the precautionary measures of fond and doting parents, and directly subsequent to his birth he was educated. He was then raised and fitted for future usefulness, and set out upon his bright career." He goes on: "This unhappy war ... found him in the army," courtesy of the Confederate Conscription Law, which "drew him forth from the modest retiracy which such a genius will ever seek." And now he can be found by visiting "one of the cabins of Gen. Lee's army." Mr. Rebelle claims that he began this poetic record during the "siege of Fort Sumter," and that he wrote many of the descriptions of battles on the actual battlefields, and in at least one case with the battle raging around him. He further informs readers, "He lost an arm at Manassas, and also one at Sharpsburg."[85] Perhaps if he had been paying attention instead of writing poetry, he would still be in one piece.

Oddly, for all his praise for the Confederate cause, Mr. Rebelle seems to be a poet with a chip on his armless shoulder. He expects that certain officers mentioned or not mentioned in the poem "will take umbrage at this performance." He also fears that he may spend time in the "regimental bastile [sic] for the hours [he is] now spending in superintending [the book's] publication." "To be an author is, I know, to be traduced," Rebelle admits. "I anticipate trouble and am prepared for it," he warns, because he is "a fighting man."[86] Unclear is the amount of criticism, if any, Mr. Rebelle and his *Abram, A Military Poem* evoked, but for some reason I cannot get the image out of my mind of the Black Knight from *Monty Python and the Holy Grail* saying, "It's just a flesh wound."

Of course, the Civil War generated shorter poems, including a multitude of "occasional" verses appearing in newspapers, magazines, posters known as broadsides, easily distributed sheets of paper, and bound volumes. One notable collection of wartime poetry published shortly after the conflict's end was edited by Richard Grant White, the author of *The New Gospel of Peace*. He titled it *Poetry: Lyrical, Narrative, and Satirical of the Civil War*. White had an ambivalent opinion of the poetry produced during the war. "It is generally true that great events do not inspire great poems," he noted, perhaps explaining why so many people have been down on Civil War poetry. "The choice of a great event as the theme for a poem is unwise," he continued, "because the poet can hardly fail to fall short of the mental elevation produced by the relation of such an event in simple prose. He will find himself compelled to assume the position of a decorator rather than that of a creator; and his decorations will only call attention to their littleness and the grandeur of the reality to which they have been appended."[87] That did not stop White from putting together this collection.

White included about one hundred and sixty verses in the volume, some of them satirical, as the title suggests, and also humorous. Few portray the big picture of the war; most focus on specific people or character types involved, specific wartime events, or the results of the conflict. Refreshing is the fact that White included no contributions from Walt Whitman, Herman Melville, or Emily Dickinson. A few specimens are noteworthy, and they tend to be aimed not at the Confederates but rather the North. "The 'Peace Democracy" by the previously discussed "Charity Grimes" attacks those members of the Democratic Party who sympathized with the Confederates. The uncredited poem "Shoddy" criticizes corruption in wartime government contracts and poor workmanship in the supplies furnished to the Union army. And worthy of a few laughs are the rants that White goes off on twice in describing the popularity of the verse he calls "John Brown's Song," usually referred to as "John Brown's Body." He calls the song "nonsensical farrago." Maybe he is onto something. "John Brown's body lies a-mouldering in the grave," the opening words inform us, three times, but "His soul is marching on!" Of course, this is followed by the well-known "Glory, halle—hallelujah" chorus, according to the rendition offered by White. Then we're told, "He's gone to be a soldier in the army of the Lord." (Oh dear.) Then, "John Brown's knapsack is strapped upon his back." (In the grave?) But he's not alone: "His pet lambs will meet him on the way." (To the grave? Or into the army of the Lord?) And then, "They will hang Jeff. Davis to a tree!" (The lambs? With John Brown?) "Now, three rousing cheers for the Union!" closes the verse. Of course, there would be many other versions of this song with different lyrics, including Julia Ward Howe's.[88]

According to White, the lyrics to the John Brown song were "sung to a degraded and jiggish form of a grand and simple old air." I can only imagine what he had to say about the "Battle Hymn of the Republic." Yet White reluctantly acknowledged the tune's popularity. "No song was sung so much during the rebellion," much to his chagrin. The song "was heard everywhere in the streets; regiments marched to it, and the air had its place in the programme of every barrel-organ grinder." It even had become popular in London among the "street boys." White asserted that the origins of the lyrics were "quite unknown." In actuality, the original lyrics were produced by members of the 2nd Massachusetts Infantry, and the John Brown to which the lilt refers was not the martyred abolitionist, who would be the subject of later versions of the song, but rather a popular sergeant with the same name in the regiment.[89]

While I have tried to stay away from verse that has been known primarily in the form of song, one ditty stands out that's worth attention, and it also appears in White's volume of poetry. In 1862 the prolific song writer Henry Clay Work put forth the song titled "Kingdom Coming," although White identified it as "The Year of Jubilee." Using a form of minstrel-style African American dialect similar to that used by Charles Graham Halpine in "Sambo's Right to be Kilt," Work's lyrics tell the tale of a planter who disguises himself as a displaced or contraband slave as the Yankees approach, leaving his slaves with the run of the plantation. It begins:

> SAY, darkies hab you seen de massa,
>   Wid de muffstash on he face,
> Go 'long de road some time dis mornin'
>   like gwine to leabe de place?
> He see de smoke way up de ribber
>   Whar de lincum gun-boats lay;
> He took he hat and leff berry sudden,
>   And I 'spose he's runned away.

Of course, now the tables are turned, and the master rather than the slave is the runaway, something amusing to the slaves, as seen in the chorus: "De massa run, ha! ha! / De darky stay, ho! ho! / It mus' be now de kingdom comin', / An' de yar ob Jubilo." The slaves next poke fun at the master's girth, "six foot one way and two foot todder, / An' he weigh six hundred poun'," and the fact that he's trying to pass himself off as one of them. The slaves then "move dere tings into massa's parlor / For to keep it while he gone," and help themselves to the master's "wine and cider in de kichin" before the "Lincum sojers" arrive, and it is all "'fiscated."[90]

In the last verse, the slaves get their revenge on the plantation's overseer. They "lock him up in de smoke-house cellar, / Wid de key flung in de well." They also hide the whip that once punished them and break the handcuffs that once shackled them. Finally, the slaves blame all their shenanigans on the master: "He big an' ole enough for to know better / Dan to went an' run away." Work's song could carry different meanings for different people, which helps explain its popularity. The comic nature of the slaves taking over the plantation, presented in the stereotypical voice of African Americans commonly heard in minstrel shows, made it acceptable to racist Northerners not ready to tolerate emancipation. The message of slavery breaking down and enslaved people being freed by a combination of Union military might and their own agency could please those of abolitionist leanings, who probably did not think twice about the use of the minstrel dialect. A version of the song even became popular in the South, minus the last verse about the overseer and the whip and the handcuffs.[91]

Henry Clay Work also wrote two of my favorite Civil War songs: "Grafted into the Army," a complaint about the draft written in Irish dialect, and the much better known "Marching through Georgia," written in early 1865 and inspired by William Tecumseh Sherman's romp from Atlanta to Savannah. Ironically, while the latter song remained extremely popular among veterans of the Union army, Sherman himself was not a big fan.[92]

The vast majority of the items in White's *Poetry* was produced in the North and by Northerners. Most of it is sympathetic to Union cause, although some poems are critical and some even subversive. Several items originated in the English press, including the verse "The Run from Manassas Junction," that appeared in the publication *London Punch* and could be sung to the tune of Yankee Doodle. The lyrics make fun of the Union for its loss at the Battle of Bull Run but also suggest that the Northerners had greater ambitions than defeating the Confederacy: annexing Canada. Not a good idea, especially considering the rout the Union army suffered at the hands of the Confederates. Of course, no such plan to conquer Canada existed.[93]

A separate appendix at the book's end contains twenty-two pieces identified as "Rebel Poetry." "The secessionists fought much better than they wrote," White noted. "I have read all that I could discover of the war-poetry written by the confederate enemies of my government, and have preserved here all that in the most catholic spirit I deemed of any intrinsic merit or incidental interest." The result was fewer than two dozen verses. A few of them are worth a chortle. The poem "Call All! Call All!" provides some interesting imagery: "Whoop! the Doodles have broken loose, / Roaring round like the very deuce / Lice of Egypt, a hungry pack,— / After 'em boys, and drive 'em back." The poem, attributed to "Georgia," also pokes fun at the John Brown of the popular song, as well as Abraham Lincoln: "Old John Brown is dead and gone! / Still his spirit is marching on,—/ Lantern-jawed, and legs, my boys, / Long as an ape's from Illinois!" The poem "Flight of the Doodles" (it seems that "Doodle" was a popular poetic insult thrown at Northerners) begins with a recap of the Battle of Bull Run: "I come from old Manassas with a pocket full of fun; / I killed forty Yankees with a single-barrelled gun: / It don't make a niff-a-stifference to neither you nor I, / Big Yankee, Little Yankee, all run and die."[94]

Evidently, it did not make a niff-a-stifference to White that many of the more humorous poems he included reflected poorly on the North.

Shortly after White's volume appeared, another collection of poetry, this one specifically Southern poetry, hit the market. This anthology, titled *War Poetry of the South*, was gathered by William Gilmore Simms, a prominent Southern poet and novelist of the mid-nineteenth century. According to one literary scholar of the early twentieth century, Simms "did much to bring on" the Civil War—in 1852 he published *The Sword and the Distaff*, a response to Harriet Beecher Stowe's *Uncle Tom's Cabin*—and from the war "he suffered severe losses." Thus, after the war, "he tried in vain to make good his losses," and *War Poetry of the South* was one such attempt. Simms definitely felt he had something to prove with this compendium. "This volume," he wrote in the introduction, "constitutes a contribution to the national literature which is assumed to be not unworthy of it, and which is otherwise valuable as illustrating the degree of mental and art development which has been made, in a large section of the country, under circumstances greatly calculated to stimulate talent and provoke expression, through the higher utterances of passion and imagination." Simms had quite a chip on his shoulder. After years of being overshadowed by the literati of the North, many Southern writers fixated on proving they could match the quality of their Northern counterparts.[95]

Thus, Simms shied away from poems considered "popular," where one usually found the funny stuff, in favor of the more artsy poems. "It is believed that the numerous pieces of this volume will be found credible to the genius and culture of the Southern people, and honorable, as in accordance with their convictions," Simms clarified. "Many of these pieces are distinguished by fire, force, passion, and a free play of fancy." Fire? Force? Passion? Free play of fancy? Okay, but funny? I think not. Simms intended to prove the honor of the South; the merit of their cause; the bravery with which their soldiers fought; the virtue of the Southern people; and, of course, how terrible the South's foe was. These poems are serious, sentimental, melodramatic, even maudlin and melancholy. Missing is any self-reflection or self-critique, often the substance of satire and humor. Simms had no place for humor in this serious endeavor. Even absent is any depiction of the Northern enemies as inferior, foolish, corrupt, and/or cowardly buffoons. After all, those buffoons were the folks to whom the Southerners lost. In short, what we see in Simms's work is the emerging romanticized ideal of the "Lost Cause" myth.[96]

Simms included over two hundred poems in his collection and referred to many more that he received or came across in preparing the volume but could not include for one reason or another. His search seems quite thorough. Surprisingly, however, Simms made no mention of Richard Grant White's volume, published almost half a year before Simms completed his work.[97] Simms may have been miffed at White's characterization of Southern wartime poetry, or at White's failure to include any of Simms's poems in his anthology. And considering all of Simms's efforts to argue the greatness of the South's Civil War poetry, Simms never could agree with White that great events could never generate great poetry. Of course, Simms remained bitter about the outcome of the war itself and probably never got over it before his death in 1870.[98]

Thomas C. De Leon published another volume of Confederate poetry a few months before Simms' work appeared. Called *South Songs: From the Lays of Later Days*, it had similar content and tone. De Leon had served in the Confederate army during the war and then edited the *Mobile Register*. After losing his sight, he became known as "the Blind Lauriat of the Lost Cause." Anyone searching for humorous Southern poetry is more apt to find it in Frank Moore's *Rebel Rhymes and Rhapsodies*, which appeared in the North in 1864. Better known for his compilation and publication of wartime material under the title *The Rebellion Record* in twelve volumes, Moore also produced a companion book of Union poetry titled *Songs of the Soldiers*, which has its share of comical verses.[99]

In my search for humorous and satirical Civil War poetry, I also consulted several indexes of Southern wartime poetry titles, which contained the first two lines of each poem. Rest assured, there is a body of funny rebel poetry out there for interested readers, as there is of Union poetry. But this section has gone on far too long already. I will note, though, that I did not find a single wartime poem that begins with the phrase "There was a young man from Nantucket." However, in 2014 a volume of poems titled *Civil War Limericks* by Charles H. Hayes did appear. Hayes presents ninety-six rhymes, each centered on a Civil War-related figure, most well-known and some obscure. The limericks are usually entertaining, but the explanatory notes that accompany them, while well-crafted and usually accurate, are decidedly neo-Confederate in leanings. One must admit that Union failures early in the war gave Hayes plenty of fodder to poke fun at, and he did.[100]

Two Fremantles, a Mule, and the Civil Wargasm

In the spring of 1863, Lieutenant Colonel Arthur Fremantle, a member of the Coldstream Guards, decided to take a leave of absence to see the war for himself. Curious about the gallantry of the Confederate army that he had been reading about in newspaper dispatches from the United States, the British officer decided to tour the South, engaging in a three-and-a half month odyssey that carried him through nine of the seceded states and reached its zenith in Pennsylvania at the Battle of Gettysburg. Upon his return to England, he prepared and published the diary he kept under the title *Three Months in the Southern States: April-June 1863*. According to historian Gary Gallagher, the book "eventually earned a reputation as one of the best personal accounts of the war." He added, "Few books in all the vast literature on the Civil War have proved to be more durable, fewer still have supplied historians and other students with more drama and insight."[101]

Fremantle began his Forrest Gump–like adventure south of the border. He arrived by ship in Mexico to avoid the Federal navy's blockade of the rebel states and crossed the Rio Grande into Texas. He then took nearly a month to traverse the Lone Star State, primarily by stagecoach and mule wagon. Along the way he met many colorful people. Of the Texans he wrote: "In spite of their peculiar habits of hanging, shooting, &c., which seemed to be natural to people living in the wild, thinly-populated country, there was much to like in my fellow-travellers [sic]." One of those he chanced to meet was Sam Houston, the onetime Tennessee U.S. representative and governor before turning hero of the Texas war for independence and the Republic of Texas's first president, followed by stints as a Texas U.S. senator and governor. Houston's opposition to secession and joining the Confederacy made the one-time hero a pariah in the republic turned state that he helped to create. That was probably why Fremantle had a negative opinion of him, calling him "egotistical and vain, and much disappointed at having to subside from his former grandeur" and criticizing him for "blowing his nose with his fingers."[102]

Eventually, Fremantle made his way into Louisiana and quickly crossed that much smaller state to reach the Mississippi River. Ulysses S. Grant's plan to capture Vicksburg, Mississippi, thwarted his plan to visit that river town, so with his agenda upended, Fremantle made his way to the Joseph Johnston's idle Confederate army east of Grant's campaign before heading for Tennessee. There he chanced upon Confederate General Braxton Bragg and the Copperhead congressman Clement Vallandigham, who had been banished to the South by the Union army for his disloyalty. He then went to Atlanta by train, on which he observed "a goodish-looking woman" whom he was told had "served as a private soldier in the battles of Perryville and Murfreesborough [sic]." According to one source, the woman may have been the famous, or infamous, Loreta Janeta Velazquez, alias Lt. Harry Buford, who according to the book she published after the war, served at various times as a soldier in male disguise as well as a spy for the Confederates.[103]

In Charleston, South Carolina, Fremantle visited Ft. Sumter; met General Pierre Gustave Tutant Beauregard; then learned of a new invention being crafted in the city, a submarine, of which a naval captain he met told him they expect "great results." On to Richmond, and what trip to the Confederate capital would be complete without meeting President Jefferson Davis? From there, our observer trekked to the Shenandoah Valley, joining the Army of Northern Virginia near the Maryland border just in time to push into Pennsylvania. Fremantle enjoyed the hospitality of General James Longstreet. He met many of the staff officers and generals of Lee's army, some who would die within days, and finally the famed Confederate hero himself. Quite infatuated with Lee, Fremantle described the general as "the handsomest man of his age" that he had ever seen. "He is fifty-six years old, tall, broad-shouldered, very well made, well set up—a thorough soldier in appearance; and his manners are most courteous and full of dignity."[104] Fremantle accompanied Lee's men into Pennsylvania, where before long he witnessed at least part of the largest battle ever fought on the North American continent.

As Lee's Confederates negotiated their way back through Maryland, Fremantle parted company with them so that he could make his way to New York City and gain passage on an England-bound ship before his leave ran out. In the process he was captured by Union soldiers and held as a spy. Released from custody, he arrived in New York, staying long enough to witness the city's infamous draft riots of the summer of 1863.

While entertaining and informative, Arthur Fremont's diary also has its share of humor. A few passages stand out, particularly in light of twenty-first-century values. In the "How Many People Can You Insult in One Passage?" category, Fremantle wrote while in Mexico:

> Some of the women are rather good-looking, but they plaster their heads with grease, and paint their faces too much.... When I went to the cathedral [it was Good Friday], I found it crammed with kneeling women; an effigy of our

Savior was being taken down from the cross and put into a golden coffin, the priest haranguing all the time about His sufferings, and all the women howling most dismally as if they were being beaten.

Matamoras is now infested with Jews, whose industry spoils the trade of the established merchants, to the great rage of the latter.[105]

Mexicans, women, Catholics, and Jews all in a blurb that would fit in a Tweet.

Later, Fremantle related a story he heard about Confederate General William J. Hardee, a reputed womanizer. Hardee, our observer explained,

is a widower, and has the character of being a great admirer of the fair sex. During the Kentucky campaign last year, he was in the habit of availing himself of the privilege of his rank and years, and insisted upon kissing the wives and daughters of all the Kentuckian farmers…. On one occasion, General Hardee had conferred the 'accolade' upon a very pretty Kentuckian, to their mutual satisfaction, when, to his intense disgust, the proprietor produced two very ugly old females, saying 'Now, then, general, if you kiss any you must kiss them all around,' which the discomfited general was forced to do, to the great amusement of his officers.[106]

One wonders how long General Hardee would have fared in the "Me Too" movement era. Hardee's fate here probably served as a greater deterrent to future liberties taken on vulnerable women than any amount of public shaming.

Finally, on a train traveling between Mississippi and Alabama, Fremantle witnessed some "negro nurses" tending some unruly children, "who were terrified into good behavior by threats … of being given to the Yankees."[107] What the children thought the Yankees would do with them is unspoken, but clearly, the children, presumably white, perceived the Yanks as a boogie man of sorts who would do terrible things to them.

While one might find these stories humorous in an anachronistic sort of way, Fremantle's experience on the third day of the Battle of Gettysburg made me laugh out loud. The lieutenant colonel wanted to see as much action as possible, and he did so on the battle's first two days. On the third day, knowing that there would be an advance on the center of the Union line under the direction of General Longstreet—Pickett's Charge—Fremantle maneuvered his way towards the center, dodging Union cannon fire and stray minié balls, making and negotiating heavily wooded areas. When he finally reached Longstreet, he announced, "I wouldn't have missed this for any thing."[108] Except, HE MISSED IT! By the time Fremont reached Longstreet and the field of battle, the Confederate advance had pressed across a mile of open field, reached the Union defenses under heavy fire, engaged in hand-to-hand combat, and been repulsed. Instead of seeing all the glory of what Fremantle believed would be a Confederate victory on that fateful afternoon, all that he saw was the Confederate retreat. Unfazed by the rebels' failure to break through the Union line and the withdrawal from Pennsylvania that transpired soon thereafter, Fremantle remained confident that the Confederate army would prevail and that the Confederate States of America soon would enjoy its independence.

One hundred-and-thirty-eight years after Arthur Fremantle made his journey across the Confederate South, his descendant, author Tom Fremantle, decided to retrace the lieutenant colonel's steps. To make the adventure more Civil War-ish, he decided to walk it, or at least what he could of it. In addition, he would be accompanied by a mule named Browny as he made his way from the Texas-Mexico border to New York City. Like his ancestor, Tom wrote about the experience, publishing his story as *The Moonshine Mule: A 2,700-Mile Walk from Mexico to Manhattan*.[109]

Tom came from a lineage of British military men yet knew very little of Lieutenant-Colonel Arthur Fremantle until he read Michael Shaara's Pulitzer Prize winning 1974 novel *The Killer Angels* about the Battle of Gettysburg. Arthur is a secondary character who is used as a sounding board for major figures like Longstreet to explain what the war is about and what victory will mean for the South. Arthur also appears in the movie version of the film, titled *Gettysburg* (1993). In it the character stands out wearing a bright red military tunic and black cap; in reality Arthur brought no such outfit with him. Having read Shaara's book, Tom turned to Arthur's *Three Months in the Southern States* and quickly became fascinated with the story. "During his rip-roaring, three month adventure," Tom wrote, "the 28-year-old soldier experienced all the rough and tumble of frontier life. He ate polecat, drank moonshine, played poker, dodged bullets, flirted with saucy belles and was arrested as a spy before finally witnessing the heroic but devastating Battle of Gettysburg."[110] Thus, Tom decided to make this quest.

Tom followed Arthur's path as well as he could, although barriers such as urban growth, private property, fences, routes where one cannot travel comfortably with a mule, and routes and rail lines that just do not exist anymore caused the need for some modification. Tom did make some detours off his main path to visit places that Arthur reached more easily via train or stage coach. In these cases, Tom left Browny behind, always in someone's capable hands, and travelled by bus or car. *The Moonshine Mule* is quite entertaining but much of it has little or nothing to do with the Civil War. Like Arthur, Tom arrived in Mexico and then crossed over the Rio Grande into Texas, where he met the owner of Browny. It also took Tom a considerable time to traverse Texas into Louisiana. Crossing over the "Father of All Waters" by bridge instead of rowboat and not having to avoid Union gunboats, he wended his way through Mississippi, then

Alabama, and on to Georgia and the Carolinas. He bypassed Arthur's visit to Tennessee, but traveled to Atlanta and Charleston before reaching Richmond. His real intent was to get to Gettysburg as quickly as possible. That is, as quickly as one can on foot with a mule in tow.

Having reached Gettysburg on March 16—he'd been travelling since September 1—Tom and Browny stayed at the home of a local journalist. The next morning, he met a Lieutenant Colonel Arthur Fremantle reenactor names Roger Hughes, decked out in an outfit similar to the one the Fremantle character wore in the movie *Gettysburg* (the red coat!). Hardly anyone would have recognized Hughes as Fremantle had the reenactor worn clothes similar to what Fremantle actually wore, but EVERYONE recognized him as the lieutenant colonel (or as he probably pronounced it, leftenant colonel) in the red coat. A native of England, Hughes resided in Orlando, Florida, but appeared at reenactments at Gettysburg and elsewhere on a regular basis. Hughes gave Tom a guided tour, covering the first two days before lunch, where Hughes arranged to be joined by a descendant of James Longstreet. After lunch it was on to the third day of the battle. They decided "to do Pickett's Charge in reverse, starting at the High Water Mark, where the most dogged Confederates had managed to briefly break through the Union lines before being repulsed for good."[111] Hughes narrated the events capably, but for Tom, I suspect it was a bit disappointing. Rather than being a sunny, sweltering day like July 3, 1863, March 17, 2002, was cloudy and cold with snow turning into sleet. Tom gave little of his own impressions in his text as Hughes narrated, and Hughes reminded Tom that Arthur had missed the attack. HE MISSED THE ATTACK!

Like Arthur, Tom made his way safely to New York City, although he did not get arrested for spying, and then back to England to write about his adventure. In *The Moonshine Mule*, some of Tom's most insightful and critical (with a splash of sarcastic humor) observations have to do with his cousin, author of "one of the best personal accounts of the war." As his journey progressed and he learned more about the American Civil War, Tom concluded that Arthur's diary was "a highly readable adventure but strongly laced with Southern propaganda." He explained, "The fact that Colonel Arthur becomes such a Confederate stooge is one of his greatest weaknesses as a diarist—especially over slavery." He elaborated, "Although clearly an observant and at times sensitive man, Arthur continues to accept lock, stock and barrel whatever the Southerners fire at him [about slavery]. Worst of all, he does not once try to see things from a slave's perspective." As for Arthur and the greatest hero of the Confederacy, Tom wrote, "At times he lapses into fawning prose, especially when he first meets noble, vice-free Robert E. Lee at Gettysburg.... Lee was undeniably a great General but this sort of adulation just makes Arthur sound like a star-struck teenager."[112]

In comparing the experiences of the two Fremantles, I'm struck by the following observation: On his journey, Arthur met many Southerners who felt deeply bitter about the Union army and the North in general, yet were certain that the Confederacy was one big win away from victory and independence. Tom, on the other hand, met many Southerners who felt deeply bitter about the Union army and the North in general, yet were certain that the Confederacy had been one "what if" away from victory and independence.

A few other humorous travelogue visits down Civil War memory lane are worth mentioning. In 2007, Andrew Ferguson published *Land of Lincoln: Adventures in Abe Lincoln's America*, investigating all things Lincoln (or at least many things Lincoln) in American Culture. In one chapter he describes the vacation he took with his wife and two adolescent children touring the "Lincoln Heritage Trail," a tourism feature created by the involved states and the petroleum industry in the 1960s to encourage travel to those destinations and the guzzling of gas. The trail, which Ferguson had followed four decades earlier on vacation with his parents, connected the various places where Lincoln once lived. By the time he made this second visit, the trail itself had not been maintained for a long time, and several of the sites along it were in a woeful state of deterioration. At least his kids, who had to be bribed to go on the trip, got to visit a few more kid-friendly and fun tourist spots along the way. Ferguson also discussed his visits to Lincoln museums, Lincoln-related national parks and historic sites, as well as Lincoln myths and hagiography, and a convention of Lincoln impersonators.[113]

Sarah Vowell also took up Lincoln as part of her book *Assassination Vacation*, covering the lives and deaths of the three nineteenth-century presidents who were assassinated and the men that killed them. Journalist and author, public radio contributor, and the voice of Violet Parr of the animated superhero family *The Incredibles*, Vowell visited locations related to the assassinations, the assassins, and the assassinated. In writing about this bit of "dark tourism," she used lively prose, razor-sharp insight, and superhuman sardonic wit.[114]

I would be remiss if I did not discuss Tony Horwitz's best-selling *Confederates in the Attic: Dispatches from the Unfinished Civil War*. A Pulitzer Prize–winning journalist and foreign correspondent, Horwitz gained a fascination for the Civil War as a child. He rekindled this interest upon returning to the United States in the 1990s after an extended absence to learn that while most Americans had limited interest and knowledge of U.S. history in general, there existed a growing attraction to the Civil War, sparked by Ken Burns' multipart documentary *The Civil War* and films like *Glory* and *Gettysburg*. The idea for his investigation of this Civil War phenomenon developed after he met a group of Civil War reenactors—or living historians—outside his Virginia home being filmed for part of a documentary on the Battle of Fredericksburg. (Evidently his street resembled what Fredericksburg looked like in the 1860s.) Self-proclaimed "hardcores," these men remained not only fixated on the war, but also on representing it authentically. Unlike the non-hardcores, or "farbs," a term about whose origin the hardcores are unsure, these men rejected anachronistic items like wrist watches, machine-made clothes, foods that would not have been available to the soldiers of the 1860s, daily hygiene practices, and so forth, at least while they were "living" history, and their living history activities were not always related to reenacting the past for others. They invited Horwitz to a two-day encampment where members of this hardcore group drilled, marched, and acted like soldiers in winter camp. And of course, they talked Civil War. The experience prompted Horwitz to explore the "places and people who kept memory of the conflict alive in the present day."[115] So Horwitz visited battlefields, museums, historic sites, libraries, and graveyards, while encountering many Civil War aficionados and groups such as the Sons of the Confederate Veterans, the United Daughters of the Confederacy, and the Ku Klux Klan.

Horwitz also introduces readers to the "Civil Wargasm." No, this is not some randy Civil War–era sexual practice. The phrase was coined by one of Horwitz's hardcore acquaintances to describe a "power tour," or pilgrimage, to several dozen Civil War battle sites carried out in a whirlwind way by car, a concession to modern living to pack as much into the trip of a week or so as possible. Horwitz goes on one of these high-speed treks, covering hundreds of miles. According to his hardcore guide, they had time for only about an hour at major battle sites and just a few minutes at minor ones. Horwitz includes a long chapter describing his "Gasm," as they called it. As the journey neared its end, Horwitz's hardcore travelling mate described the experience as "Very productive. New dimensions. Holy. Spiritual. Humorous. Educational. Maximizing time. Intense. Peaked many times."[116] Okay, maybe it was a little randy.

A few days after the Gasm, Horwitz joined some of his hardcore friends at Gettysburg, where on the anniversary of Pickett's Charge, they planned to relive the event, not as part of a reenactment but for their own pure joy. Of course, these hardcores tried to carry out the task as authentically as possible. They first situated themselves in the trees across from the center of the Union line on Cemetery Ridge, the high-water mark, emulating the Confederates who waited until their army's artillery barrage ended before making their advance. At the appropriate moment, they pushed off to assault the Yankees. "As we left the shaded woods," Horwitz explained, "the midafternoon sun felt blindingly hot and bright." Clearly the weather conditions matched more closely those of July 3, 1863, than when Tom Fremantle visited Gettysburg. Horwitz continued, "Cemetery Ridge shimmered in the distance, about a mile away across an undulating field that tilted gently upward. As we marched silently through the tall grass, I could feel the ground crunching beneath my cracked boots." So far, so good. Horwitz's "heart began thudding more from excitement than exertion." Caught up in the moment, he thought that maybe he was beginning to experience the feeling that reenactors called a "period rush."[117]

But then his concentration was broken, but not by the burst of a cannon shell or a minié ball whizzing past his head or a chorus of rebel yells breaking out. "I heard whirrs and clicks just off to our left. A skirmish line of tourists had formed about fifty yards off, aiming cameras and binoculars at us. Several others approached from our right flank." Then the tourists engaged the rebel reenactors. Horwitz described the exchange: "Are you guys reactors?" asked one. The questions kept coming. "Which one of you's Pickett?" "You gonna win it for us this time?" When one of the men pointed out that "the Tourists of Northern Virginia are close on our rear," the advancing combatants picked up their pace, eventually making their way to the top of the ridge. At first Horwitz felt uncomfortable with all the attention they had attracted, but then he reconsidered: "By charging across the landscape in our rebel uniforms, we'd given a flesh-and-blood boost to the imagination [of the observers], a way into the battle that the modern landscape didn't easily provide."[118] He felt that their charge and interaction with the tourists gave the latter a better sense of what happened on that day in 1863. If only Arthur Fremantle could have seen Horwitz and the hardcores (great name for a band) reenact the charge that he missed in 1863.

Horwitz related one more story worth retelling. While visiting a Vicksburg museum, he saw an exhibit that included a minié ball and a picture of a Civil War–era Vicksburg doctor. The sign with the exhibit read:

> During the battle of Raymond, Miss., in 1863 a minié ball reportedly passed through the reproductive organs of a young rebel soldier and a few seconds later penetrated a young lady who was standing on the porch of her nearby home. The story was written later by Dr. Le Grand G. Capers of Vicksburg for the American Medical Weekly. Capers claimed that he tended their wounds, that the girl became pregnant from the fertile minié ball, that he delivered the baby, introduced her to the soldier, that the two were married and had two more children by the conventional method.

Horwitz found the tale of an immaculate minié ball conception laughable, as did Tom Fremantle, who also heard the story during his journey. The account did in fact appear in the professional publication *American Medical Weekly* in 1874, written by Capers, a legitimate doctor from Vicksburg. According to the article, this "Miraculous Bullet" not only passed through the soldier's genitals and then penetrated the reproductive organs of the young lass (who insisted she was a virgin), it eventually lodged itself in the scrotum of the baby, a boy. Capers, it turns out, wrote the whopper as a spoof of the many exaggerated tales of valor, glory, and in some cases medical heroics appearing in the postwar period. He meant for it to be published anonymously, but the journal's editor recognized his handwriting and gave him the by-line.[119]

In a subsequent issue, the editor revealed that Capers' article was a hoax. Nevertheless, in 1959 a doctor argued in a respectable OB-GYN journal that a pregnancy could have occurred in this way, and in 1971 the popular magazine *American Heritage* published an article telling of a similar event, with a different location and cast of characters but the same conception.[120] Whatever the case, the story lives on in the Vicksburg museum and in Civil War memory. One last point: if it is true that a young woman did become pregnant about the time of the Battle of Raymond in Mississippi, is it a coincidence that Lieutenant Colonel Arthur Fremantle was passing through that neck of the woods right at that time?

This Book Is Brought to You by the Committee to Elect George McClellan

Several historians have observed that upon returning from the war, Civil War soldiers proved reluctant to discuss their experience in word or print. The soldiers, it seemed, wanted to put behind them the memories of battle, of the harshness of military life, and return to their peacetime pursuits. Besides, soldiers felt, civilians and family members who had not experienced war would never understand a realistic portrayal of what the men in uniform knew first hand. Thus, when it came to their wartime involvement, the former soldiers entered into what historian Gerald Linderman has characterized as a hibernation of sorts.[121] Perhaps the soldiers' reticence helped to prompt Walt Whitman's lament about the "real war."

This assessment has been subject to debate; in fact, some former soldiers did not wait for the guns to fall silent. One was Ashbel Fairchild Hill. A native of Fayette County, Pennsylvania, at nineteen years old Hill enlisted in the 8th Pennsylvania Reserves, later called the 37th Pennsylvania Infantry. As part of the force that would become the Army of the Potomac, Hill gained promotion to sergeant and participated in most of the major engagements and campaigns in or near northern Virginia until he received a wound during the Battle of Antietam that would necessitate the amputation of his left leg. Sufficiently recovered but no longer able to serve, Hill received a discharge from the army in December 1862.[122]

Prior to the war, Hill had shown a talent for writing, having an amusing poem called "The Watermelon Riot"—based on an actual incident—published in a local newspaper.[123] Once back in civilian life, Hill returned to the pen to sustain himself. His first effort would be an autobiographical account of his military service titled *Our Boys: The Personal Experiences of a Soldier in the Army of the Potomac*, which appeared in 1864.[124] Detailed, lucid, candid, realistic, not overly sentimentalized, and unfortunately at times extremely racist, the tome covers from Hill's enlistment through his wounding, roughly about a year and a half. Hill wrote with a style at times reminiscent of several well-known later satirical fictional accounts of war such as Joseph Heller's *Catch-22* and Richard Hooker's *MASH: A Novel About Three Army Doctors* (upon which the 1970 movie and subsequent TV show were based).

Through Hill we meet distinctive and eccentric characters—not fictional but real, mind you—such as Dave Winder the habitual liar; Major Clark the chronic drunkard; a young, "saucy and impudent" stuttering brawler named Jim Hare; the slow-moving Jim Troth; "the clown" James Gaskill, who liked to frighten people with his pet black snake; Heinrich Rouschenschwacker, the German of Hill's company who nearly came to blows with a pine tree that had the misfortune of having Heinrich run into it in the dark; and more. We learn that Hill had little tolerance for incompetence, hypocrisy, and "idiots." He also harbored a healthy lack of respect for military authority. Hill related stories about regularly disobeying regulations: going AWOL; helping himself to local farmers' produce against orders; stealing an officer's rowboat for his own pleasure cruise. And the list goes on. How much of his account is true, or at least not suffering from embellishment, is hard to tell, but at least the stories are often funny, making the volume an enjoyable read. Plus, Hill's narrative concerning his unit's combat actions gives every appearance of being accurate, enough so that a recent history of his regiment cites Hill heavily.[125]

None of Hill's contempt for military rules interfered with his loyalty to the Union, however, and in that respect, *Our Boys* serves as pro–Union propaganda. Nevertheless, Hill embedded in his book a propaganda of a different sort, one that comes across loud and strong from the work's dedication through to its last pages: a defense and vindication of his former commanding officer and 1864 presidential candidate, George B. McClellan. "As a Mark of Respect and Esteem, and as an acknowledgment of his manly qualities and soldierly bearing," Hill professed at the book's outset, "I dedicate this work to General George B. McClellan, our loved and honored commander, who has led the Army of the Potomac in battle on many a bloody field."[126] Of course, by the time Hill penned these words of praise, "Little Mac" had long since been removed from command of the Army of the Potomac, and although still a commissioned U.S. Army officer, he appeared to be the odds-on favorite for the Democratic Party's nomination to run against Abraham Lincoln in the upcoming election. Hill no doubt knew this, and while he may have been compelled to write this memoir for a number of reasons, glorifying his former leader definitely was on his agenda.

Hill took many opportunities to describe the general in gushing terms that would resonate with the typical mid-nineteenth-century American readers. When he and his comrades had their first encounter with McClellan after he gained command of the main Union forces in and around Washington, Hill explained, "We expected to see a man of stern, hard features, wearing a look of conscious importance. But instead of anything like this, we saw just the pleasantest countenance I ever beheld. Nothing of arrogance was written there! Nothing of pomp or show! He was the very *beau ideal* of, 'A nobleman of Nature's own.'" Thus smitten, Hill went on, "We at once learned to love, were indeed irresistibly drawn toward him." A deconstructionist scholar would have a field day with the homoerotic overtones of Hill's prose. Manly, faithful, able, and patriotic were terms Hill often used to depict "the noble, generous, brave, true-hearted McCLELLAN." "The very mention of his name was sufficient to inspire us with a ready desire to meet the enemy," he proclaimed in describing the events on the eve of the Battle of Antietam, "for when McCLELLAN was with us we knew that all would be well." The next day Hill was shot in the hip, the wound that would lead to the amputation of his leg.[127]

Losing a limb did not sour Hill's opinion of McClellan. The general could do no wrong. Hill described his first entry into battle in December 1861, nearly five months after McClellan took command. In a minor engagement near the town of Drainesville, Virginia, Hill's regiment "arrived upon the scene just in time to see the rebels disappear down Centreville road." He added, "This was the last battle fought in 1861; and it was the first victory our arms had achieved for some time." Hill probably would have disagreed with President Lincoln that Mac's reluctance to engage the enemy in a serious way, despite the president's urging, probably had much to do with the lack of victories through 1861. Then, Hill foreshadowed, "from that time forth, the rebels met with nothing but defeats, until late the following summer, when the tide of victory was again reversed, in consequence of a change of commanders." Here, Hill referred to the disastrous sequel to the war's first big battle, the Second Battle of Bull Run, where Union forces fought and lost under the command of General John Pope while McClellan sat in the time out corner.[128]

Lincoln, on the other hand, would have disagreed with Hill's assessment that the Army of the Potomac had racked up a string of victories under McClellan prior to Second Bull Run. True, McClellan orchestrated the successful, if excruciatingly slow, advance on Richmond at the outset of the Peninsula Campaign, yet once reaching the outskirts of the Confederate capitol, his army suffered a series of reverses—the Seven Days' Battles—in which Hill participated. In this case, however, Hill described his own regiment doing the skedaddling, all the way to Harrison's Landing, where McClellan and his army settled in for a rest. Hill inaccurately depicted the boys in blue being greatly outnumbered at the gates of Richmond, at least two to one and in one assessment even three to one, similar to the excuses McClellan used to explain his failure to take Richmond. According to Hill, McClellan informed the troops, "You have been attacked at your position in front of Richmond by far superior numbers; and, there being no hope of reinforcements, you have succeeded in changing your base of operations by a flank movement." What Mac termed "changing your base of operations by a flank movement," others might label heeding the call to "Run Away! Run Away!" Then, as Hill recalled, McClellan asserted, "You have repulsed the enemy in every encounter, always holding the field at night." Neither McClellan nor Hill explained why with all that attacking and repulsing and holding the field and changing base, Richmond then was safer than it had been just two weeks earlier.[129]

One would have been hard pressed to find a more vigorous defender of Little Mac or a critic of his critics than Ashbel Hill. "There *are* many who have never seen him," Hill wrote after describing his first impression of the general's appearance, "many who have never been within hearing of the hostile cannon, who take great pleasure in censuring him, and in condemning his every action! But why speak of them?" After all, Hill later insisted of Little Mac, "Who could doubt *him*? None! No one doubts him even now." Except for the people that doubted him. McClellan "has many enemies who say they doubt him—doubt his ability—his loyalty." So according to Hill, no one doubted the Young Napoleon, except of course for the people who doubted him, about whom Hill chose not to discuss, except, of course, when he chose to discuss them. Who were these enemies of McClellan? "Snarling politicians AT HOME," Hill revealed. Any enemy of the general was an "inveterate civilian," definitely not a soldier. Hill attacked the Committee on the Conduct of the War, whose members slandered his "loved commander ... the noble, generous, brave, true-hearted McClellan!" He also castigated "army contractors ... who, as a matter of course, will be in favor of any measure that will prolong the war, and dead opposed to any man who is likely to end it soon."¹³⁰ Evidently the contractors would have preferred a general who kept his troops in camp and put them through countless drills while also resting them up for some future but unspecified advance on the enemy and Richmond instead of McClellan's strategy of.... Oh, that *was* McClellan's strategy.

Hill made no direct mention of the election of 1864 or Little Mac's presidential bid in the book. Surprisingly, in his last chapter, a rundown of the status of various people encountered in the book as of the time of the work's writing, Hill was silent on McClellan. Hill certainly would have been aware of the impending electoral contest, and that Little Mac was the favorite for the Democratic nomination. Perhaps he decided to abstain from giving an overt endorsement and let his depiction of McClellan speak for itself. To his credit, Hill did not use the book as a vehicle to tarnish the president. Lincoln made a brief appearance in the text, reviewing the troops with McClellan; this was McClellan's first review and the first time his troops would lay eyes on him. Hill's initial impressions of the general are described above. As for the commander-in-chief, Hill had nothing to relate, except that when the review was completed, the soldiers gave "three loud and long cheers" for the president. Then three cheers went up for their new commanding officer: "The cheers that our regiment sent forth were wild and stirring indeed. Three times three cheers rang out; nor did we stop at that." In a scene reminiscent of the one portrayed by Hawthorne's Peaceable Man, Hill described, "We continued to shout and yell till our lungs were exhausted, and our voices subsided and died away like the sound of many waters. Thus early we began to love our general." If Hill is to be believed, Little Mac definitely won this popularity contest. After that scene, President Lincoln is noticeably absent from the narrative. Of course, McClellan is the butt of one of the funniest stories attributed to Lincoln; when frustrated with what Lincoln referred to as the general's "case of the slows," the president allegedly said to Little Mac something to the effect of "If you are not using the army, may I borrow it?"¹³¹

Hill also made no mention of slavery as a cause of the war or emancipation as a result. However, it is clear that Hill had little empathy for African Americans, enslaved or otherwise. Hill regularly used epithets like "sable Sambo" and "ignorant darkey" in reference to African Americans and he generally saw them as people to be mistreated, humiliated, and abused to generate a laugh or two from him and his comrades. Hill's animosity toward African Americans continued to show in a book he published after the war, an autobiographical, or semi-autobiographical, work titled *John Smith's Funny Adventure on a Crutch, or the Remarkable Peregrinations of a One-Legged Soldier after the War*.¹³² Hill used the generic "John Smith" name for his protagonist and never admitted to being the inspiration for the stories told, but the tales he weaves parallels his own biography in numerous ways, starting with Smith losing a leg at Antietam.

The book begins with a description of one particular rifle shot fired during that bloody engagement, the one that lodged a one-ounce lead ball in John Smith's hip. "That rifle," the narrator acknowledged, was "evidently fired by some one whom I would have shot first, if I had a good chance—and therefore I couldn't blame him much for shooting me." Having made his peace with the man who shot him, Smith (or Hill) reasoned, "that if the man who had fired the rifle—allowing him to have been one hundred yards distant, and the barrel of the piece to have been four feet long—had moved the muzzle one-hundredth part of an inch to the right, I should have been missed; if he had elevated it about the same distance I should have been *missing*. My next thought was that whereas my antagonist had discharged his rifle, I must request the government to discharge *me*."[133] Like Hill himself, his Smith character had a healthy disrespect for authority, military and otherwise, and refused to suffer fools, preferring to make them suffer. Yet while *John Smith's Funny Adventure* starts out rather humorously, despite its racism, the book becomes tiresome about half way through. In fact, I saw this as more proof that *Funny Adventures* was autobiographical, as no accomplished author would choose to be so dull when he or she had the liberty of making things up. I suspect that Hill himself lost interest in writing the book and completed it only because he had an obligation to the John E. Potter publishing company, which produced his first two books.

As well as harboring no grudge against the man who shot him, Hill through John Smith revealed no malice against the South, no anger for secession or the rebellion, no condemnation of the defeated Confederacy. He also excluded from the book any discussion of the end of the war or the assassination of President Lincoln. Instead, Hill reflected a heavy nostalgia for the time he spent with his fellow Pennsylvania boys who served as the subject for his first book. As for *Our Boys*, despite its undue glorification of George McClellan and its racism, Hill's memoir is entertaining. Unfortunately, if Hill indeed did intend to sway voters to support his idol, he failed. McClellan lost the election, 212 electoral votes to 21. Lincoln took fifty-five percent of the popular vote, and among soldiers voting, McClellan won only twenty-two percent. Even voters from the Army of the Potomac supported Lincoln, preferring him to their old commander by a ratio of seven to three.[134] After the war, Hill produced two more books and wrote for several Democratic Party newspapers. Active in local politics, he campaigned for Samuel Tilden for the presidency in 1876, only to die from natural causes on the day of the election. A few years later, Civil

War veterans awoke from their hibernation and began telling their stories. Thus, the nation witnessed a flourishing of first-hand accounts of the Civil War from the perspective of the men who fought it.[135] Had it not been for the presidential campaign of George B. McClellan in 1864, perhaps Ashbel Hill never would have committed his story to the public record. Unfortunately for McClellan, Hill's endorsement did not give him a leg up.

Appendix (or Is That Appendage?)

In *John Smith's Funny Adventure on a Crutch*, Ashbel Hill makes fun of the fact that he is missing one of his lower extremities and uses his leglessness as a vehicle for poking fun at or pranking others. Some might find his willingness to mock what for many veterans proved to be a devastating loss rather insensitive. Yet this was not the first time that an author placed amputation at the center of written humor. In 1866 Silas Weir Mitchell published a short piece of fiction in *The Atlantic Monthly* called "The Case of George Dedlow."[136] Mitchell, a physician who treated Union soldiers with war-related nervous disorders, studied amputees and identified the condition known as phantom limb pain. He also wrote this anonymously published story about Dedlow, who as a young lieutenant in an Indiana infantry regiment loses both arms and legs. The story is told in three parts. First, our protagonist joins the Union army, is wounded in both arms while being ambushed by guerrillas, and loses one arm while under the care of Confederate doctors as a prisoner. After benefiting from the prisoner exchange, Dedlow rejoins his regiment only to have both legs amputated after being wounded at the Battle of Chickamauga. Then he loses his last extant limb to gangrene while recovering from his other removals. To recover, Dedlow is sent to a hospital in Philadelphia—the so-called "Stump Hospital" specializing in treating amputees—and then to the United States Army Hospital for Injuries and Diseases of the Nervous System in Washington. This brings us to the second section of the story, where the narrator describes Dedlow's continued sensations of feelings in the limbs that are no longer attached to him, what Dr. Mitchell as a scientist famously dubbed phantom limbs.

Thus far, Mitchell's tale is compelling, well written, and very dramatic. His prose exposes the trials and tribulations of those soldiers who literally gave a piece, or pieces, of themselves in the fight to preserve the Union. It is in the last section of the essay that "George Dedlow" turns from the serious to the humorously absurd, as Mitchell takes a swipe at the popular nineteenth-century spiritualist movement.[137] The armless, legless Dedlow is invited by a fellow patient to visit "the New Church," where one is "able to turn away from earthly things and hold converse daily with the great and good who have left this here world." Along with several people seeking to reach the dearly departed, at the church Dedlow encounters a quack doctor, described as "a flabby man, with ill-marked, baggy features and injected eyes," and "Sister Euphemia," a female-authoress "of two somewhat feeble novels," depicted as a "pallid, care-worn young woman with very red lips, and large brown eyes" who had left her husband to devote herself to the quack. Then there is the star of the event, the medium named Brink, a jewelry-clad, side-whiskered charlatan with a large nose and full lips.[138] As the meeting progresses, we are told, Brink is able to communicate with the deceased young son of a woman in mourning clothes, who becomes overwhelmed and carried from the room. The medium then contacts lost loved ones of several others in attendance through a series of raps supposedly emanating from the afterworld. Two raps mean yes.

The attention finally turns to George Dedlow, with the medium now assisted by the quack doctor and his big-eyed devotee. The doctor instructs Dedlow to think of a spirit whom he wishes to contact from the beyond. Struck by an idea, the skeptical Dedlow agrees, and after a pause more rapping commences. Two raps, then two raps. The quack posits that there must be two spirits present. Then the rapping counts out two sets of numbers, 3-4-8-6, then 3-4-8-7. In a moment worthy of the ending of a *Twilight Zone* episode, Dedlow cries out "Good gracious! ... they are *my legs—my legs!*" It turns out that Dedlow decided to try to make contact with his lost lower limbs. The raps represent the numbers assigned by the United States Army Medical Museum to his severed legs, now part of the museum's collection. Where Rod Serling would have wrapped up the story with a sardonic coda, Mitchell carried the narrative a bit too far. Feeling "reindividualized," Dedlow then "arose, and staggering a little, walked across the room on limbs invisible" to him or to the others. While the staggering may have been a product of disuse of the legs for so long, the museum had been storing the actual legs in a vat of alcohol, thus the limbs may have been a bit tipsy. Whatever the case, after a few seconds the unseen legs disappear, and Dedlow sinks safely to the ground, after which he "fainted and rolled over senseless."[139]

In the wake of the piece's publication, an outpouring of sympathy and support emerged for the fictional George Dedlow. People contacted or visited the real "Stump Hospital" on the outskirts of Philadelphia trying to locate "the unhappy victim." Others attempted to raise money for his benefit. Despite the phantasmagoric ending, people believed the tale to be true and Dedlow to be real. In 1871, Mitchell issued a disclaimer of sorts, not in *The Atlantic Monthly*, but rather as a passing mention in an essay on phantom limb pain that appeared in a different popular magazine. Never taking credit for writing the essay on Dedlow, Mitchell noted that the story's author "could never have conceived it possible that his humorous sketch, with its absurd conclusion, would for a moment mislead anyone." It did. In an age when many clung to the idea that the living could contact the dead, especially in light of the death toll of the Civil War, many may have seen the George Dedlow story as evidence that loved-ones lost were just a rap or two away.[140]

Another Civil War story worthy of *Zone* treatment is Minnie Hite Moody's "The Ghost of General Jackson," which first appeared in *The Saturday Evening Post* in 1946.[141] Serling's introduction could read something like this: "Meet Miss Lucy Trevilian, a well-to-do 'unreconstructed' elderly Virginian living eight decades removed from the Civil War. She resides in 'lone spinsterhood,' except for her octogenarian African-American butler Uncle Enoch, and, of course, her long-time house guest, the ghost of Confederate General Thomas Stonewall Jackson." Each meal, Enoch sets a place at the dinner table for both Miss Lucy and the general, and each year Miss Lucy and her houseguest celebrate the anniversary of Virginia's secession from the Union in 1861. Enoch goes along with this, for "he had enjoyed better raising than to stick his nose now into white people's business." Through a series of events, Miss Lucy decides to have a proper tea party and to invite her friends from "the Daughters," that is, of the Confederacy, and her guest of honor will be none other than her house guest, "Virginia's most beloved general," Stonewall Jackson. Formal invitations go out, and "the town is agog." But no one challenges her claim, for "Miss Lucy's family name was one of such integrity that not even the most uncouth of her fellow townsmen or sister townswomen dared defile it with the suggestion that she might have gone bats." The big event arrives, and everyone who is anyone is there. However, after a reporter with a camera disrupts the gathering before the guest of honor appears, it is decided that the general, who was upstairs resting in a closed room, will not appear as planned. Rod Serling could wrap things up by stating that it was best not to disturb the dead, a lesson George Dedlow learned.[142]

"A delightful denunciation of Federal commanders"

In his contribution to *The Cambridge Companion to War Writing*, Will Kaufman noted, "War novels such as Henry Morford's *Shoulder Straps* (1863), *Coward* (1863), and *the Days of Shoddy* (1864) are largely unremembered."[143] Kaufman wrote too soon, as recent scholarship by J.

Matthew Gallman and Chris Walsh have un-unremembered Morford's Civil War fiction.[144] Nevertheless, Morford *is* largely remembered as the author of *Red-Tape and Pigeon-Hole Generals*. Unfortunately, Morford did not write that book.

It is unclear when this misidentification first came to be. A *Catalogue of Miscellaneous Books of the Pennsylvania State Library* published in 1878 accurately identified the actual author, William H. Armstrong, a native of that state. Actually, the book lists the author as "Armstrong, W.H." A half a century later, in *Descriptions of Maryland*, an extended bibliography of published works that contain—you guessed it—a description of Maryland, Bernard C. Steiner identified the author of *Red-Tape* as "Morford, H." I would guess he meant Henry Morford, the unauthor of the book. That still does not prove when this misidentification first occurred. Since then, many have made the same mistake, for example, two prominent reference works of the last half century. Calling the book a "delightful denunciation of Federal commanders by a Federal private in the East," Civil War scholar James I. Robertson credits Morford as the author in the 1967 compilation *Civil War Books: A Critical Bibliography*. More recently, *The Chronology of American Literature: American Literary Achievements from the Colonial Era to Modern Times* makes the same error.[145]

Indeed, many have made this misidentification in their scholarly articles and books, and some not-so-scholarly ones, too, and I am sure the mistake will continue to appear. My purpose is not to call the mistaken out. Rather, it is to look at this "delightful denunciation of Federal commanders by a Federal private." Actually, Robertson had that wrong, too, in that the narrator, and the actual author William H. Armstrong, was a lieutenant-colonel, not a private. Robertson also erred in his assessment that "the book borders on satire."[146] When it comes to its treatment of Union officers, *Red-Tape* undoubtedly is satire, and rather biting satire at that.

Like Ashbel Hill's *Our Boys*, Armstrong's book appeared in 1864 under the title *Red-Tape and Pigeon-Hole Generals: As Seen from the Ranks during a Campaign in the Army of the Potomac by a Citizen Soldier*.[147] A lawyer by trade, Armstrong had served in the 129th Pennsylvania Infantry, a regiment raised for a nine-month stint in the summer of 1862. After completing his tour, Armstrong returned to his law practice and Republican Party politics. In the Forward to the 1999 edition of *Red-Tape*, Charles T. Joyce notes, "For the better part of 133 years the book you are about to read lay on the library shelves mislabeled as fiction, wrongly attributed to a hack nineteenth-century novelist, and largely ignored or overlooked by historians." "Largely ignored or overlooked [or unremembered] by historians"? This is true. "Attributed to a hack nineteenth century novelist"?

Maybe, but to Henry Morford's credit, newspapers deemed his three wartime books worthy of reviewing, and they went through several printings. "Mislabeled as fiction"? That I take exception to, not that the book is not based in fact or that it is not autobiographical. Frederick Arner, who published this edition with his own extensive commentary, makes a compelling argument for that. But he also admits that "because the author and major characters were deliberately disguised [the book] has been miscatalogued" as fiction.[148] While it looks very much like a memoir, the book is a pseudo-memoir. Plus, Armstrong provides contrived dialogue to further the story, and I suspect some of the lesser characters are contrived, too. In other words, it qualifies as fiction, historical fiction, but fiction nonetheless. *Red-Tape* technically is a novel and a satirical one at that.

While William Armstrong and Ashbel Hill shared much in common, there was definitely one big thing that they did not share, and it's not the number of legs each had. Ashbel Hill adored George McClellan. Apparently, William Armstrong did not. Armstrong's regiment joined the Army of the Potomac too late to participate in the Battle of Antietam, McClellan's swan song. Not long after that, the general was gone for good. In *Red-Tape*, the narrator, the "Lieutenant-Colonel" of the 210th Pennsylvania Infantry, introduces McClellan as "the Commander-in-Chief." Armstrong writes: "While the troops were *en route* [to Antietam], the Commander-in-Chief in his hack and four, followed by a staff imposing in numbers, passed. The [army] Regulars cheered vociferously. The applause from the Volunteers was brief, faint, and a most uncertain sound." Definitely not the response from the volunteers that Hill described. Through the Lieutenant-Colonel, Armstrong explains, "Volunteers ... are in the field from what they consider the necessity of the country, and ... are bent on a speedy, honorable, and victorious termination of the war," unlike regulars, who are apt to become blindly attached to their commanders, losing sight of the outcomes of the orders they obey. Armstrong makes his opinion of McClellan's talents even clearer in the three-page screed the officers of the 210th Pennsylvania launch into after the regiment arrives at Sharpsburg the night of September 17 and are told that even though the Confederates had been defeated that day and that the enemy is surrounded on three sides by a river (I assume Antietam Creek) with the Army of the Potomac on the fourth, no Federal attack on the rebs is forthcoming. Says the Lieutenant-Colonel, "I have always thought ... that the test of a great commander was his ability to follow up and take advantage of a victory."[149] Abraham Lincoln probably would have agreed, which is why Lincoln soon relieved McClellan of his command.

Armstrong definitely fell into the camp of the detractors that so angered Ashbel Hill. Armstrong was not alone, if his pseudo-memoir is to be believed. Upon the occasion of McClellan's last review of his army, the Lieutenant-Colonel relates, "Little Mac, once so great a favorite through efforts of the Press and officers with whom he had peopled in places in his gift, received his last cheers from some Divisions of that same Army *by word of command*." Not exactly the spontaneous outpouring of affection described by Hill during McClellan's first review of the troops. The Lieutenant-Colonel adds, "The sympathies of the Rebel residents [near their encampment] seemed strangely in unison with those of the chieftain's favorites."[150]

Armstrong certainly had no love for George McClellan. According to Frederick Arner, however, McClellan was not Armstrong's main target. Rather, according to Arner, Armstrong wrote *Red-Tape* to lambaste Brigadier General Andrew A. Humphreys. A career officer, Humphreys had been the commander of the division that Armstrong's brigade and regiment served in during the existence of the 129th Pennsylvania. Before that, Humphreys had been on McClellan's staff and had never held an actual troop command.[151] Armstrong portrays Humphreys as a bureaucratic paper pusher, capable only of doing administrative work, and incompetently at that.

We first meet the Humphreys character, referred to as "the Division General" or "Old Pigey," when he calls for the Lieutenant-Colonel because someone had made a mistake in a hand-written copy of a certain order that originated in the Division General's headquarters. The particular copy in question had been written by the Lieutenant-Colonel, and the Division General demands to know how such a mistake could be made. Furthermore, he is at a loss to know what to do about it, having "consulted authorities the greater part of last night, French and American," on the proper remedy. (He regularly obsesses with the "French authorities" concerning proper procedure.) Assessing the document and the mistake it contained, the Lieutenant-Colonel informs the Division Commander that "the copy is a faithful one of the order issued from your Head-Quarters." Disbelieving that such an "infernal blunder" could be made in HIS headquarters, he demands to see the original copy. The Lieutenant-Colonel, it is proven, is almost correct, setting the Division General off on a diatribe against the mistake maker: "Captain, this is too G-- ---- bad after all my care and trouble in giving you full instructions. Is it possible that the simplest order can't be made out without my supervision, as if, by G-d, it was my business to stand over your desk all day long, see every paper folded, endorsement made, and the right pigeon-hole selected? This won't do. I give full instructions, and expect them carried out. By G-d," he emphatically repeats, "they must be carried out." What was the mistake? Something that exposed military secrets? Put lives in danger? Delayed important transactions from taking place? No. It is a simple mistake in one verb being written in the past tense instead of the present. And even then, the change in tense does not change the context of the word or the meaning of the order.[152]

After the incident, the Lieutenant-Colonel wonders "if the Government would not have been the gainer if it had made it the business of the General to fold and endorse papers, and dust pigeon holes. It was generally understood that this occupation had been, previous to his being placed in command of the division, the sum-total of the General's military experience." This was not completely true. Andrew Humphreys, a West Point Graduate, had seen brief action in the Seminole War in Florida. He also spent more than two decades in the army's Corps of Topographical Engineering, becoming an accomplished specialist in hydrographic studies, not exactly the "quiet clerk in the Topographical Department" Armstrong makes the Division General out to be. For the first year of the war, however, Humphreys had been a staff officer for McClellan before getting this divisional command. The Lieutenant-Colonel ponders how far the "red-tapism" exhibited by the General extended into McClellan's staff and wonders if it was these "trifling details" that were "detaining the grand army of the Potomac from an onward movement in this most favorable weather, to the great detriment of national finances, the encouragement of the Rebellion, and the depression of patriots everywhere." He concludes that "red-tape was a greater curse to the country than the rebellion." These "trifling details ... delay the movements of great armies, and the striking of heavy blows." Where the General demands that "t's must be crossed and i's carefully dotted," the Lieutenant-Colonel believes that "t's must be crossed when they ought to be crossing the Potomac; i's dotted when we ought to be dotting Virginia fields with our tents."[153]

Back at his tent but a few minutes, the Lieutenant-Colonel gets summoned by the Division General to account for other mistakes in records. Once aware of one miscue, the General sees them everywhere. Flustered, the General directs the Lieutenant-Colonel to a document related to a court martial that the Lieutenant-Colonel presided over as judge advocate. The document lists "Private John W. Holman" as the defendant, but then "not two lines below," refers to the soldier as "John W. Holman, Private." The General exclaims, "Now, by G-- Colonel, one is certainly wrong, and *that* blunder did not come from Division Head-Quarters." The General is unable to identify which is wrong, or to accept that the discrepancy is "a mere clerical error." "There is no such thing in military law as a mere clerical error. Every thing is squared here by the regulations and military law."[154]

Calling the Lieutenant-Colonel back to headquarters a third time, the General continues to unhinge, this time insisting that the verdict of the case involving the seventeen-year-old "Private John W. Holman," or "John W. Holman, Private," be changed from a reprimand to death. "What will General McClellan say with that record before him?" the General asks. "By G--! [Holman] is a soldier in the Army of the United States," the General exclaims, "and must be tried and punished as a soldier." In the exchange between the two officers, the Lieutenant-Colonel intentionally remains calm as he explains why the court decided that the boy deserved the sentence he received, which only infuriates the General all the more: "Colonel, if your manner was not respectful, I would think that you intended insulting me by your d---- provoking coolness." As the discussion continues, the Lieutenant-Colonel's "cool contempt" further angers the General. Perhaps the Lieutenant-Colonel's calm demeanor, which fuels the General's rage, is informed by the knowledge that an officer charged with reviewing the decisions of a court martial cannot make the sentence harsher. All that he could do by army regulation was to submit a statement detailing why he disagreed with the court's decision.[155]

In the end, the court reconvenes, and the judge advocate—the Lieutenant-Colonel—reads and rereads the General's statement or parts thereof. "After considerable laughter over the document, and some little indignation at the unwarranted dictation of 'their commanding General,' of which title the General had taken especial pains to remind them at least every third sentence," the narrator related, "the court decided not to change the sentence." They send all the court documents on to the War Department, and that is the last they hear of it. Unfortunately, Private Holman, who had previously fallen ill and received a doctor's request for a medical discharge, died in camp, awaiting the discharge which was tied up in red tape in the General's headquarters. If the discharge had been delayed in his headquarters, the General remarks in bureaucratic fashion, then "it is because it was not properly folded or endorsed."[156]

The Lieutenant-Colonel reveals many other shortcomings of the General through his own observations or stories related by others, including evidence of incompetence and cowardice on the battlefield. On a lighter note, according to one story the Lieutenant-Colonel heard, a private known among his comrades as a bit of a slacker settled in to fish in a pit originally dug as a latrine. Along comes the General, which the soldier probably expected, who asks the man what he is doing. "Fishing," the soldier replies. The General tells him that there are "no fish in there," calling him "crazy." The soldier answers, "I've caught them in smaller streams than this," then adds, "but then I had better bait." Incensed and convinced that the private is "demented" and a danger to have in camp, the General storms off. Shortly after, a squad of guards arrives and takes him into custody, bringing him to the Surgeon of the Division. In a scene that would have made the

4077 M*A*S*H unit's Corporal Max Klinger envious, a few days later the private receives a discharge on account of his mental status.[157]

Despite its fictionalized nature, Armstrong's narrative very much resembles a typical Northern veteran's Civil War memoir, complete with discussions on topics such as life in camp and on the march; foraging; battles; the disloyalty of Southerners; officers liked and disliked; complaints over regulations; tensions between regular soldiers and volunteers; the efficacy of emancipation and arming Black men; and so forth. While the attack on Andrew Humphreys is only a portion of the story, it is what makes the narrative memorable. Certainly, Armstrong had an axe to grind against the general. One wonders whether Frederick Arner, who resurrected and republished *Red-Tape*, complete with his commentary pointing out Armstrong as the story's villain, also had an axe to grind. Whatever the case, whether or not he based his "Old Pigey" on Humphreys, Armstrong presents a comical caricature of a by-the-book (including the French authorities), over-reacting, tightly-wound, unreasonable, paranoid, intemperate, incompetent, cowardly bumbler, a combination of *Beau Geste*'s Major Lejuane, *Catch-22*'s Colonel Cathcart, and *Hogan's Heroes'* Colonel Klink. And he did it without the help of Henry Morford.

Are "Two Federal Pens" Mightier Than Two Swords?

Other soldiers produced memoirs before the guns fell silent. In early 1865, Confederate veteran and recent prisoner of war Anthony M. Keiley anonymously published a short volume titled *A Rebel in Two Federal Pens, by A. Rifleman, Esq., Gent.* It recounted his time as a prisoner of war from the first day of Ulysses S. Grant's assault on Petersburg in June 1864 until his release and exchange five months later. Keiley is better remembered as the author of an expanded version of *A Rebel in Two Federal Pens*, which appeared a year later under the titled *In Vinculis; or, The Prisoner of War. Being the Experiences of a Rebel in Two Federal Pens, Interspersed with Reminiscences of the Late War; Anecdotes of Southern Generals, Etc.* For this version, he dropped the pseudonym "A. Rifleman, Esq., Gent." and adopted the less creative alias "A Virginia Confederate." A lawyer, newspaper publisher, and postwar diplomat, Keiley had served in the 12th Virginia Infantry, rising to the rank of lieutenant, until he was elected to the Virginia state legislature in 1863. In his home town of Petersburg on June 9, 1864, when the advance forces of Grant's troops approached the city, Keiley volunteered to join the home guard in the city's defense. That did not go well for him.[158]

Part I. "Crude partisan versifying on both sides"

In the Preface to *A Rebel*, dated "Petersburg, January 2, 1865," Keiley promised "a plain and unembellished account" of his experience, an "unvarnished tale" of what he "*saw* and *knew*." He saved the embellishment and the varnish for *In Vinculis*, in which he made no such pledge. A review of *In Vinculis* called the memoir "rich, rare, racy, and refreshing ... entertaining ... instructive.... [and] full of humor." Unfortunately, the book does not live up to the hype completely, at least about the humor part. The two versions of Keiley's memoir have their moments when it comes to laughs, although essentially, the story is a prisoner of war narrative. Civil War historian David Blight observed, "No other experience ... caused deeper emotions, recriminations, and lasting invective than that of prisons. Civil War prisons were, by and large, hellholes of disease, misery, and death."[159] Under these conditions, any author would be hard pressed to find much that was truly funny. Thus, much of what could be considered humor in Keiley's *A Rebel* comes off ranging from bitterly sarcastic to rancorously snarky. This is even truer for *In Vinculis*, which is Latin for "in chains."

Sent to the Point Lookout Prisoner of War camp in Delaware after his capture, Keiley remained there for a short while before being shipped to a new prison camp in south-central New York at Elmira with several hundred other prisoners. Shortly after his capture but before arriving at Point Lookout, he had an interview with Union Major General Benjamin Butler. Butler became notorious and hated throughout the South in 1862 when, as commander of Union-occupied New Orleans, he issued General Orders, No. 28 in response to the treatment Federal soldiers had been receiving from Confederate women in that city. According to the so-called "Woman Order," any "women (calling themselves ladies) of New Orleans" who should "by word, gesture, or movement insult or show contempt for any officer or soldier of the United States" would be "regarded and held liable to be treated as a women of the town plying her avocation"—in other words, a prostitute.[160]

Keiley's description of Butler, one of the oddest looking characters of the Civil War, indeed, perhaps in all of American history, merits attention. "The first thought that crossed my mind [upon meeting the general] was one of profound gratitude to God who creates no mortal enemy to man, without clothing it with features that excite the instant and instinctive aversion of the entire human race," he begins. "How deadly would the cobra and tarantula be, if providence had not made them as loathsome as they are venomous." Keiley found that the general bore such characteristics:

> To Benjamin F. Butler's face scarce an element is wanting of absolute repulsiveness. Rapacity finds appropriate expression in his vulture nose—sensuality in his heavy pendant jaws—despotism in his lowering eye-brow, and to

these facial charms is added an optical derangement which permits him to scrutinize you with his left eye—the one he seems to place most dependence on—while the right, revolving in a different plane, and concerned, you would imagine, about separate objects—wanders away in another field of vision.[161]

Personally, I've always thought that Butler resembled the Warner Brothers' cartoon character Droopy the Dog, but this description of Butler and his chameleon-like, independently-mobile eyes gives me a fresh impression of him.

A second passage worthy of note concerns the policy at Point Lookout relating to prisoners' clothing. According to Keiley, prisoners were allowed to possess only one item of each type of clothing: one shirt, one pair of pants, one jacket, etc. Thus, when prisoners received care packages from home that contained new clothes, they had to turn over their old clothing. As Keiley explained, "No one [is] allowed to take any articles of outside wear, from hat to shoes ... unless he deposits the corresponding article of his existing stock" with prison personnel. Prisoners were not always ready to relinquish those older items, however, and so it became necessary "to find some method of evading the laws," which Keiley assured "was not very difficult." One only needed "to buy or beg or 'flank' a suit of clothes, to surrender which would involve no other sacrifice than that purely emotional one which founds our attachment to certain things, on account of an absurd veneration for antiquity." One day, Keiley learned that he had received a package from home. Anticipating that it contained clothes, he went about buying, begging, and flanking an outfit that he could hand over for the new togs. As he described it, he "*accumulated* a suit that would have entitled [him] to an exalted position among the raggedest vagrants in Naples and Constantinople." "My shoes had to be coaxed to stay on," he expounded, while the hat he found deserved the name only because "in some mythical era of the past," it had been a hat. As for his coat, he concluded, "It being a warm summer day, ... it would excite no suspicion to appear without" one. That left his pants, or his "pantaloons" as he calls them. (He and Abraham Lincoln.) "Verily, verily, never since the martial ancestors of the gay Parisians invented these indispensable institutions of dress ... did such a travesty on costume, disgust the eye and taste," he asserted. "Innocent of buttons, both legs out at the knees, stained by time and less tender agencies out of all approach to its original color, with an enormous quadrilateral, carved out of it in a location which indeed could best spare so large a tax, but which modesty forbids me to make particular reference to." I'm guessing the seat of his pants. "It was only by a diligent and scientific application of pins, that I could induce [the hole] to preserve even a bifurcated appearance, while the assistance of one hand was necessary to keep the entire compilation from demolition."[162]

Thus attired, Keiley made his way across camp to the office where his package awaited, along the way receiving verbal jabs from his fellow prisoners. Upon his arrival, he learned that his "preparations turned out to be all in vain." Rather than holding new clothes, the package contained "a beef tongue and a can of 'solidified cream.'" Disappointed, he returned to his quarters and gave himself "a denuding shake," after which he shared his largesse with his mess mates, which helped him to forget "both the troubles and the farce of costuming."[163]

For humor, the two versions of Keiley's memoir do not match the wit of Ashbel Hill's *Our Boys*. They do, however, reflect three things that Keiley and Hill shared in common. First, both ignored slavery as the root cause of the clash between North and South. In *In Vinculis* (but not in *A Rebel*), Keiley asserted that the war was one of independence for the South. It was "the war of the people. In it every hope and interest and energy and affection of a brave people were centered." Northerners refused to admit this. Their "effort to prejudice the cause of the South by declaring the war to have been the act of a few discontented politicians, was necessary to justify the North before the eyes of the world. If it had once been admitted that *the people* of ten States with great unanimity desired independence, the unexampled wickedness of a war for their subjugation by a people themselves the creation of a revolution which asserted the people's right to change their governments at will, would have been manifest to the world." "The Southern war for liberty," Keiley insisted, "was *the people's war*." He did acknowledge emancipation as a consequence of the war, but added that "the North, in liberating four millions of blacks, enslaved eight millions of whites."[164] Keiley is not specific on why Southerners sought their independence, but his portrayal of Northerners sheds some light. He writes in *A Rebel* (but not in *In Vinculis*): "The cruelty, blood-thirstiness, avarice, hypocrisy, vulgar despotism and brutality, which characterizes so many of our enemies, need only to be once seen, and above all once *felt*, to summon every Southron to the altar, that he may take the Carthaginian oath of undying hate to his enemies."[165]

Second, Keiley shared Hill's disdain for African Americans, whom he often encountered as guards. He described the first Black guard placed over him while in custody: "An odorous Congo, with a claymore two-thirds his length, a Nubian nose, boundless buttons, and the port of Soulouque [a Haitian general and then president until he was proclaimed emperor of Haiti in 1849] was strutting up and down before me in most amusing enjoyment of his responsible position." This is one of the more complimentary descriptions Keiley provides. (I'm unaware of Union soldiers ever being armed with large medieval-era Scottish swords.) He later explains that Africans "have written no books, painted no picture, carved no statue, built no temple, established no laws, launched no ships, developed no language, achieved no invention," and so on.[166] Of course, these things are untrue. Where Hill and Keiley differ is that as a Union soldier, Hill often vented his dislike for African Americans in verbal and physical abuse. As a prisoner of the Union army, Keiley dared not, which certainly enflamed his rancor.

Finally, despite his nasty characterization of Northerners, Keiley's positive comments about "McClellan men" suggests that he too supported the former general for president in 1864.[167] Had *A Rebel in Two Federal Pens* appeared in print in time for the election, however, it probably would have had the same impact on the contest that *Our Boys* did.

Works like those produced by Ashbel Hill, William H. Armstrong, Andrew Keiley, and Silas Weir Mitchell at times graphically confronted the grittiest and most unpleasant aspects of the war with humor, what historian Jon Grinspan identified as "hard humor."[168] Hard war humor definitely appears in later soldiers' memoirs. Perhaps through the use of hard war humor, some of Whitman's real war did slip into at least some of the books.

PART II

"The war was a draw game, and ... both sides were whipped"
The Post-War Writers

In "Chiefly About War Matters," with the war just a year old, Nathaniel Hawthorne predicted that "even supposing the war should end to-morrow, and the army melt into the mass of the population within the year, what an uncalculable preponderance will there be of military titles and pretensions for at least half a century to come!" Hawthorne's Peaceable Man tells the reader, "Every country-neighborhood will have its general or two, its three or four colonels, half a dozen majors, and captains without end,—besides non-commissioned officers and privates, more than the recruiting offices ever knew of,—all with their campaign-stories, which will become the staple of fireside-talk forevermore." Hawthorne overestimated the number of officers per community, no doubt, but his conclusion that these soldiers would have stories to tell proved very accurate. Although veterans at first may have been reluctant to commit their stories to paper, by the 1880s veteran-authored works on the Civil War began to flourish and would continue to do so for decades to come. Veterans told their stories in many forms, but particularly common was the memoir or reminiscence.[1]

Writing about the war helped many veterans to come to terms with what they had experienced as well as to shape the memory of the conflict. An old saying claims, "History is written by the victors," but evidently there is another old saying: "The winners forget and go about their business, while the losers spend the rest of their lives remembering and explaining their, or their ancestors,' exploits, motives, and failures." For Civil War veterans, both statements are part true and part false. Both sides remembered and wrote about the war in their own way. Historian David W. Blight argued that Northern veterans often portrayed themselves and their comrades as "saviors, the deliverers of the nation." Because of them,

Part II. "The war was a draw ... both sides were whipped"

"The republic had survived and been renewed by their blood." At the same time, Union veterans downplayed slavery and emancipation as a cause and consequence of the conflict. Former Confederates, on the other hand, regularly denied that they had fought for slavery and that they had taken part in a rebellion against the Federal government at all. Rather, theirs was a war for independence, which "failed only because it was overwhelmed by numbers and resources." Thus, the veterans had attained a "manly reconciliation," agreeing that "they had all fought heroically and deserved recognition, regardless of which side of a stone wall they had stood upon. The culture of veterans' reminiscences," Blight concluded, "acknowledged a distinction between the causes for which North and South had fought, but no difference in the moral righteousness and valor with which they had performed their duty."[2]

Leading the way in this spate of memoir production was *The Century Magazine*, a popular publication of the day. In 1883, *Century*'s editors devised a plan to publish a series of firsthand accounts of the major battles of the war, written by officers who played key roles in them. The magazine initially intended eight or ten pieces and had to convince, coax, and cajole the former officers to contribute. The project took on a life of its own, however, and eventually the *Century* "Battles and Leaders of the Civil War" series, as it became known, occupied about one third of each monthly issue. This success also prompted the editors to publish most of the articles, along with additional material, in a separate four volume series titled *Battles and Leaders of the Civil War*, which debuted in 1888. Introducing the series, the editors stated that its purpose was "to clear up cloudy questions with new knowledge and the wisdom of cool reflection." The essays, they believed, would also "soften the controversy with that better understanding of each other, which comes to comrades in arms when personal feeling has dissipated, and time has proven how difficult are the duties and how changeable are the events of war—how enveloped in accident and mystery." "No time could be fitter," the editors opined, "for a publication of this kind than the present, when the passions and the prejudices of the Civil War have nearly faded out of politics, and its heroic events are passing into our common history where motives will be weighed without malice, and valor praised without distinction of uniform."[3]

Not everyone embraced the *Century*'s "Battles and Leaders" series. In 1887, as the series was completing its run, Union veteran George W. Peck published his memoir. The Wisconsinite began the work with the observation, "For the last year or more I have been reading the articles in the *Century* magazine, written by generals and things who served on both the Union and Confederate sides, and have been struck by the number of generals who fought them and saved the country." Peck continued:

It seems that each general on the Union side, who fought a battle, and writes an article for the aforesaid magazine, admits that his battle was the one which did the business. On the Confederate side, the generals who write articles invariably demonstrate that they everlastingly whipped their opponents, and drove them off in disorder. To read those articles it seems strange that the Union generals who won so many decisive battles, should not have ended the war much sooner than they did, and to read the accounts of battles won by the Confederates, and the demoralization that ensued in the ranks of their opponents, it seems marvelous that the Union army was victorious. Any man who has followed these generals of both sides, in the pages of that magazine, must conclude that the war was a draw game, and that both sides were whipped.[4]

Thus, Peck decided to write his own history of the war, from the perspective of a "private soldier."

Writing of those soldiers, who were drawn from the "great mass of plain people" of both North and South, Bell Irvin Wiley observed, "One of the engaging qualities of the lowly folk as they revealed themselves in the crisis of war was humor."[5] This trait continued in at least some of the post-war accounts of soldiers and officers. Whether or not the memoirs helped to reconcile North and South or create a better understanding between the two, some of the stories told by the veterans did, and still do, make us laugh.

How I Put Down the Rebellion

When George Peck published his account of the Civil War, *How Private Geo. W. Peck Put Down the Rebellion, or the Funny Experiences of a Raw Recruit*, the explosion of veterans' wartime memoirs was well underway. Enlisting in the Union army in December 1863, Peck admitted that while other men joined "from patriotic motives," he did so "for the bounty." Each volunteer received a three-hundred-dollar bounty payment from the Federal government upon joining the military. Just a day after signing up, however, Peck learned that had he enlisted in a neighboring town desperate to fill its quota of volunteers, he could have received additional money from that community for a total of twelve hundred dollars. "I never suffered much more than I did when I found out that I had got to go to war for a beggerly three-hundred dollars bounty," he complained indignantly, "when I could have had twelve hundred dollars by being credited to another town." Peck's candidness provides a droll counterpoint to the altruistic reasons usually put forward by veterans for their enrollment in the army. Nevertheless, Peck committed himself to "putting down the rebellion," as he reminds his readers over and over. The "South had no right to secede," he asserted, adding, "that is all the South is fighting for," ignoring slavery and its protection as the South's motivation. In fact, slavery played no role in his decision to enlist. Rather, for some time it had been a hindrance for him. "I had always been a Democrat, at home, and not very much mashed on our colored brothers, and one thing that prevented me from enlisting before I did was the idea of making the colored men free," he confided. That's the entirety of what he has to say about emancipation. As for African Americans, he admitted, "I had nothing against a colored man, and got to think a great deal of them afterwards." That did not stop him from using derogatory terms in reference to them throughout the book.[6]

Despite Peck's criticism of *Century*'s "Battles and Leaders" series, his memoir serves as the kind of vehicle for the reconciliation that the magazine's editors hoped to provide. Peck expressed his desire to let bygones be bygones in his dedication:

> To the "Boys in Blue" and the "Boys in Gray," Who got real spunky at each other, some years ago, while playing in their adjoining door-yards, threw tomato cans and dead cats back and forth, called each other names, pulled hair, and snubbed noses until they got into real, actual war, in which such bravery was shown on both sides, as the world had never seen before, and who have decided to be neighbors and friends again, ready to protect and defend each other against all the world.[7]

Peck ended up as a replacement in the 4th Wisconsin Cavalry, a veteran unit created early in the war. This happened despite the fact that Peck claimed never to have ridden a horse before enlisting. In contrast to the assurances Peck received from his recruiting officer that because the war was so close to its end that his life would be one continued picnic for two or three months, he experienced many unexpected tribulations, such as sleeping outside and on the ground; eating soldier's rations and at times going without; rudeness from officers whom he had known and had been on an equal footing with before the war; regular abuse and teasing from the veteran soldiers because he was a "raw recruit"; and suffering the "meanest horse in the regiment." It did not take long for Peck to realize that "war was no picnic."[8]

Nevertheless, Peck's first encounter with the enemy turned into a pleasant affair. Sent to keep watch on a nearby road, Peck spied a dark figure coming around a bend and approaching him, a Confederate, also sent to watch the road. Peck thought, "What sense was there in picking a quarrel with him? Why should I want to shoot a total stranger, who might have a family at home, somewhere in the South, who would mourn for him[?] He might be a dead shot, as many Southern gentlemen were, and if I went to advising him about halting, it would very likely cause his hot Southern blood to boil, and he would say he had just as much right to the road as I had." Before Peck could resolve his dilemma, his horse startled and began to run, prompting the approaching man's horse to run. Unable to stop their horses, the two soldiers raced along, unsuccessfully exchanging shots from their revolvers until they both emptied their guns. Before long Peck realized that the two were moving in circles. The road was not a road, but rather an old horse racetrack. After several times around the track, both horses stumbled, sending the two to the ground. Then they argued with each other over who was whose prisoner. The matter unresolved, they decided to wait until sunrise. In the meantime, they played cards, shared some food and tobacco, and got some rest. After sun up, they decided to "call it a stand-off, and agree that neither ... should be a prisoner." Instead, they agreed that "each should go hunt up his own command, and tell the biggest lie we could think of as to the fight we had had."[9]

Peck described several other incidents that advance the process of reconciliation. For example, when ordered to kill thirty worn out horses to keep them from falling into the hands of the Confederates, he instead gave them to some destitute Southern farmers who could use the horses to provide for themselves and their families. And Peck saw to it that a prisoner, the brother of a young Southern woman who spent a week nursing the Wisconsinite through a serious illness, got special attention and was allowed to be paroled. Despite this, Peck acknowledged that the Confederates were his enemy. In the book's only notable discussion of battle, Peck wrote, "All idea of being sorry for the enemy, all charity, all hope that the war might close before any more men were killed, was gone. After looking in the upturned faces of our dead and wounded on their field, the more of the enemy that were killed the better. It is thus that war makes men brutal, while in active service. They think of things and do things that they regret immediately after the firing ceases." Then of the specific battle that inspired this observation, he explained, "The next ten minutes was the nearest thing to hell that I ever experienced, and it seemed as though my face must look like that of a fiend. I felt like one."[10]

Besides this one instance, Peck rarely mentioned engaging the enemy. Instead, in several places he expressed his desire not to fight, at times bordering on cowardice. Nevertheless, Peck remained committed to "putting down the rebellion," and carried out many tasks that he argued would aid in doing just that. He foraged for food (despite an initial reluctance to steal from others). He led a detachment to unload supplies from a steamboat. (His men refused to do this, so he hired some former slaves to carry out the task.) Finally, he supervised the building of a bridge across a bayou (although he erected it in the wrong place and had to have it taken apart and moved.) While he often found himself getting in trouble, Peck developed a reputation for carrying out unusual missions. To save a general from embarrassment, Peck was tasked with stopping and searching a beautiful female rebel to whom the general had given a pass to travel back and forth through the lines. The woman, who used her feminine wiles to get the pass, took advantage of the situation to smuggle quinine and other contraband to the Confederates. Peck received orders, which he was not to share with the other men posted with him, to halt the woman, bring her into a nearby schoolhouse, and search her for the illegal goods. Then he would bring her to the general, who would reprimand him for acting without orders in a way insulting to a lady, even though he had those orders and she was indeed smuggling. She would be let go, but her smuggling halted.

The encounter proved comical. Having found newly printed Confederate bonds hidden in her hat, Peck ordered her into the schoolhouse and told her to go behind a pulpit and disrobe so that her clothes could be searched. All the while the woman protested, insisting that searching her was inappropriate, and all the while Peck insisted that he was just doing his job. With each layer of clothing the woman removed, more contraband appeared. The search exposed bottles and packages of quinine, all sorts of pills, salves, ointments, and plasters, plus about "a pint of gun caps" in her corset. He even uncovered one letter, destined for her rebel officer husband serving in Virginia, after she took off her shoes. In the letter she expressed her fears about smuggling, her guilt for betraying the kindness of the general who gave her the pass, and her plan to go to New Orleans to join their children after she completed this last mission. Touched by the letter, Peck decided to allow the woman to escape, as long as she stopped smuggling and went to New Orleans. Upon returning to camp, Peck informed the general of their success in confiscating the contraband goods and showed him the letter. He then informed the general that the woman had escaped, at which the general expressed his relief that he did not have to confront her, and probably that his duplicity, or the fact that he was duped, would not be exposed.

Word of Peck's encounter with the female smuggler spread through camp, leading to another adventure for the raw recruit. Fearing that men on picket duty would take liberties with any females authorized to pass through the lines, the general engaged Peck to disguise himself as a woman and try to pass by a particular corporal while he was on picket duty because they suspected that he would inappropriately take advantage of the situation. He did. Peck played the part of the Southern lady to the letter, and no one, especially the corporal, suspected that she was a he. When the corporal attempted to unbutton madam Peck's dress, the ersatz lady punched him in both eyes, knocking him to the ground. Just then an officer aware of the sting underway arrived on the scene and ordered the accused smuggler, the corporal, and his men to return to camp with him. Still playing the part, Peck mounted the horse astraddle like a man, and as they moved toward camp, he pulled out his pipe and had a smoke, much to the bewilderment of the unsuspecting men. Only when they arrived in camp did Peck reveal his true identity. These were the kinds of assignments that George Peck was willing to undertake in putting down the rebellion.

Peck's narrative ends rather abruptly months before the war's end and with the rebellion yet to be put down. A journalist and editor after the war, perhaps Peck was planning for his successful run for mayor of Milwaukee in 1890 followed by his successful bid for his state's governor's office that same year. Or perhaps he was just being a bad boy. Prior to writing his war memoir, Peck had gained fame as the author of numerous stories featuring a rascally trouble making fellow known as "Peck's Bad Boy."[11]

The so-called "Bad Boy" genre of literature has had a long history and can be traced forward to iconic fictional characters such as Dennis the Menace and Bart Simpson. Peck did not originate the genre, however. That distinction goes to Thomas Bailey Aldrich, who in 1869 published *The Story of a Bad Boy*, about, obviously, a bad boy and loosely based on his life experiences. Soon, Aldrich had many imitators, including Peck. According to scholar Kenneth B. Kidd (an appropriately named specialist in "boyology"), "A hallmark of the Bad Boy genre is the town fight, in which contending groups of boys reenact and practice war," and that Aldrich "retells the Civil War as a great winter snow fight" pitting the rival North End Boys against the South End Boys.[12] I'm not sure if Peck ever depicts a Civil War reenactment in any of his "Bad Boy" books, but he does mention his Pa having served in it on several occasions, doing his part to put down the rebellion.

My Real Story Will Never Get into the Century's Battles and Leaders Books

In December 1885, the *Century Magazine* published a contribution to its "Battles and Leaders" series penned by the increasingly famous author Mark Twain. A few years later, the editors decided to leave Twain's essay, "The Private History of a Campaign That Failed," out of their four volume *Battles and Leaders of the Civil War*. Twain admitted at the essay's outset that he did not represent the many men who joined one army or the other and committed themselves to their cause to the end. Rather, he was one of the "thousands [who] entered the war, got just a taste of it, and then stepped out again, permanently." That group, he asserted, was "entitled to a sort of voice,—not a loud one, but a modest one; not a boastful one, but an apologetic one," and "they ought at least to be allowed to state why they didn't do anything, and also to explain the process by which they didn't do anything." Twain then described the two weeks he spent in the summer of 1861, back when he was known as Samuel Clemens, as part of a "military company" joined by friends from his boyhood in Marion County, Missouri, and dubbed the Marion Rangers. Fifteen men comprised the company, including Twain, who was selected lieutenant, the second in command of the group next to Captain Tom Lyman. Titles and rank did not mean much, though, as these men had known each other for years and saw each other as peers, which usually meant that one was very resistant to taking orders from another. According to Twain, this was commonplace: "There were scores of little camps scattered over Missouri where the same thing was happening. These camps were composed of young men who had been born and reared to a sturdy independence, and who did not know what it meant to be ordered around by Tom, Dick, and Harry, whom they had known familiarly all their lives, in the villages or on the farm."[13]

Shortly after the company formed, a colonel swore the men into service. The men pledged themselves "to be faithful to the State of Missouri and [to] drive all invaders from her soil, no matter whence they might come or under what flag they might march." This oath did not specify just what service they had joined and who the invaders might be, but according to Twain, the colonel "knew quite clearly that he had invested us in the cause of the Southern Confederacy." Whatever the case, Twain disclosed that he and much of his group saw "this military expedition" whether consciously or not, as "simply a holiday." Much of the time they "had been having a very jolly time, that was full of horse-play and school-boy hilarity." The Marion Rangers spent most of the two weeks reacting to rumors that the enemy was approaching them by retreating. There was a reason why the men chose Tom Lyman as their captain, as he devised a strategy to avoid the enemy. "All we had to do," Twain explained, "was not to retreat *toward* him." They proved pretty adept at this. "We kept monotonously falling back upon one camp or another," Twain, related, although they had one encounter that Twain called the "Engagement at Mason's Farm," during which the men were attacked by a pack of dogs.[14]

Finally, the Marion Rangers met the enemy, or at least a man they thought was the enemy. One night while camped out, the men heard someone approaching on horseback. As the stranger neared, several of the men including Twain grabbed their guns. Then someone yelled, "Fire!" and the man dropped. Twain painted a graphic picture of the scene. The soldiers gathered around the man, who "was lying on his back, with his arms abroad; his mouth was open and his chest heaving with long gasps, and his white shirt-front was all splashed with blood." Many things went through the author's head at this point. "The thought shot through me that I was a murderer; that I had killed a man—a man who had never done me any harm." Twain was not alone in this sentiment. "All the boys seemed to be feeling in the same way," he confessed. "They had forgotten all about the enemy; they thought only of this one forlorn unit of the foe." After the man died, Twain rationalized the death. "He was killed in war; killed in fair and legitimate war; killed in battle, as you may say; and yet he was as sincerely mourned by the opposing force as if he had been their brother." The man wore no uniform, carried no weapon, and had no identification. "He was a stranger in the Country," Twain reckoned. "It seemed to me an epitome of war; that all war must be just that—the killing of strangers against whom you feel no personal animosity; strangers whom, in other circumstances, you would help if you found them in trouble, and who would help you, if you needed it." With this realization, Twain concluded, "My campaign was spoiled."[15]

Soon after, the Marion Rangers agreed to disband. Serving as a catalyst for this decision was word that "a Union colonel was sweeping down on us with a whole regiment at his heels." Twain added, "In time I came to know that Union colonel whose coming frightened me out of the war and crippled the Southern cause to that extent—General Grant. I came within a few hours of seeing him when he was as unknown as I was myself." With this, Samuel Clemens ended his military career and decided to head west, where Clemens became Mark Twain.[16]

Over the several decades after the war ended, Twain told and retold his story, or variations thereof, in speech and in print. For instance, in October 1877 Twain spoke at a dinner of an honorary military organization in Hartford, Connecticut, where he presented what scholar David Rachels identifies as "Mark Twain's First Civil War Autobiography." After concluding "the history of the part which my division took in the great rebellion," he invited the attendees to raise a toast to the "neglected and forgotten heroes, my footsore and travel-stained paladins, who were first in war, first in peace, and were not idle during the interval that lay between." Twain also briefly mentioned his service in his 1883 book *Life on the Mississippi*, if only to compliment his retreating skills: "I had done no advancing in all that campaign that was at all equal to it."[17]

Twain returned to the retreating theme on many occasions. For example, in an interview with an Australian newspaper given while he was on a round-the-world tour, Twain recounted, "My company became so fatigued that we couldn't retreat any more, and I resigned. I should have got fatigued earlier," he added, "had the company marched in the other direction." A few months later he elaborated in an interview with the *New*

Zealand Mail, this time tying Ulysses S. Grant back into the story. "Grant and I were very near coming to violent collision during that two weeks," he told his interviewer. When asked how the collision was prevented, he explained, "by my retreating. When we got to that point there was another point in view—somewhere out of danger ... and I retreated to that point. I was very fond of exercise in those days; had to be to keep in health. But fourteen retreats in two weeks; two retreats a day was too much exercise." So, he resigned.[18]

Implicit or explicit in many of Twain's recollections of the war is the theme of reconciliation and reunion. Nevertheless, there remained a bit of a rebel in the "Lost Cause" vein in Twain, as evident in the 1901 comments he made at a Lincoln's birthday commemoration. "We of the South were not ashamed of the part we took" in the war. "We believed in those days we were fighting for the right—and it was a noble fight, for we were fighting for our sweethearts, our homes, and our lives. To-day we no longer regret the result, but we of the South are not ashamed that we made an endeavor."[19]

Twain was an inveterate storyteller, and one must always ask where facts end and fiction begins in assessing his autobiographical writings. Twain's best-known work of fiction is *The Adventures of Huckleberry Finn*, his follow-up to *The Adventures of Tom Sawyer*. Both can be considered Bad Boy books, although only a long-unpublished story contains a hint of a war reenactment characteristic of the Bad Boy genre. In "Tom Sawyer's Conspiracy," an unfinished installment of the Tom Sawyer saga, set a year after the Huckleberry Finn story, Twain has Sawyer suggesting the idea of starting a civil war to "make the summer buzz, and worth being alive." When Tom proposes instigating a civil war to the no longer enslaved Jim, Jim asks what "civil" means. Tom replies: "Well, it means—it means—well, anything that's good and kind, and polite, and all that—Christian, as you might say." Jim then asks how something could have those characteristics, or be civil, if it entails killing people. "*Civil* war!" Jim exclaims. "De ain' no such war. De idear!—people dat's good en kind en polite en b'long to de church a-marchin' out en slashin' en choppin' en shootin' one anther—lan,' *I* knowed dey warn't no sich thing. You done 'vent it uo' own self, Mars Tom...." Thus, at Jim's urging, Tom agrees to "countermand the civil war." Twain tells the reader, Tom decides to

> give up the civil war, and it is one of the brightest things to his credit.... And it don't seem right and fair that Harriet Beecher Stow and all them other second-handers gets all the credit of starting that war and you never hear Tom Sawyer mentioned in the histories ransack them how you will, and yet he was the first one that thought of it. Yes, and years and years before ever they had the idea. And it was all his own, too, and come out of his own head, and was a

bigger one than theirs, and would a cost forty times as much, and if it hadn't been for Jim he would a been in ahead and got the glory.[20]

If Tom Sawyer deserves the credit for inventing the Civil War, as Twain suggests, then Jim merits recognition for putting down the rebellion.

Twain wrote a few other short stories related to the war, including "Lucretia Smith's Soldier," satirizing men who joined the army to win the hearts of women and the role women played in encouraging men to enlist to prove themselves worthy. Four years before Twain's "Private History" appeared in the *Century Magazine*, he published in that periodical a short spoof titled "A Curious Experience" about a quirky and bored teen boy taken in by the commander of a Federal fort in Connecticut during the war and then suspected of being a spy. And there is the not necessarily funny but definitely "feel good" narrative, "A True Story, Repeated Word for Word as I Heard It," about an elderly formerly enslaved woman who recounts her experience living in bondage, having her family and herself separated by sale, and thirteen years later during the war being reunited with her youngest son, Henry, who is now a member of the United States Colored Troops.[21] Mark Twain spent only two weeks as a participant in the Civil War. Nevertheless, he left his mark on the real war as it has been told in the books.

After a While They All Sound the Same...

Civil War veterans produced a plethora of memoirs and histories that provided fodder for Civil War historians for years to come. Because of their usefulness and popularity, soldiers' first-hand accounts continued to appear in print. To be honest, after a while, these reminiscences start sounding the same. Whether Northern or Southern, soldiers had the same material with which to work. Soldiers shared similar experiences and many of the same values. To be sure, not all memoirs are really alike. Some soldiers expressed their thoughts and related their experiences better than others. And whether intentional or not, some were funnier than others.

While many former officers from both sides put pen to paper to record their daring deeds, rank and file participants echoed George Peck that privates, and occasionally non-commissioned officers, could best tell the story of their war. Tennessee Confederate Sam Watkins "proposed to tell of the fellows who did the shooting and killing, the fortifying and ditching, the sweeping of the streets, the drilling, the standing guard, picket and videt, and who drew (or were to draw) eleven dollars per month and rations, and also drew the ramrod and tore the cartridge." Why not, Watkins reasoned in a rather democratic way: "The histories of the 'Lost

Cause' are all written out by 'big bugs,' Generals and renowned historians, and like the fellow who called a turtle a 'cooter,' being told that no such word as cooter was in Webster's dictionary, remarked that he had as much right to make a dictionary as Mr. Webster or any other man; so have I to write a history." Watkins's 1882 memoir *Company Aytch* has made its way into the footnotes of an army of historians; in fact, nearly a century and a half after the war's end, author Roy Blount, Jr. observed that *Company Aytch* was "the book Mark Twain might have written if he had stayed in, and survived, the war."[22]

Fellow former Confederate Alexander Hunter seconded Watkins's assessment in his not as often cited 1905 publication *Johnny Reb and Billy Yank*: "No officer high in rank dared write the exact truth." Knowing "something of the art of war through tough experience," men who served as privates "can afford to tell the truth as to what he saw, heard and thought without fear or favor. And above all, a private in the ranks, having no grievances, can be fair and just."[23] Right. Soldiers never had grievances, except for all the things they complained about during and continued to complain about after the war. It's in their complaints that some of the funniest writing resides.

Nevertheless, not every soldier who left a first-hand account for posterity believed that theirs was the final say on the war. Samuel A. Swiggett, formerly of the 36th Iowa Infantry, informed readers in his Preface that he "does not intend to permit the possible deception of a confiding public into the belief that they cannot exist without reading" his book. "It is without plot, moral, historical value, mystery, romance, horrors and murderous scenes." He only wrote it because his friends pressured him to do it.[24]

Sam Watkins correctly points out that lowly soldiers like him did "the shooting and killing." That's why he shot at privates rather than officers. "It was they that did the shooting and killing, and if I could, kill or wound a private, why, my chances were so much the better." It was usually in the things they did while not shooting and killing that humor can be found, however, such as griping about not getting a chance to shoot and kill. When Watkins's regiment arrived too late to participate in the Battle of Manassas, he revealed, "We felt that the war was over, and we would have to return home without even seeing a Yankee soldier." Even more, he continued, "How we envied those that were wounded. We thought at the time that we would have given a thousand dollars to have been in the battle, and to have had our arm shot off, so we could have returned home with an empty sleeve. But the battle was over, and we were left out."[25]

Readers might detect a note of sarcasm in Confederate John S. Robson's lament about missing the Battle of Manassas. His regiment, "the 52d Virginia was sorely disgruntled," he carped. "Jealousy rankled hot in our hearts at sight of the battery boys, and others, from Staunton, who were sporting around town with bullet-wounds and bloody bandages, the idols of the girls and made heroes of by everybody. Fate was against us, for we had not even seen the smoke of that first great battle from afar, and we would have resigned a kingdom without a murmur to have had one of those wounds; even a very small wound would have been thankfully received." Robson wanted to be a hero, but questioned whether the battle produced any real heroes: "Every one of these veteran heroes of that battle was supposed to have slain at least four Yankees, and fought Sherman's battery with bowie knife. 'Charging' the batteries of the enemy was the favorite amusement of the lucky fellows who were at Manassas, and every one of them had 'charged,' more or less, batteries that day."[26]

Some veterans were a bit more circumspect about missing that first big battle, or at least most of it. Before completing his medical training to become a surgeon in the Confederate army, Ferdinand Eugene Daniel served in a Mississippi regiment. While the clash began around sunrise, Daniel admitted, "Our regiment was not engaged until late in the afternoon.... I'm glad of it. I might have been killed, and see what the world would have lost if I had!"[27]

While it's doubtful that Sam Watkins in hindsight actually wished he had lost a limb at Manassas, he probably did regret missing his chance to "see the elephant." Considering that so many people overoptimistically thought that the war would be short in duration, he probably believed that his chance had passed. Texan William A. "Bill" Fletcher felt even more anxious about missing out on the war. Then in his early twenties, the young man learned that war had begun while on the roof of a two-story house putting on new shingles. Immediately, he knew he would enlist, but he also knew that he had to finish the job. "It made me very nervous thinking the delay of completing the roof might cause me to miss a chance to enlist," he fretted. The roof finished, he enlisted and was off to Richmond.[28]

Young men going off to war for the first time little knew what to expect, as shown by the things they carried. Ferdinand Daniel "took along a sole-leather valise ... full of broadcloth suits, patent leather shoes, linen shirts, fancy socks and ties." He had thought, foolishly, "that both armies would march out in an open space and meet by a kind of understanding, and after a few selections by the band, go to fighting; and at sunset or sooner, the one that whipped would have some more music by the band, and then we'd retire." Ever the optimist, he added, "We were to be the ones that whipped, of course." Afterwards, there would be "the social part of it, and that is where the good clothes were to come in." The last that Daniel saw of his valise and his good clothes was at Manassas Junction, when all things the soldiers could not carry were sent to the rear in anticipation of the fight.[29]

Most soldiers brought more practical baggage, but over-packed nonetheless. According to Sam Watkins, "Every soldier had enough blankets, shirts, pant and old boots to last a year.... In addition, everyone had his gun, cartridge box, knapsack and three days' rations, a pistol on each side, and a long Bowie knife." One can imagine relatives and friends of recruits giving them what the civilians thought the soldiers might need, often several times over, and the soldiers, not wanting to offend, graciously taking the things with them. Plus, there were those entrepreneurs who sought to make a fortune by providing the new recruits with needful things. New Hampshire native Freeman Colby wrote that his training camp in Woburn, Massachusetts, was visited regularly by "venders of pies, cakes, fruit, cutlery, and many small wares which each assured his customers would be absolutely necessary to their health and comfort at the front. Many of the boys loaded up with these articles," he related, "until they needed a donkey apiece to carry their luggage."[30]

On top of what they left home with, the soldiers had their army issue to carry or wear. Union veteran Warren Lee Goss revealed, "My first uniform was a bad fit: my trowsers were too long by three or four inches; the flannel shirt was coarse and unpleasant, too large at the neck and too short elsewhere. The forage cap was an ungainly bag with pasteboard top and leather visor; the blouse was the only part which seemed decent; while the overcoat made me feel like a little nib of corn amid a preponderance of husk." The one piece of government issue that many soldiers agreed proved useless for its intended purpose was the bayonet. "The first and last time I ever saw blood from the stick of a bayonet," Bill Fletcher, remembered, was when a drunk soldier carrying his rifle with the bayonet affixed tripped and accidentally grazed an officer on the cheek with the blade. For cooking food, bayonets proved very useful, however. The bayonet served well for roasting meat over a fire.[31]

Civil War soldiers with their democratic and egalitarian sensibilities often complained about their officers and military regulations. Ashbel Hill peppered *Our Boys* with jabs at his former officers, except, of course, George McClellan. Warren Lee Goss grumbled, "Our colonel is a strict disciplinarian," and specifically protested "his efforts to drill out of us the methods of action and thought common to citizens, and to substitute in place there of blind unquestioning obedience to military rules." Goss tried to bring a complaint to his colonel, approaching him as "one gentleman calling upon another," about his drill sergeant, who had inflicted on Goss "a blast of profanity at which [his] self respect rebelled." That didn't go well.[32]

Freeman Colby believed that his captain did not like him because the New Hampshirite was not from Woburn, Massachusetts, where most of his regiment resided. He received some relief when his colonel took a shine to him and told the captain to knock it off. Nevertheless, Colby did not hesitate to criticize his colonel. For example, he described how the colonel ordered a shipment of care packages sent to the men to be brought to headquarters first. "Before being delivered to their owners each box was opened by the officers," he explained. "For this, a fee of five cents was charged and to promote the cause of temperance among the privates they took out all the liquor they found and saved it for themselves." A "fine drunk they had that night," Colby confided. "More than half the crowd was unfit for duty the next day. But the object of their care for our good was accomplished for every private remained perfectly sober."[33]

Sometimes it was even more personal, like William Armstrong's thinly disguised attack on the "pigeon-hole general" Andrew Humphreys. Frank Wilkeson, a teenaged New York artillerist with sociopathic tendencies, despised the quartermaster sergeant of his battery. When the sergeant confronted Wilkeson and the other privates in the battery who had been harassing him, Wilkeson confessed, "I was wicked enough to wish that he would get shot. He swaggered up and down behind the guns, talking loudly, and ignorant of the danger" from nearby Confederate sharp-shooters. "I, with high-beating heart, looked eagerly at him, hungrily waiting for him to jump and howl" from being shot. Wilkeson would be disappointed. The bullet that killed the sergeant entered his throat and severed his spine. The sergeant "simply fell on his back dead."[34] The scene could have been written for a Quentin Tarantino film.

Beyond his immediate superiors, Frank Wilkeson showed real contempt for the leadership of the entire Army of the Potomac from Ulysses S. Grant on down. "Under a tree stood Generals Grant, Meade, and Hancock, and a little back of them was a group of staff officers. Grant looked tired," he observed. After describing the general in unflattering terms, he continued, Grant "gazed steadily at the enlisted men as they marched by, as though trying to read their thoughts, and they gazed intently at him. But the men did not evince the slightest enthusiasm. None cheered him, none saluted him."[35] At least Wilkeson was not wishing a bullet to drop the general.

Many Union soldiers objected to orders they received to protect civilian property, especially when they knew that those civilians supported the Confederacy. "The policy of the Government was to whip the rebels without hurting their feelings," observed Wisconsinite Melvin Grigsby. "It seemed ... that the government gave more thought and care to the protection of the property and rights of rebels than to the safety and comfort of the men who had enlisted to fight for the Union." That did not stop Grigsby and his comrades from helping themselves to the Southerner's property—foraging—when they had the chance: "All that summer [1862] we carried on a warfare of that kind against what we believed to be a mistaken policy of the government." Grigsby was not the only Union soldier to disagree with the army policy against foraging. Most soldiers seem to have disregarded it at least some of the time when the opportunity arose. Frank Wilkeson lifted it to an art form. In fact, Wilkeson stole liberally from everyone. He was quite a kleptomaniac. He felt remorse only when he thought he had been caught. Sent for by the adjutant-general of the Army of the Potomac, Wilkeson bemoaned, "I was tortured with the belief that I was to be punished."[36] It turned out to be a false alarm, and Wilkeson went back to his thieving ways. Like I said, he was a sociopath.

Sometimes soldiers came to blows over attempts to protect civilian property. One night two members of Freeman Colby's company, brothers, received orders to guard the store owned by a local who also sympathized with the Confederates. When members of a New York cavalry regiment attempted to enter the store and to liberate its stock of whiskey, the brothers resisted, not because they agreed with their superior's order, but rather because they were "sons of temperance." They held the rambunctious cavalrymen off until help arrived, although one brother was "almost unroofed." Nevertheless, their actions proved, "At least this once, prohibition *prohibits*!" (Where were the brothers when their officers helped themselves to the alcohol in the men's care packages?) Besides saving the liquor, the men had one other thing to celebrate. To this point, Colby's regiment had yet to see battle. The wound the one brother received on his noggin was proclaimed "the first case of bloodshed for the regiment!"[37]

Prohibition does not always prohibit, however. While some soldiers shunned the fruit of the vine, others gave in to temptation. Melvin Grigsby drank because he liked to break rules for the sake of breaking the rules. Stationed on the outskirts of Memphis, the men of Grigsby's regiment continually found ways to elude the guards that had been posted around their camp to keep them from going into the city. Then came the order barring the sale of alcohol to the soldiers. "Before that order was issued," Grigsby confessed, "I seldom thought of drinking anything. After the order was issued, I never went into the city without finding a place where the order could be evaded. Such rules and orders," Grigsby concluded, "have that effect on men."[38]

Soldiers usually developed close bonds with their peers because of their shared experiences, but tensions between the men in arms did exist. "The infantry were good at guying the cavalry and thought the boys had little to do but to find the Yankees for them to fight, and as the Yankees were so plentiful, they had an easy job," Bill Fletcher explained. That didn't stop Fletcher from seeking a transfer to the cavalry when a wound to his foot threatened his place in the infantry. Specifically, Fletcher feared becoming a "wagon dog," one of the soldiers who ended up riding in the supply wagons for one reason or another because he could not keep up. "The cavalry boys vented their feelings" about the infantry, according to Fletcher, "mostly at the wagon dog when passing the wagon train." That was unacceptable to Fletcher: "I would prefer desertion, and desertion with me would have meant the passing of life with the unknown with a changed name." Fletcher got his wish, avoiding both wagon dog status and desertion.[39] Now he could make fun of the wagon dogs.

Wagon dogs got a bad rap because some of them were faking it, plain and simple. They "played sick," Fletcher revealed, and "were ingenious cusses in their mode of deception." Confederate surgeon Ferdinand Daniel made a similar complaint of many "convalescents," also known as "the hospital soldiers." These men "had convalesced so long ago that they had forgotten they were ever sick." "Omnipresent and all pervading," the doctor continued, "about town and village, they were simply everywhere." The hospital soldiers "invaded premises on any and all pretexts; loafed, stole fruit...." Wait a minute, stole fruit? Lots of soldiers stole fruit. They called it foraging. In fact, Bill Fletcher, the critic of the malingering wagon dogs, who spent a considerable amount of time convalescing in military hospitals himself, boasted of the clever way he and a fellow hospital soldier, Wild Bill Pemberton, for several days stole "nice ripe fruit" from a vendor in the street below the window of his third-floor hospital room. They fashioned a fishing hook into a harpoon, speared pieces of fruit and pulling them up. After the vendor caught on, the two devised another way to purloin fruit, going about town and village to do it. Feeling no guilt, they called it a "foraging trip." "'Foraging' was the word applied for such outings during war," Fletcher insisted. It's only in "civil life" that it's called "shoplifting." Fletcher spent a considerable amount of time in the hospital. In fact, in the first chapter of his memoir alone he was beset by and treated for measles, mumps, a plague of lice, an injury from a fall, jaundice, food poisoning, and "camp diarrhea." Maybe he should have laid off the fruit.[40]

While many soldiers' memoirs crow about the camaraderie in the ranks, Frank Wilkeson oozed with enmity. Not quite sixteen years old when he enlisted in late 1863, Wilkeson called his fellow new recruits "as arrant a gang of cowards, thieves, murderers, and blacklegs as were ever gathered inside the walls of Newgate or Sing Sing." A man's "social standing in the barracks was determined by the acts of villainy he had performed," Wilkeson complained. Substitutes, who served in lieu of someone who paid to be exempted, were worse: "Many of them [were] unable to speak English, vermin infested, rough-shinned, stinking with disease, their eyes running matter, their legs and arms thin and feeble, their backs bowed, and their rat-like and idiot-like heads hanging low."[41] Wilkeson basically held everyone in contempt, except for the volunteers who joined early in the war and fought with McClellan in 1862, whom the teenager idolized. He would have loved Ashbel Hill. Besides those veterans, this nineteenth-century Holden Caulfield believed himself superior to just about everyone else. Considering Wilkeson's dislike and disrespect for others, the wise-ass remarks he made, his hot-headed temper, his devil-may-care demeanor and know-it-all attitude, it's surprising that he didn't get his butt kicked on a regular basis.

One soldier named Stewart, a "sturdy, blue-eyed, black-haired Scotsman" known for being "a marvelous shot with a Napoleon gun," did seem to impress Wilkeson, however, and not for his artillery prowess. Ordered punished for getting drunk, the still inebriated cannoneer "ran at the top of his speed to a large tree ... nimbly swung himself upward into its lower limbs, and speedily climbed to the top. Once there, he drew his heavy revolver and promptly opened fire on the sergeant of the guard and his detachment. Then he howled and swore" and shot at others. The officer who ordered Stewart's arrest approached the tree, upon which Stewart "emptied his revolver" in the officer's direction. Missing with the bullets, Stewart then threw the pistol at the officer, also missing with that. Stewart still refused to descend. Only after the officer ordered that the tree be chopped down did Stewart decide to come down and face the music.[42]

One might wonder if alcohol alone fueled Stewart's behavior, or if he might have been a bit mentally disturbed. Some soldiers acted crazy to try to get discharged, like the latrine fisherman described by William Armstrong. Freeman Colby depicted a similar soldier who simulated insanity "so perfectly that there is a pretty general agreement he has lost his head. He stations himself on the parade grounds in the stillness of the night hours and declaims the entire contents of the 'American First Class Reader,'" a school book used to teach elocution, "from memory." According to Colby, many had become convinced that the soldier was nuts, even their colonel. But then the soldier went too far. After his recitation, the man went to a barrel used for "night refuse"—think a big chamber pot for the whole company—and began "soberly" bobbing "for bites in the filthy liquid." After watching for a bit, the colonel approached the soldier and asked, "What are you doing?" "Fishing, sir," came the reply. "What do you expect to *catch*?" asked the colonel, and here is where the conniver slipped up. He answered, "My *discharge*, sir."[43] The soldier should have read *Catch-22*.

One wonders what Frank Wilkeson would have thought of refuse barrel fisherman. Wilkeson probably would have critiqued his elocution and then his bobbing style. Sam Watkins had a disdain similar to that of Wilkeson for the militia men that Georgia governor Joseph Brown sent to help the Confederate Army of Tennessee fend off William Tecumseh Sherman's drive onto Atlanta. Known for his rigid states' rights views, even by Confederate standards, Brown had been notorious for holding back men as home guard rather than sending them to fight with the main Confederate armies. Watkins's description of these inferior soldiers was worthy of Wilkeson's acerbic observations:

> Every one was dressed in citizen's clothes, and the very best they had at that time. A few had double-barreled shot-guns, but the majority had umbrellas and walking-sticks, and nearly every one had on a duster, a flat-bosomed "biled' shirt," and a plug hat; and, to make the thing more ridiculous, the dwarf and the giant were marching side by side; the knock-kneed by the side of the bow-legged; the driven-in by the side of the drawn-out; the pale and sallow dyspeptic, who looked like Alex. Stephens, [who resembled an extra from the TV show *The Walking Dead,*] and who seemed to have just been taken out of a chimney that smoked very badly, and whose diet was goobers and sweet potatoes, was placed beside the three-hundred-pounder, who was dressed up to kill, and whose looks seemed to say, "I've got a substitute in the army, and twenty negroes at home."[44]

In general, however, Watkins thought highly of his fellow soldiers. Wilkeson did not. Both wrote their books three decades after the war. Nevertheless, time did not temper Wilkeson's scorn for his comrades. The thought occurred to me after finishing his book that maybe Wilkeson used his experience to craft a parody of the memoir genre. Maybe as a soldier he had been a nice guy who got along with others, who had high opinions of his officers and respected other people's property. Maybe he was just spoofing the "band of brothers" accounts like that of Watkins. After all, he came from an impressive background. His father had been a famous journalist, his mother's sister was women's rights activist Elizabeth Cady Stanton, and his grandfather once served as mayor of Buffalo, New York.[45] Yet despite his fine pedigree, in his memoir Wilkeson describes himself acting like a middle-aged curmudgeon. By the 1880s, Wilkeson was truly one, evidently unabashed by the way he carried himself during the war.

One thing that did escape Wilkeson's vilification was lice, commonly referred to as graybacks. Not so with other authors. It took Bill Fletcher just a few days in the army and six pages into his memoir to encounter the little vermin. Dealing with lice proved to be a constant battle with the soldiers. "Our principal occupation" at his regiment's summer quarters, Confederate Sam Watkins divulged, "was playing poker, chuck-a-luck and cracking graybacks. Every soldier had a brigade of lice on him, and I have seen fellows so busily engaged in cracking them that it reminded me of an old woman knitting." Having lice became both a plague and also the norm. "Pharaoh's people, when they were resisting old Moses, never enjoyed the curse of lice more than we did." But Watkins and his compatriots made the most of the infestation by holding lice races. Freeman Colby describes a similar condition in the Union army camps. Each camp "became overrun with these little pests and only by constant industry could they be kept down in our tents and personal effects." Not all men seemed to care, though. Colby continued: "Some men who took little pains to keep clean were lousy all the time they were in service. Neither the ridicule and scoffs of their fellows or the tongue lashing of the officers were of the slightest effect." In fact, some seemed rather proud of the little creepers. In the face of criticism, one soldier, "in bravado," would "unbutton the front of his shirt and show a hairy front covered with crawling graybacks which he never seemed to mind in the least."[46]

In a way, soldiers became a prisoner to lice. Some also became prisoner of the enemy. As discussed in relation to Anthony Keiley's two versions of his memoir, soldiers found it difficult to find humor in the prison experience. But bless his heart, Samuel Swiggett tried in his publication *The Bright Side of Prison Life*. An officer in the 36th Iowa Infantry, Swiggett wasted little time on the early part of his military career in his book, as his "object" was "to chronicle only the principal events which led up to the prison life and efforts to escape." Unlike most of the veterans who used their prison memoir to vilify their captors, Swiggett chose to "drop the hardships from the story ... and to treat the thing as a huge picnic." Why? He attributed it to his "natural disposition ... to see the bright side only."[47] Thus his "Always Look on the Bright Side of Life" approach.

Captured in Arkansas in 1863, Swiggett spent two years as a prisoner in a camp in Texas. Well, some of that time he spent as a prisoner. A good portion of the time he spent on the lam, having attempted to escape many times. During his stint in the hands of the Confederates, Swiggett got along so well with enemy soldiers and the Southern civilians he met that it was startling to be reminded that they were at war. Most rebel soldiers were kind to the prisoners; civilians offered food and other supplies, even when Swiggett was at large or being brought back to the camp after being caught. Guards even helped in carrying out escapes. Swiggett acknowledged that "there were cases of personal ill-treatment which came under my notice, but they were the great exceptions." At the heart of Swiggett's depiction may be his desire to promote reconciliation and reunion. These attitudes emerge in several places in the text, and at the book's end, he sounds like a virtual apologist for the Confederate prison system. How "bright" Swiggett's story is I'll leave to other readers, but the exploits he relates, sanitized as they are, are entertaining.

To be sure, it was hard but not impossible to find humor in the prison experience. Most authors chose to focus on the harsh conditions and poor treatment in a growing sub-genre of Civil War memoir in which former prisoners tried to prove that the other side's prison system was worse than theirs. Such was not the case with Griffin Frost, who published his memoir *Camp and Prison Journal* in 1867 before this contest of prison narratives evolved.[48] Frost intended no "bright side" retelling of his experience and did not shy away from the more negative aspects he encountered in his stays in the Gratiot Street Prison in St. Louis and the Alton Military Prison in Alton, Illinois. Yet his discussion of prison life lacks that bitter edge that later depictions embrace. That's not what evokes a chuckle in Frost's *Journal*. I'm a bit embarrassed to say what it is for me. It's Frost's cluelessness, at least by twenty-first-century standards. Frost, a captain in the 2nd Confederate Missouri infantry, introduced readers to his "mess mates," the men he shared quarters and meals with while in the Gratiot Street Prison. They included Joseph H. Elliott, known affectionately as "Feminine Joe." Feminine Joe, according to Frost, "can do nearly everything that ladies claim as their work."[49]

Frost gave the following description of Joe Elliott (Frost spelled the name with one t): "He is quite good looking, medium size, blue eyes, and glossy black hair—which he curls." Frost added that Joe "embroiders like a lady; and has a great fondness for teasing his fellow prisoners by catching them and hugging them and kissing them." Definitely not conduct allowed in today's workplace, yet Frost found this behavior acceptable. He noted that the other mess mates were "all fond of him," and labeled Elliott "a noble generous fellow." He also called him "the lady of the house." One must wonder if Frost would have tolerated Joe's hugging and kissing in civilian life. Perhaps if Feminine Joe had taken more of a shine to Frost, as he did with mess mate Joe Soward, Frost would have felt differently. Elliott called Soward "my Joe," and he "declared himself in love" with Soward. According to Frost, Elliott tormented Soward "almost to death—if 'my Joe' starts for a drink of water, the feminine is sure to follow; if he lies down, he is clasped in the loving arms; at table the 'feminine' refuses to eat unless 'my Joe' helps his plate." It's not that the mess mates ignored the situation. They got "provoked" sometimes, and gave the offending Joe "a genuine scolding lecture." Joe Soward, too, "occasionally" got "exasperated" and gave Elliott "a severe tongue lashing." Elliott would respond by accepting the rebuke "in a regular lover like pouting manner." The two then "won't speak for several days, and won't sleep together." Eventually, the reader is left to assume, the two made up. (Kissed and made up?) When the mess hired another prisoner to do their cooking, Frost celebrated the additional time the mess mates would have to do other things, especially Feminine

Joe. He "will have nothing to obstruct the free course of his embroidery and crocheting, while his 'lovyer' will receive more devoted attention than ever." As "provoking" as Elliott's behavior was, Frost felt, "Our two Joe's, with their odd conceits and witty sallies are the life of the mess."[50]

Now, if one were to witness this type of behavior today, one might assume that Feminine Joe was homosexual, and probably Joe Soward, too. The notion that the relationship between the two Joes, or at least the source of Elliott's behavior toward Soward, might be real romantic or sexual attraction and not just an odd conceit doesn't seem to cross Frost's mind. To be sure, the concept of homosexuality and same-sex attraction as we understand it today did not develop until the late nineteenth century.[51] But in an age when men were men, and masculinity was expected, especially in the army regardless of the need to carry out domestic tasks, the behavior of the two Joes was quite out of place. Frost never suggests a sexual relationship between the two besides maybe some heavy petting. Homosexuality was unknown but homosexual behavior, i.e., sodomy, was, and it was not acceptable. With the evidence at hand, there is no way of knowing how physical the relationship was. As for the behavior of Feminine Joe, Frost's portrayal is reminiscent of the depictions of gay men in pop culture of the 1970s and 1980s, when homosexuality was beginning to be acceptable by at least some, but it still could be made fun of (think Jack Tripper pretending to be gay in the 1970s sit-com *Three's Company*, or the Lamar character in the *Revenge of the Nerds* movies). Whatever the case, if the two Joes found momentary happiness with each other, whatever the nature of their relationship, I say good for them. Frost and his mess mates tended to agree.

One thing is certain: many Civil War soldier soldiers commented that while in camp and prison, they missed the company of women. When soldiers did experience the opportunity to interact with females, the results could be comical. While making their way back home to Texas at the war's end, Bill Fletcher and his pal John asked an elderly woman whose farm they stopped at to bake them some bread. Her farm had been overrun with rats, and for the woman's kindness, the two soldiers agreed to help her two daughters kill the pests. What ensued turned into a sort of double date. "On our way to the house," explained Fletcher, "John and I settled our claims to the young ladies—the older one was mine and the younger, John's." So far so good. "The young ladies proved to be nice, mannerly and sociable," he continued. However, "after we had pleasantly conversed a short time, we reminded the young ladies of their promise" to their mother. "The girls were more used to the fun" of slaying the critters "and seemed to enjoy the conversation" more. The boys, however, wanted to kill more rats. In fact, Bill noted, they had "rats on the brain."[52] Thus, the date ended with a lot of dead rodents but no plans for a second get together. Evidently, Bill and Joe had spent far too much time in the company of only men and really needed to brush up on their romance skills before wading into the dating pool again.

Sometimes discussing the possibility of a romantic connection could cause trouble. After being captured in Mississippi, Melvin Grigsby found himself temporarily under guard on a cantankerous old rebel's property. Challenging Grigsby on his attitudes toward African Americans, the old man queried, "I suppose you would just as soon marry a nigger wench as to marry a white woman, wouldn't you?" Grigsby replied, "I wouldn't want to marry any nigger wench that I have seen around here, for fear that I would have some of you rebels for a daddy-in-law." The old man went into a rage, stormed off, and returned with a loaded shotgun. Had it not been for the intervention of his guard, Grigsby felt certain that he would have been shot.[53]

Not all memoirs that showed comical promise lived up to expectations. LaSalle Corbell Pickett, the widow of Confederate General George Pickett, began her memoir *What Happened to Me*, in a droll way by explaining her "advent into earthy existence." She was born unexpectedly, "in the middle of the night, the middle of the week, the middle of the month, almost the middle of the year, near the middle of the century, and in the middle of a hail-storm." She was also born a girl when everyone expected a boy. When she arrived a bit prematurely, the delivering doctor said, "A girl! Why! Damn him!" "Thus my first greeting upon arriving on earth was one of profanely expressed disapproval," she remarked. Eventually the doctor and her family got over the disappointment of her gender, but from there the memoir devolves into a semi-factual, often fib-filled and not very funny fairytale about how her husband was the greatest general next to Robert E. Lee.[54] It's too bad, considering the paucity of women's voices among the humorous memoirs and other writings.

No doubt many people who wrote Civil War memoirs exaggerated, embellished, stretched the truth, told white lies, and even spun a few whoppers. A couple of spurious publications are notable primarily because of the funny comments others made about them. Ralph O. Bates claimed to have enlisted in the 9th Ohio Cavalry, later joining the 129th Indiana Infantry as a second lieutenant. After the war, Bates toured the country lecturing about his exploits. After his death in 1909, according to historian Robert Scott Davis, his wife published Bates's "purely imaginary memoirs in what amounted to a novel" under the title *Billy and Dick from Andersonville Prison to the White House*. (Ralph is allegedly the "Billy" in the book.) According to Davis, the book tells of Bates's "service as a teenager in the 9th Ohio Cavalry, his imprisonment in Camp Sumter [Andersonville], a daring escape with a friend, an interview with President Lincoln, and his testimony in the trial of Captain Wirz—none of which actually happened!" William Hesseltine, an innovator in the study of Civil War prisons, pointed out that Bates's stay in Andersonville, according to *Billy and Dick*, took place a year before the prison actually opened. Hesseltine called the book one of "a few freakish works" in "the list of prison literature." On the other hand, Allen Nevins called the book simply "bad fiction masquerading as fact."[55]

Lawrence S. Thompson argued that Thomas Berry's *Four Years with Morgan and Forrest* "deserves a place in the humorous literature of the war, for Berry's vehement insistence on the veracity of his whoppers is in the best tradition of the tall tale as she was cultivated on the western frontier." Thompson described one of the more memorable scenes from the book: "At Chickamauga a yankee minié ball plowed into [Berry's] intestines; and when the Confederate field surgeon refused to remove it, Berry himself extracted the missile, trimmed the bowel neatly, and put six stitches into it." Thompson added, "If the Confederacy had been able to produce a dozen such Münchhausens and get their stories into print before 1865, the South would have won the war hands down, for every yankee general who could read would have died laughing."[56]

Finally, there is Bartlett Yancy Malone, of whom I say with confidence, wrote a diary published after his death completely devoid of falsehoods. I assert this with such confidence because the book, first published as *The Diary of Bartlett Yancy Malone* in 1919, and later with the catchier title *Whipt 'em Everytime*, is the most boring firsthand account of the Civil War that I have ever read. Unless he (or she) had no imagination whatsoever, a person fabricating a Civil War story for oneself or even just padding his (or her) life story would be able to come up with some details more interesting and exciting than what Malone left behind. So, three cheers for Bartlett Yancy Malone and what very well may be the most honest firsthand account of the Civil War ever printed.[57]

... But This One Looks Like a Comic Book

At the age of nineteen, Freeman Colby, a native of New Hampshire working in a currier shop in Woburn, Massachusetts, enlisted with his younger brother in the 39th Massachusetts Infantry in July 1862. He produced a diary noting many of the details of his experience, which at some point after the war was transcribed and made its way into the Henniker Historical Society in Colby's home state. There it sat untouched, perhaps for a century, until discovered by Marek Bennett. Despite its lack of exciting battle scenes, Colby's prose is written much better than many of the first-hand accounts of the war that have made their way into print. Impressed with the narrative, Bennett went to work, and in due time he produced *The Civil War Diary of Freeman Colby*.[58] What makes the published Colby diary unique is that Bennett is not an historian or genealogist; rather, he is a graphic artist. The diary he saw through to publication is now in the form of a graphic history.

Bennett, a teacher and accomplished artist, used Colby's text, his "words, spelling, even punctuation," except for small changes for consistent formatting. Bennett's drawings, over three hundred pages of them, look like a cross between early *South Park* animation and Matt Groening's *Life in Hell* characters. I mean that as a compliment. The drawings Bennett produced suit Colby's story and dry humor very well. In many ways, Colby's tale is a typical wartime memoir, with the same types of incidents and complaints as other veterans' narratives. But he also has a few unique experiences. After its initial round of training back in Massachusetts, Colby's regiment headed south toward Washington. While it experienced a layover in Baltimore, people offered the men coffee, a common incident. But Colby knew Baltimore as a "hotbed of rebellion," no doubt remembering the mobbing of another Massachusetts regiment passing through that city during the first few days of the war. Some of the coffee had been laced with strychnine. "A couple hours after" receiving the tainted coffee, "several of the men were suddenly taken sick." One died, and others fell gravely ill. Not knowing who provided the poisoned coffee, nothing could be done. Colby wrote about the incident to his parents, wryly assuring them that if he and his brother were poisoned, they "would surely escape being shot."[59]

Colby's diary reminds us that Civil War soldiering was not all battles and glory. Through the first two years of Colby's enlistment, his regiment passed time encamped in one place or another, performing picket duty or other non-life-threatening tasks. In fact, despite being encamped around Washington, Colby's regiment appears not to have engaged in any major battles until May of 1864 with Grant's campaign that led to the siege of Petersburg. Soldiers will be soldiers, however, and Colby described a "sham fight" the artillery battery and the cavalry assigned to his brigade staged to break up the monotony. They called it the "Second Great Battle of Poolsville," the first being the clash between the two brothers guarding a Poolsville general store and some soldiers looking to steal whiskey from its inventory just days earlier. "The cavalry took the battery with the loss of one man's coat [which caught fire], the hair which was burned off one side of his horse," both of which occurred when the artillerymen fired a blank cartridge at their opponents, "and the breaking of a sword in the attack."

Besides the coat and the horse hair, the only casualty was a gunner, who stood too close to a cannon when another blank cartridge went off and had his arm broken in two places plus some of his clothes blown off.[60]

Colby's diary ends abruptly in early 1863, but several letters that he wrote also made their way into the Henniker Historical Society's holdings. Bennett used these letters along with writings of "several other historical eyewitnesses" to splice together a second work titled *The Civil War Diary of Freeman Colby. Volume 2, 1863*. "Where Colby falls silent," Bennett explains, "these other voices have stepped in to supply vital perspectives on one of the most consequential years in our nation's history." Whether this approach allows the "real war" to get into the book is open for debate, but it did allow Walt Whitman to get into the book, with a long passage from Whitman's poem "The Wound Dresser."[61] Some might quibble with Bennett for turning Colby's story into a graphic narrative, but a graphic representation of a Civil War memoir might appeal to a younger audience more accustomed to visual stimulation. As a teacher, I'm all for that.

Before the age of the graphic work, both fictional and factual, there was the comic book, and the Civil War made it into this literary form. In the 1950s Gilberton publishers included three Civil War-related items into their *Classics Illustrated* collection: *The Red Badge of Courage* by Stephen Crane (1952), the turn-of-the-century best seller *The Crisis* by Winston "I'm the American author not the British statesmen" Churchill (1958), and an unattributed biography titled *Abraham Lincoln* (1958). They also put out a special issue titled *The War Between the States*, just in time for the war's centennial. These comic books appeared at a time when the industry faced extreme scrutiny because critics accused comic books of causing juvenile delinquency and a host of other social woes. Gilberton escaped this attack, however, because of the respectable literary basis (meaning unfunny) of its publications. Gilberton also published a version of Harriett Beecher Stowe's *Uncle Tom's Cabin* in 1967, but by then the comic book scare had passed.[62] By then, too, middle-class comic book readers (and their parents) were a little more likely to accept a comic book that had black protagonists. (Just wait until they see *Black Panther*!)

In 1952, E.C. Comics began releasing a series of comic books telling the story of the Civil War in its Frontline Combat series. The comics featured the artistic talents of several illustrators, including Jack Davis, who would go on to become a famed cartoonist for *Mad* magazine. Born in Georgia, Davis developed a liking for drawing Civil War images, both as realistic portrayals as seen in the Frontline Combat series and in caricature as seen in *Mad* and elsewhere. In 1961 Davis launched a Civil War-themed comic strip titled *Beauregard!* featuring a comical Beetle Bailey-type Confederate soldier. Unfortunately, it ran in syndication for only four months. The short life of the strip is surprising considering that it appeared in the first year of the Civil War centennial with all its heightened interest in the conflict. One source blamed Northern newspapers for the failure, arguing that they took a pass on carrying it because it was from a Southern point of view. Another source blamed Southern papers; Southerners did not consider the Civil War a joking matter.[63] Thus began a civil war among fans of Jack Davis over who deserved the onus for the failure of *Beauregard!*: Northerners or Southerners.

Oddly, the Civil War in comic form has met with success in Belgium of all places. Written in French, *Les Tuniques Bleues* (*The Bluecoats*) first appeared in 1968 in *Spirou* magazine. Four years later, the first portion of the strip appeared in book form released by the publisher Dupuis. Since then, successive volumes in the series, over sixty so far, have met with bestselling success among comic books published in French. Written by Raoul Cauvin and illustrated by Willy Lambillotte (shortened to Lambil), *Les Tuniques Bleues* features the adventures of the short-tempered Union sergeant Cornelius Chesterfield and his sidekick, the lazy and usually cowardly Corporal Blutch. They belong to the 22nd U.S. Cavalry, known as the "Suicide Regiment" because its colonel always wants to charge into battle. Many volumes start and/or finish with the lethal outcome of some charge. For a humorous comic book, there are a lot of dead bodies. Several story lines feature real historic figures (no Walt Whitman so far) and actual events, with of course, some poetic license. In 2008, a British publisher began issuing translated volumes of the series. The British volumes are not appearing in order, but that works because the series is not a vehicle for telling the history of the Civil War.[64]

The first British release begins with our heroes being captured and sent to Robertsonville Prison. In the next issue, the men join the navy, followed by their aerial adventures as balloon observers. To be honest, I've read only the first four English installments, but one observation is that the artists behind the comic do not feature slavery as a central part of their story lines. In those issues, African Americans rarely appear, and slavery is not discussed. At least one volume still appearing only in French and bearing the unfortunate subtitle *Black Face* does focus on slavery and has an African American soldier as a lead character.[65]

In *Black Face*, the army's high command employs an African American Union soldier known only as Black Face to spark a slave rebellion behind the lines, and appoints Sergeant Chesterfield and Corporal Blutch to escort him. Chesterfield and the equally short-tempered Black Face have already clashed, and Black Face's resentment toward the sergeant and the army in general because he and his fellow African American soldiers are used only as manual laborers only deepens. While our heroes dressed in civilian clothes are mistaken for doctors and forced to treat a seriously injured Confederate colonel, Black Face recruits slaves to rise in rebellion, not just against Southern whites, but against all whites. Facing a race war that has now turned against the Union army, the generals enlist a psychotic lieutenant to lead an expedition to kill Black Face and his followers. To make a long story short, the two groups exterminate each other. Did I mention that lots of people die in these stories? Chesterfield and Blutch end up back with the suicide regiment and engage in another deadly charge. And more dead people.

Mind you, this is a fictional comic book primarily produced for laughs. A single issue of *Les Tuniques Bleues*, whether in French or English, has many more casualties than Colby Freeman's actual diary from his wartime service. And evoking a race war? There's no doubt which graphic publication is the more graphic.

The Pen Is Mightier Than the Sword (or Is That the Pin?)

The Civil War affected the life of just about every person living in the United States at the time, and not every person who left a note-worthy personal account served as a soldier. One such narrative came from the pen of Junius Henri Browne, a journalist serving as a war correspondent for the *New York Daily Tribune*. In *Four Years in Secessia: Adventures Within and Beyond Union Lines*, Browne provided colorful and detailed depictions laced with Unionist sentiments. At times he offered straight-forward factual accounts, at others sentimental and/or impressionistic descriptions. He was able to turn a phrase, and at times could be serious, candid, humorous, ironic, satirical, and sarcastic, and occasionally he slipped in a bad pun. (After spending the night in a barn, he and his fellow travelers woke up "expecting ... we might be a little hoarse." Da-Dum.) He wrote the book as the war drew to a close and finished it shortly after Lee's surrender while Jefferson Davis was still on the run.[66]

As a member of the "Bohemian Brigade," the newspapermen who covered the war at the front, Browne saw the conflict in a somewhat different way than soldiers did. He began his book by explaining that serving as a war correspondent was a thankless job. "The ill-starred Bohemian has a most delicate and difficult task to perform," he noted. "He must do his duty, and yet offend no one. He must praise, but not censure.... Few give him commendation; yet many are willing to denounce him. What he does well passes in silence; what he does ill is blazoned to his shame." If that wasn't enough, he went on, the "correspondent may do, and dare, and suffer; but who yields him credit? If he die in the service by disease or casualty, it is thought and declared by many that he had no business there. The officers frequently dislike him, because they have not received what they conceive to be their meed of praise; and the people do not appreciate him."[67] He goes on with six more pages in defense of his work.

Despite his journalistic credentials, Browne experienced and wrote about many of the same things as did the soldiers he travelled with in the Western Theater: cantankerous officers; the tedium of camp life; the disappointment that came from missing the fight; the fear evoked from coming under fire; and even capture and imprisonment. Then there were the vermin. Browne encountered a variety of nasty swarming, biting, stinging, and otherwise annoying insects. And in vivid detail he described them all! His first experience came early in the war. "Until I began to follow the camp," he wrote, "I had never known, save by auricular evidence, of those unpoetical insects known as fleas." He then painted a picture of an insect onslaught that equaled the one Texan Rensalear Reed Gilbert created. Fleas weren't the only bugs that beset Browne. "The countless musquitos in the vicinity of Fort Pillow, during the month of April, 1862, must have had strong Secession sympathies," he conjectured. "They certainly were bitter enemies of the Nationalists, and phlebotomized them without mercy." And then there were the gnats. "The winged pests covered us in swarms, and for five minutes our motions resembled the wild movements of dancing Dervises. Indeed, I doubt if the Dervises ever danced as we did."[68]

Surprisingly, Browne seemed reluctant to discuss the one type of vermin with which so many soldiers contended: lice. It appeared that the Bohemian had his first bout with the little buggers after he reached Libby Prison in Richmond, two years into his adventure. First, he witnessed others combatting the crawlers. "What first shocked me in the Libby more than aught else was, that my fellow-prisoners, at least once a day, thoroughly examined their garments, for what purpose I will not be unpoetic enough to state—and accompanied their researches with much profanity and considerable phlebotomy." He would not even mention them by name. Soon the experience became more than vicarious. "A few hours proved the urgent necessity of the custom, and from that time until after my escape I made a quotidian investigation—in which, like a jealous husband, I looked for what I feared to find—that never failed to fill me with aversion and disgust."[69]

Most nineteenth-century Americans saw lice as a sign of uncleanliness and inferiority. Proper, hygienic, and moral people did not get lice. To do so evoked shame and humiliation. Yet, as historian Evan A. Kutzler has pointed out, "The Civil War was a great boon for lice." While some Civil War soldiers and later memoirists came to accept, acknowledge, make fun of, and write about lice as a reality of war, others did not. Browne falls somewhere in the middle, willing to acknowledge the little creatures but not to the extent that he would call them by name. As for the lice, this boon also proved detrimental. Hans Zinsser, a prominent bacteriologist of the first half of the twentieth century, pointed out in his book *Rats, Lice and History* that lice passed diseases like typhus to humans, and that "camp epidemics ... have often determined victory or defeat before the generals know where they are going to place the headquarters' mess." But in order to pass typhus, Zinsser's main interest in his book, to humans, the lice had to contract the disease from humans. And typhus WILL kill lice. "If lice can dread," Zinsser empathized, "the nightmare of their lives is the fear of some day inhabiting an infected rat or human. For the host may survive; but the ill-starred louse ... is doomed beyond succor."[70] Unfortunately, we only have Zinsser's word on this. Civil War–era lice left no memoirs. If they did, they surely would be from the perspective of "The Louse Cause."

While writing little about lice, Junius Browne saved some of his harshest terminology for Southern women. Union soldiers commonly depicted Southern women in negative terms. Browne was no different. "Secession women are amusing," he observed, "and, so long as they confine themselves to talking, do no harm, unless to some false reputation they may have acquired for understanding." He acknowledged, though, that they did do harm. "Every Southern woman exercised her influence in the cause of the Rebellion; bade her husband, brother, father, lover, friend, make another struggle for his fireside and country, and victory would reward his efforts." Perhaps he exaggerated, but many women in the South did encourage men to enlist, as did women in the North. Browne particularly attacked rebel women he witnessed in Missouri and Arkansas. In Missouri, "fine women did not appear indigenous to the disloyal soil.... They were in the rough, as sculptors phrase it; lacking the refining chisel of Art and Culture to fashion them into loveliness." These "brown and brawny women ... offended his taste ... chilled his gallantry ... [and] repressed his chivalrous sentiment." Moving further south, Browne's opinion became only firmer. "The women" of Arkansas "were only such in name; their sex, in their absence of physiological demonstration, requiring to be taken on faith. Tall, meagre, sallow, with hard features and large bones, they would have appeared masculine if they had not been too attenuated to suggest the possibility of health or strength. They drank whisky and smoked as freely as men; often chewed tobacco, and went about swearing in discordant tones, and expectorating skillfully."[71]

I should note that Browne's attitude toward women in general could not be described as enlightened. To be sure, Browne was not averse to women. In fact, during his trek to reach Union lines after escaping prison, he had a romantic moment with a North Carolinian lass who helped him hide when they feared the local home guard was approaching. As they hid in the darkness with the young woman clinging to one of his arms, Browne confessed in terms worthy of a romance novel, he threw the other "about her waist—a taper one, even though she had always lived in North Carolina, and had never worn a corset—and drawing her plump figure to my bosom, kissed her long and closely." The romantic prose quickly disappeared, as Browne admitted that he kissed her, "long and closely," mind you, "more for gratitude than gallantry, more from a sense of duty than affection." How honorable. Fortunately, he acknowledged, his "duty just at that moment appeared not disagreeable to discharge." In fact, he added, "The sensation was not unpleasant to me." Oh, and she was sixteen.[72]

Browne's opinion of Southerners in general differed little from that of Southern women (except maybe sixteen-year-olds). The Southern people were "uneducated, coarse, ignorant, vulgar people, who have no idea of comfort or convenience; but live in wretched cabins, on pork, corn-bread, and hominy, thanking God they are not negroes, but having no conception of a higher or worthier existence." As for the slave-holding class, "even the oligarchs, the privileged few, who hold slaves, and rule the whites as thoroughly, though in a different way, as they do their human chattels, have little to boast of." And he goes on for two chapters.

Considering that Browne spent a year and a half as a captive in Confederate prisoner of war camps, one can understand his acrimony toward Southerners. During the war, captured journalists routinely were released and passed through the lines. Not Browne and his colleague Albert D. Richardson. The two worked for the notoriously abolitionist *New York Tribune* and its famed, or if you were Southern infamous, editor Horace Greeley. Browne and Richardson suffered from guilt by association. There would be no release for them, except by escape. Capturing the two journalists near Vicksburg, the Confederates shipped them off to Virginia. They spent time in Libby Prison and Castle Thunder in Richmond and then Salisbury Prison in North Carolina. Like so many Civil War memoirists who faced prison, Browne found little funny to relate. Except tunnels. Browne became fixated with tunnels and the possibility of escaping through a tunnel. But tunnels so often were unreliable. They collapsed. They failed to extend far enough beyond the prison. They were discovered. Indeed, he explained, "A woman's humor is not more uncertain than a Tunnel," not missing an opportunity to belittle women. Given the chance to escape with others by means other than a tunnel, however, Browne took it: "A Tunnel is a Tunnel; but Liberty is Liberty; and the latter is acceptable in any form, while the former alone is but an abstraction."[73]

Once on the run, a bit of Browne's humor returned. At one point on the lam, he and his party hid under beds in the home of a Unionist when they feared the approach of Confederate authorities. After explaining that they "crept under the beds," Browne commented snidely, "Some of our party may have been compelled to indulge in that kind of thing before; but I conjecture it was under very different circumstances." Browne may have had in mind his old friend, Albert D. Richardson, who had a reputation as a bit of a womanizer before he married.[74]

Elizabeth Keckley also never put on a uniform, never toted a musket, never served picket duty, and never marched long distances to set up a new camp only to be ordered to pack up for a march to yet another location. Keckley had a more critical, high pressure, and potentially dangerous job during the war. Keckley made dresses for Mary Todd Lincoln. Born into slavery, Keckley became a talented seamstress, which helped to support the family that owned her. After earning money for herself, she purchased her freedom as well as that of her son. She moved to Washington, D.C., and began a dressmaking business, employing several other seamstresses and including among her clientele many of the capital's elite women, such as the wives of Jefferson Davis and Robert E. Lee. After the Lincolns came to town, Keckley became the modiste for and confidant of Mary Todd Lincoln, an experience she chronicled in her autobiographical *Behind the Scenes, or, Thirty Years a Slave and Four Years in the White House*, which focusses mostly on the titular four years and several afterward.[75]

While not meant to be funny, *Behind the Scenes* was written with candor and subtle wit. Keckley paints a not always flattering portrait of Mrs. Lincoln and reveals how she had to handle the first lady delicately, like an unexploded shell. When she arrived a bit later than expected with the dress she made for Mary for the inaugural ball, she found Mary in a frenzy because she thought it was too late for her to dress and she would not be able to go to her own husband's celebration. "You are not in time, Mrs. Keckley; you have bitterly disappointed me," Mary complained. "I have no time now to dress, and, what is more, I will not dress, and go down-stairs." When Keckley assured her that there was plenty of time, Mary responded, "No, I won't be dressed. I will stay in my room. Mr. Lincoln can go down with the other ladies." Handling Mary like Mr. Rogers might handle an incorrigible child, Keckley convinced her to dress, with time to spare.[76] Keckley never editorialized on Mary's behavior, but it is hard not to draw conclusions about the first lady. Keckley revealed that Mary disliked many of the capital's women, seeing them as rivals for attention, and that Mary told the president which women he should not speak with at a White House reception. Keckley further suggested that Mary failed to give Abraham the affection he deserved. While she stressed that Mary sought to save money by dressing herself thriftily, Keckley discussed Mary running up a huge debt with New York merchants while keeping her husband in the dark. To be sure, Keckley intended no behind the scenes exposé, despite her book's title, but she did leave us with a tale of a first lady whose bratty and self-centered behavior in hindsight can only spark a chuckle.

Keckley's *Behind the Scenes* tells another story, that of the struggles African Americans both enslaved and free faced in the Civil War era. Keckley handled this subject with equal grace. In a memorable scene, after the president's assassination, Keckley met Mary in New York. Strapped for money, Mary thought that she could sell some of the wardrobe she bought that put her in debt in the first place. Travelling under an assumed name to fend off attention, Mary arrived at the hotel first. When Keckley got there, Mary tried to obtain a room for her. The hotel's clerk responded, "We have no room for her, madam," without explanation. "But she must have a room." said Mary. "She is a friend of mine, and I want a room for her adjoining mine." He came back, "We have no room for her on your floor." "That is strange, sir. I tell you that she is a friend of mine," Mary insisted, "and I am sure you could not give a room to a more worthy person." "Friend of yours, or not, I tell you we have no room for her on your floor. I can find a place for her on the fifth floor." Keckley never directly addressed why a room could not be had next to Mary's on a lower floor, but it was unnecessary. Keckley did get a bit of revenge in her description of the offensive counter worker: "The clerk, like all modern hotel clerks, was exquisitely arrayed, highly perfumed, and too self-important to be obliging, or even courteous." Keckley had another clash with the rude clerk and some other staff when they refused to allow her to eat in the dining room because she was a "servant," even though she was not. When Mary tried to intercede, Keckley stopped her, not wanting the true identity of the former first lady exposed.[77] Keckley responded to these encounters with aplomb and dignity. Had she reacted angrily when it happened and then, more importantly, written angrily about in her book, many white readers would have dismissed her sentiments.

Only six months after Keckley published *Behind the Scenes*, a parody appeared. While imitation may sometimes be the sincerest form of flattery, *Behind the Seams* was not intended to flatter. Published anonymously, *Seams* is a blatantly racist attack on Keckley and *Scenes*. Authorship is attributed to "A Nigger Woman Who Took in Work from Mrs. Lincoln and Mrs. Davis," later identified as "Betsey Kickley. (nigger)." "I was born a nigger slave," asserts the ersatz author. "My parents were slaves and niggers, and I came upon the earth done up brown, that is to say a dark mulatto." *Seams* author depicts the hotel check-in scene that Keckley describes, which while intending to belittle Keckley, in actuality, unintentionally reveals the clerk's real motivation, only validating Keckley's initial grievance. This version revolves around the clerk's blatant admission, "We don't board niggers."[78]

Seams' author has been identified as Daniel Ottolengui, a native of Charleston, South Carolina, from a slave-owning family. Unfortunately, the author had an audience ready to consume such racist portrayals; the era certainly had its share of deplorables to provide a readership. Nevertheless, *Seams* stands as stark evidence of the racism Keckley sensitively described. Fortunately, Ottolengui's *Seams* has been all but forgotten except by a small number of unsympathetic academic specialists,[79] while Keckley's *Behind the Scenes* continues in publication in numerous versions and for free through sources like Google Books. More importantly, *Scenes* continues to be remembered. Now if that wouldn't needle Daniel Ottolengui, I don't know what would.

The Many Lives of the Jordan Anderson Letter

In August 1865 a letter from Jordan Anderson, a recently emancipated Black man now living with his family as a free man in Dayton, Ohio, to his former master, Colonel P.H. Anderson in Tennessee, appeared in the *Cincinnati Commercial*. In the letter, purportedly recorded verbatim as it was dictated by the formerly enslaved man, Jordan Anderson cleverly declined the colonel's request to return to his farm to work there. At times the letter is serious and poignant, but it is also quite humorous and sarcastic in an innocent, or perhaps passive aggressive, sort of way. Since its first publication, the letter has experienced many lives; it has been reprinted, excerpted, cited, or discussed in myriad textbooks, monographs, article-length essays, stage plays, and in recent years on the web. Many of the scholars who have utilized the Anderson letter have praised its author and its content. In his Pulitzer Prize-winning study of Reconstruction, *Been in the Storm So Long*, Leon Litwack attested that "few individuals—white or black—have ever articulated the meaning of freedom more clearly or more precisely than Jourdon Anderson." Ralph Ellison biographer Lawrence Jackson described the letter as "full of bravery, wit, and self determination," while civil rights activist John Yancy Odom used the term "exquisite." "It is clear," Odom added, "that Mr. Jourdon Anderson was not only literate, he was articulate." And the Huffington Post reported one hundred and forty-seven years after the penning of this letter, that Jordan Anderson, "in the most genteel manner," told his "Old Master to Shove It."[80] Despite its modest origins, the Anderson letter has experienced much more exposure than its author ever could have imagined and continues to find a place in academic and popular publications and on-line outlets. It can be accessed easily on the internet, and if you have not read it yet, I highly recommend it. I'll wait.

Jordan Anderson's letter first appeared in the *Cincinnati Commercial* on August 12, 1865.[81] The editors titled the document "Letter from a Freedman to his Old Master" and preceded it with the comment, "The following is a genuine document. It was *dictated* by the old servant, and contains his ideas and forms of expression." Over the next few weeks, many newspapers—not surprisingly all Northern—reprinted the letter. Most, but not all, cited the *Cincinnati Commercial* as their source and included the *Commercial*'s editorial comment on the letter's authenticity. The *New York Daily Tribune*, however, identified the author of the letter as "Jourdon" Anderson, even though his correctly-spelled name appears in the letter's first sentence. Other publications copied the *Tribune*'s version, thus the spelling disagreement on Jordan's name. Abolitionist William Lloyd Garrison's weekly newspaper *The Liberator*, which published the letter in its September 1 edition, also misidentified the author, in this case as "George" Anderson, again despite the author's self-reference.[82]

While the letter caught the attention of many newspaper editors, perhaps not all recognized the gravity of its content and the sarcasm of its tone. For example, the *Boston Daily Advertiser* and the *Lowell Daily Citizen and News* both describe the item as "A Quaint Letter from a Freedman to His Old Master." It cannot be stated with certainty that the Lowell paper copied the letter (and its "Quaint" description) from the neighboring Boston paper because the former identifies the *Cincinnati Commercial* as the letter's source while the latter does not. The Boston paper, on the other hand, probably copied the letter from the *New York Tribune*, suggested by the *Advertiser*'s misspelled "Jourdon" name.[83]

Anderson's letter found outlets in places other than newspapers. For example, Lydia Maria Child reproduced it in her December 1865 publication *The Freedmen's Book*, a collection of short items written by or about enslaved people and freedmen. Child, an author and long-time advocate of abolition and women's rights, expressed her hope that those who read the book or had it read to them by others "derive fresh strength and courage from this true record of what colored men have accomplished, under great disadvantages." Anderson's letter even made its way across the Atlantic Ocean, appearing in the British periodicals *The Freed-Man: A Monthly Magazine Devoted to the Interests of the Freed Coloured People* and *The Anti-Slavery Reporter and Aborigines' Friend*, both published in London.[84]

By 1866, Jordan Anderson's letter disappeared into obscurity. The transition of formerly enslaved people to free men and women had become old news to journalists. Soon, the nation experienced a flourishing of histories and memoirs written about the Civil War, often produced by participants in the conflict. This literature had little room for the voices and stories of African Americans and usually portrayed people of color in negative stereotypes. One group of scholars and intellectuals who rejected this racist image of African Americans emerged from the "New Negro" movement, which stemmed from the Harlem Renaissance in the early twentieth century. The New Negro movement promoted African American dignity, while challenging Jim Crow race relations and segregation. Known as the Father of Negro History, Carter G. Woodson published *The Mind of the Negro: As Reflected in Letters During the Crisis 1800–1860* in 1926. Despite his stated time-frame, Woodson included Anderson's epistle in a section devoted to letters "not written for publication" and produced by "persons [who] belonged to the lower walks of life." That same year, *The Journal of Negro History*, which Woodson founded in 1916, published a large section of letters from *The Mind of the Negro*, including that of Jordan Anderson.[85]

This would not be the last time that Anderson's letter found its way into a scholarly periodical. In the spring of 1942, the inaugural issue of the journal *The Negro Quarterly* appeared as an outlet for writers who projected the "true experience" of African Americans. The editorial staff and board of the short-lived journal eventually included Angelo Herndon, Ralph Ellison, and Alain Locke. In a review of a recently-published history of the Civil War appearing in *The Negro Quarterly*'s first number, L.D. Reddick, curator of the Schomburg Collection of Negro Literature of the New York Public Library, took to task historians for their "nostalgic" depictions of "the feudal beauty of lordly masters, palatial mansions and slaves, 'sleek, fat and strumming the banjo.'" The *Quarterly* had no place for caricatures of Civil War–era African Americans such as this. It did, however, have a place for Jordan Anderson's letter, reprinting it in the same issue.[86] Two and a half decades later, Anderson's letter appeared in a 1969 issue of *Negro History Bulletin*, and in 1999 it once again found a place in the NAACP publication *The New Crisis: A Magazine of Opportunities and Ideas*.[87]

While Anderson's letter had been forgotten by all but a small number of scholars through more than half of the twentieth century, his story found a place in other print forms. Early in the century, many of the literary figures of the Harlem Renaissance saw poet and author Paul Laurence Dunbar as a role model. In 1904, the same year that he died, Dunbar published the short story "The Wisdom of Silence," which opens with its main character "Jeremiah Anderson," formerly enslaved, verbally declining an offer from his former master to return to the plantation. The resemblance of the plot to the Jordan Anderson narrative is not a coincidence, although Dunbar did not draw inspiration from the letter. Rather, Dunbar lived in

Dayton, Ohio, and was close friends with Anderson's son Valentine Winters Anderson. Dunbar no doubt knew the story from the younger Anderson, if not from Jordan himself.[88]

Jordan Anderson's letter also has made it to the stage. Inspired by the Civil Rights movement, in 1964 author, historian and social activist Martin B. Duberman wrote *In White America: A Documentary Play*, portraying the lives of African Americans from the colonial period through the 1950s. Duberman included an edited version of the letter in his script, although he presented it as if it had been written prior to the Civil War, not after. His play has been performed on many college campuses and Off-Broadway, as recently as 2015 in conjunction with its fiftieth anniversary. A half a century later, the letter inspired the multimedia play *Jordan Anderson Writes a Letter*, authored by Arthur J. Beers and first performed at the University of Detroit–Mercy. Excerpts of the letter also appear in the avant-garde play *Dead Letter Office (a prelude to Bartleby the Scrivener)*, written by Matthew Earnest and first performed at Marshall University in 2012.[89]

As Civil Rights promoters enlisted the use of Anderson's letter in the twentieth century, political activists employed the letter in the early twenty-first century to advocate for reparations to compensate African Americans for the damage done to generations of families due to slavery, discrimination, and segregation. For example, historian Robin D.G. Kelley used the letter in his book *Freedom Dreams: The Black Radical Imagination*. He argued, "By even the most elementary principles of liberal capitalism, Jourdon Anderson presents a sound, reasonable case for receiving compensation for years of unpaid labor." In the end, he concluded, Colonel Anderson probably "laughed ... dismissing his former slave's request as absurd." In *Reparations: Pro and Con*, Alfred L. Brophy described the letter as "so perfect that one thinks it must have been invented by some latter-day reparations proponent (or by someone seeking to stir up anti–Southern feelings in the wake of the Civil War)." Other authors have utilized the letter in their works on the reparations issue, including at least one who focused on seeking payments for Black Africans who suffered through the Apartheid system in South Africa.[90]

For better or worse, Jordan Anderson's letter has found use promoting other causes. In 2006, Sage Starkeeper published *The Un-Promised Generation*, a convoluted critique of the unfulfilled promises of the Civil Rights movement, which she argues have been co-opted by the ruling power structure, and of the failures of the African American community for putting faith in the government rather than their own "villages," "Elders," and "Ancestors" for answers. "The letter *'To My Old Master,'*" Starkeeper asserts, "provides guidance from the Ancestors and reveals basic insight and reasoning that is key for developing the qualifications for moral leadership necessary to guide a family, a community, a nation and a *New Age of Purification and Progress*."[91]

Of course, Jordan Anderson's letter has had a much more academic life, as well. Beginning in the 1950s, Civil War historians launched a major challenge to the prevailing notions about slavery and those enslaved and the persistent "Lost Cause" interpretation with all its racist trappings.[92] Then, starting in the 1960s and 1970s, the study of history "from the bottom up" became more commonplace with the growth of social history as a field of study. This trend would also impact the teaching of history in college and high school classes, leading to the adoption of course material such as letters and diary passages from obscure figures from the past who never held political office or played any other significant public role, yet whose prose captured a moment, a trend, or an experience that shaped the past. An unscientific survey conducted by this author found Anderson's letter appearing in no fewer than twenty-five document readers and textbooks.

This survey does not exhaust the places where Anderson's letter has appeared. Other authors have recognized in Anderson's correspondence its significance and its humor. In 1965 journalist and CBS public relations executive Philip Sterling found a place for the letter in his anthology *Laughing on the Outside: The Intelligent White Reader's Guide to Negro Tales and Humor*. In his introduction, Sterling explained, "For the purpose of this essay, humor is hereby defined as any utterance capable of making others laugh, thoughtfully, or think laughingly." Anderson's letter certainly is capable of both. Sterling, who was white, evoked the early twentieth-century African American activist and historian W.E.B. DuBois's observation that humor provided, in part, a "defense mechanism" for African Americans that gave them "inner satisfaction" in the face of discrimination and oppression. Much had changed since DuBois wrote those words, and according to Sterling, "Negroes haven't quit laughing, but they're no longer 'sitting idly by.' They're on their feet and moving in a direction that is perfectly apparent to the whole world," no doubt a reference to the Civil Rights movement and the successes it had achieved by the mid–1960s.[93]

Saunders Redding, an historian and probably the first African American to teach at an Ivy League school, added in the introduction he wrote to Sterling's book, "American Negro humor is often an escape into pride and dignity; into a sense of that human equality the substance of which was (and is) too often denied; and into a spirit of triumph that chronic adversity contradicts."[94] Jordan Anderson's letter reflects the pride and dignity that the former slave had long since been denied by his former master. Sterling includes Anderson's letter not with the section concerning the Civil War era, instead placing it in the book's last section, which embraces humor primarily from the twentieth century. What ties these selections together, according to Sterling, "is that they dwell only fleetingly, if at all, on the past, give short shrift to the present, and direct attention to the future."[95]

With the proliferation of websites, blogs, chat rooms, bulletin boards, and other social media, Jordan Anderson's letter has found new life in the twenty-first century on the internet. A search for "Jordan Anderson" (or "Jourdon Anderson") will come up with a multitude of sites posted within the last two decades reporting on the letter, the vast majority of them taking great pleasure in Anderson's response to his former owner. Many would agree with political scientist and blogger Corey Robin, who called the letter "A Most Delightful Fuck You."[96]

Jordan Anderson was more than just the name on a "quaint" letter from a freedman. And he was more than a topic for twenty-first-century bloggers to bandy about glibly. Anderson lived. Anderson spent the rest of his life living in a working-class neighborhood in Dayton, Ohio, with his family. He found employment as a hostler and then translated his talent with horses into a coachman's position. He ended his working career as a butler, but by 1900, according to the census, Anderson had "retired." Furthermore, he watched his children grow up in freedom and get the education he so much desired for them. Jordan Anderson died in 1907, outliving his former master by four decades. Anderson's letter, however, continues to live. Through this compelling document, Jordan Anderson continues to inform, inspire, amaze, and amuse. And it continues to get into the books.

Grant vs. Lee

When it came to winning civil wars, Ulysses S. Grant beat out Robert E. Lee, 1–0. When it came to producing postwar memoirs, Grant also won by the same score. While Lee never put pen to paper about his wartime experiences, Grant's *Personal Memoirs of U.S. Grant*, first published in 1885 and 1886, became what many consider the most significant first-hand account of the conflict. The work has been praised by Pulitzer Prize historians such as Bruce Catton, William McFeely, and James McPherson and literary giants like Gertrude Stein, Owen Wister, and Mark Twain (who had a personal stake in its publication). In his monumental study *Patriotic Gore*, the usually persnickety literary critic Edmund Wilson asserted, "Never has a book so objective in form seemed so personal in every line, and though the tempo is never increased, the narrative, once we get into the war, seems to move with the increasing momentum that the soldier must have felt in the field." Indeed, Wilson heaped praises on *Memoirs*, calling it "a unique expression of the national character."[97]

Memoirs was not Grant's first attempt at producing a personal war narrative. In 1884 the editors of *Century Magazine* scored a coup when the retired general and former president agreed to contribute to their "Battles and Leaders of the Civil War" series. Grant produced four well-received articles, although the remuneration he received for them proved insufficient to lessen the financial woes in which he had recently found himself, further complicated by a diagnosis of throat cancer. Grant initially planned to publish his memoir through *Century*, but when friend Mark Twain offered him a more lucrative deal, Grant decided to go with Twain's own publishing house. Grant completed the work in July 1885; a month later he died. Profits from the publication solved the family's financial situation and kept Grant's widow comfortable for the rest of her life.[98]

Despite the praise *Memoirs* received upon its release and since, the book was not without controversy. Even before publication, rumors began to circulate that Grant was not the true author of the work, and soon suspicion of being the alleged ghostwriter fell on Mark Twain. The claims traced back to Adam Badeau, a disgruntled former aide who helped research Grant's *Century* articles and fact-check the memoir. After Grant's death, Badeau even claimed that *he* did most of the writing. Badeau's accusations were baseless. "That no one can have tampered much with the original text of the *Memoirs*," Edmund Wilson insisted, "is proved by the complete uniformity of their style with that of Grant's dispatches, his letters, and his recorded conversations."[99] I have to agree.

Grant's prose is appropriate for the seriousness of the subject at hand. Yet occasionally, he placed a humorous quip in the narrative. For example, unenthusiastic about entering West Point but thrilled to see a bit of the nation, he commented on his passage through Philadelphia and New York City, "When these places were visited I would have been glad to have had a steamboat or railroad collision, or any other accident happen, by which I might receive a temporary injury sufficient to make me ineligible, for a time, to enter the Academy." Alas, no accidents occurred, and soon he "had to face the music." After graduation, he observed of his superiors at his first assignment, "It seems to me, in my early army days, that too many of the older officers, when they come to command posts, made it a study to think what order they could publish to annoy their subordinates and render them uncomfortable." Many veterans made similar observations of their Civil War chain of command. As for the officers Grant had in mind, he continued, "I noticed, however, a few years later, when the Mexican war broke out, that most of this class of officers discovered they were possessed of disabilities which entirely incapacitated them for active field service. They had the moral courage to proclaim it, too. They were right," Grant concluded, "but they did not always give the disease the right name."[100]

In his treatment of the Civil War, Grant's writing reflects a sober contemplation of the events. (Yes, I meant that pun, but I'll return to that later.) One barb aimed at his former enemies really stands out for a good laugh, however. In his discussion of the Battle of Shiloh and the critics of Confederate General Pierre Beauregard, who accused him of losing the battle the rebels surely would have won had it not been for the death of Albert Sydney Johnston, Grant wrote, "Some of these critics claim that Shiloh was won [by Union forces under Grant] when Johnston fell, and that if he had not fallen the army under me would have been annihilated or captured." In his own defense, and not Beauregard's, Grant begged to differ with this speculation: "*Ifs* defeated the Confederates at Shiloh. There is little doubt that we would have been disgracefully beaten *if* all the shells and bullets fired by us had passed harmlessly over the enemy and *if* all theirs had taken effect."[101]

At this point I must make an observation. Many memoirists who wrote about their encounters with Ulysses S. Grant commented that he had a sense of humor. Here we are presented with some specimens of that humor. Still, I can't help but hear the voice of Mark Twain in these jests. Don't get me wrong; I'm not trying to resurrect the old "Mark Twain ghostwrote the memoir" thing. I stand by my earlier position on that. Had Twain written a large portion of the book, I suspect there would be a whole lot more funny stuff. But as an author, I know that sometimes editorial suggestions from one's publisher make their way into the final work. So, while I'm convinced that Grant wrote the *Memoirs*, I suspect that Twain left his mark on them, too.

One subject that Grant does not broach in the memoir is booze. Nick Sacco, a park ranger with the National Park Service at the Ulysses S. Grant Historic Site in St. Louis, Missouri, noted, "For many, the most recognizable trait in Grant that they learned in school isn't that he was a general or president, but that he was allegedly an alcoholic."[102] This was probably true for most American school kids in the twentieth century. It was for me. Probably more influential than the works of professional historians and the lessons of teachers in crafting this image of Grant the boozer was the stereotypical besotted U.S. Grant portrayed in popular culture. I'm not sure when this image began to appear, but by 1930, the American humorist James Thurber needed little explanation in the hypothetical "If Grant Had Been Drinking at Appomattox" as the title of a short story published in the *New Yorker*. In it, Thurber portrays a terribly hung-over Grant being woken by his aide and then drinking several hairs of the dog that bit him before meeting with General Lee and his staff. In this altered state, the confused Grant offers his sword in surrender instead of vice versa.[103]

The drunken Grant has appeared on screen as recently as January 14, 2019, in a "Drunk History" segment as part of Comedy Central's *The Daily Show*. However, Grant scholar Charles G. Ellington observed in a 1987 study that the general "drank—like most soldiers of his time. But he was not a drunkard." Most recent historians agree and have worked diligently to dispel this portrayal. Grant did have issues with alcohol, but he was a binge-drinker, and his binges were few and far between. Furthermore, rarely did his drinking interfere with important matters like fighting a civil war. Plus, Grant was a light weight, so it didn't take much to affect him. Nevertheless, as historian Joan Waugh noted in a 2010 lecture, when it comes to Grant, an incompetent drunk is funnier than a sober, diligent officer, and such a stereotypical image suits the needs and interests of comedy writers.[104] Now that Ron Chernow has written a biography of Grant, the Broadway play penned by Lin Manuel-Miranda that no doubt will follow should set the record straight. After all, Grant truly was the model of a modern major general.

Grant's chief rival in gray, Robert E. Lee, never wrote a memoir that might have showcased his sense of humor, but according to Thomas Forehand, Jr., the Confederate icon, known as the "marble man" for his stoic demeanor, had a lighter side. Lee "joked, teased, punned, told humorous stories, occasionally pulled pranks, and sometimes laughed himself to tears." Biographer Roy Blount, Jr., known for his own witty writing, agreed, noting that Lee "was capable of larky jocularity in the oddest connections and the darkest times." While Lee left no first-hand account, others who knew the marble man did, and from this large body of hagiography, Forehand drew over one hundred examples of Lee light-heartedness.[105]

Probably the most bizarre story included in Forehand's collection concerns Lee's apparent fixation with his feet and having them tickled by children. A Freudian psychiatrist might say that Lee may have had a foot fetish with pedophiliac tendencies. It's actually Lee's son Robert E. Lee, Jr. who inadvertently spilled the beans in his own memoir. While fondly reflecting on his days of youth, the younger Lee recorded that his father "petted" his children "a great deal." Then junior explained that the young ones' "greatest treat was to get into [their father's] bed in the morning and lie close to him, listening while he talked to us in his bright, entertaining way." Okay, maybe it was all innocent. But then, the description gets weirder. The general, according to Robert Jr., "was very fond of having his hands tickled, and what was more curious, it pleased and delighted him to take off his slippers and place his feet in our laps in order to have them tickled." The tickling became part of a ritual. "Often," Robert reminisced, "as little things, after romping all day, the enforced sitting would be too much for us, and our drowsiness would soon show itself in continued nods." The older Lee would have none of that. "To arouse us, he had a way of stirring us up with his foot—laughing heartily at and with us. He would often tell us the most delightful stories, and then there was no nodding." The stories came at a price, however. "Sometimes ... our interest in his wonderful tales became so engrossing that we would forget to do our duty:" tickling his feet. When that occurred, Lee "would declare, 'No tickling, no story!'" With the tickling recommenced and "going on briskly," the general would continue his story, "with foot in either lap of [son Robert] or youngest sister [Annie]."[106]

Whether or not Lee let others tickle his feet is unknown. Early in the war, he wrote to his youngest daughter Annie that "my feet are entirely neglected." Robert Jr. recorded that his father did let the small daughter of a friend tickle his hands, at least once. What makes Lee's focus on his feet all the more fascinating is the fact that he had tiny feet! According to Roy Blount, by modern measurements, which did not differ from that of Lee's days, Lee had what would be a men's size 4½, which shoe producers do not make today. It would be in the children's size range. Otherwise, Lee was not a small man, standing at five foot ten or eleven inches. Such a physical characteristic, especially on someone who gained a larger than life, mythical reputation, seems rather incongruous. In his memoir, Ulysses S. Grant wrote, "The natural disposition of most people is to clothe a commander of a large army whom they do not know, with almost superhuman abilities. A large part of the National army, for instance, and most of the press of the country clothed General Lee with just such qualities, but," Grant continued, "I had known him personally, and knew that he was mortal."[107] I'm guessing that Grant had seen Lee's feet.

A Tale of Two Kleggs

In Civil War memoirs, as with all autobiographical accounts, the line between fact and fiction sometimes gets blurry. The same is true with Civil War fiction. In the decades after the war, many people put their pen to paper to write fictionalized tales of the conflict, some rather fanciful but others quite factual. Wilber F. Hinman's 1887 publication *Corporal Si Klegg and His "Pard"* definitely falls into the latter category. Hinman's long novel reads like a particularly detailed soldier's memoir written by a recruit from Indiana named Si Klegg. It traces his experience from the outbreak of the war and his enlistment to his return to his hometown after the guns fell silent. A buddy story, the book costars Si's "pard," Shorty, who is slightly more experienced at soldiering than Si, having served in a three-month regiment at the war's outset before joining Company Q of the 200th Indiana Infantry, where he and Si meet.[108]

The character Si Klegg, a naive farm boy, is a "red-cheeked, chubby-faced boy who had some distance to go before getting out of his teens" at the time of his enlistment. Tall, overweight, and not shaving yet, Klegg in the book's illustrations looks like a taller and a bit older version of Bobby Hill from the animated primetime FOX show *King of the Hill*. Personality-wise, Klegg is more like Gomer Pyle with an attitude, for those who remember the 1960s sitcom. One big difference is that Gomer Pyle spent six television seasons in extended boot camp in California (while many actual Marines were being sent to Southeast Asia); the Si Klegg character has a war to fight. Older than Si, Shorty is "lank and lean" and has a "well tanned face" that "gave evidence of much exposure to the wind and sun." He gains his nickname (his real name was Josiah) because he appeared to be tall due to the fact that he was so very thin. Shorty often keeps Si from getting into trouble and doing unwise things.[109]

Hinman's Klegg experiences many of the things that veterans wrote about in their memoirs. In fact, according to historian Allan R. Millett, "*Corporal Si Klegg and His 'Pard'* became the book of choice for Union army veterans because they believed it was the most accurate portrayal of their wartime experiences, physical and spiritual." It also became a favorite among Civil War reenactors for its detail and accuracy in describing the soldier's life. (*Corporal Si Klegg*: Fighting farbism since 1887!) Some literary scholars also credit the book with being an inspiration, perhaps THE inspiration, behind Stephen Crane's *The Red Badge of Courage*.[110]

Like George Peck, Klegg succumbs to the deceptiveness of a recruiting officer. Service would be a three-year-long "protracted picnic." Klegg does not want a picnic, however; he is anxious to join the fray, like the real recruits John Robson, Sam Watkins, and Bill Fletcher. Klegg "was burning with desire to fight the rebels. To his mind everything indicated that the commander of the Union army was only awaiting the arrival of Company Q to fall upon the enemy and smite him hip to thigh." Soon he will be "charging around on the field of battle, climbing over heaps of slaughtered rebels, and surrounding the name Klegg with a halo of immortal renown." And that is just his first day in the ranks. Shorty is a bit more circumspect about fighting. Speaking in eye dialect, Shorty tries to curb his pard's enthusiasm: "F'm what I've heern the old soldiers tell, the battle ain't such a fun thing as a feller thinks what don't know nothin' 'bout is. The boys is always hungry at fust for shootin' and bein' shot at, but I've an idee that it sort o' takes away their appetite when they gits one squar' meal of it." He adds, "It's likely we'll git filled one o' these days! I'm willin' ter wait."[111]

Like Watkins and Ferdinand Daniel, Klegg leaves home with far more stuff than he will ever need, never mind be able to carry, mostly due to the kindness of well-meaning family and friends. After a few hours of marching, Klegg starts jettisoning items one after another. And this is before the soldier receives his government issue equipment and uniform. It is then that Klegg learns the value of the haversack. When he receives it, he does not know what it is for, so Shorty informs him that it's "ter carry yer grub in!" He explains, "If ye've got 's good a appetite 's I think ye hev f'm yer looks, ye can't git 'long 'thout that, nohow.... It'll be the best friend ye'll find in the army." No matter how discolored, dirty, greasy, and fetid it became, the haversack is indispensable. "When his regiment halted, [the veteran soldier] would drop by the roadside, draw his grimy and well-greased haversack around in front of him, and from its dark and odorous recesses bring forth what tasted better to him than the daintiest morsel to the palate of an epicure."[112]

Klegg also discovers the multitude of uses of the bayonet, all of which are "unknown to military tactics." As a weapon, however, "It was a long time before he hurt any rebels with it," even in a bayonet charge. The bayonet did not evoke terror during a charge. It was the yell the men let out when charging: "A bayonet charge without a yell would be as incomplete as a dance without music. The yell itself was usually terrifying enough to bleach the hair on an ordinary man. The combined effect was to greatly stimulate the natural impulse to break to the rear. So it was that only in very rare cases was the bayonet long enough to reach for purposes of bloodletting."[113] Certainly, many rebels would agree with that yelling part.

As for the uniform he first receives, it fit as badly as the one Warren Lee Goss described. Nevertheless, he is prouder than a "five-year-old boy" who "donned his first pair of breeches" when he puts on that uniform. Despite Klegg's shiny brass buttons and his keen desire to destroy the enemy, veteran soldiers begin insulting and teasing this raw recruit, ad nauseam, as many memoirs show that seasoned soldiers were wont to do. Klegg and the other men of Company Q have much to learn. When given the simple command "right face" during their first drill, "the men faced to all points of the compass."[114] Eventually, Klegg is one of those veteran soldiers who has earned the right to humiliate the new.

Klegg also reflects a healthy disrespect for officers and for military regulations, and he and Shorty wage their own war against lice. Despite Klegg's fervor to put on a uniform and go off to war, he and Shorty show some ambivalence as to why they fight. "We ain't doin' all this eatin' hardtack 'n' trampin' 'round fer fun nor fer money," Si tells Shorty. "I 'spose it's what the spouters calls patri'tism." Shorty is a bit more unsure. "I couldn't hardly tell ye what I 'listed fer, 'cause I don't know myself," he tells Si. "I s'pose almost every man's got some o' what they calls patri'tism … I'm more 'n half thinkin' 't when they distributed it 'round I didn't git quite my sheer on it; an' it hain't growed any sence I've bin soljerin', nuther." Nevertheless, they are both committed to fighting "t'll we gits them rebils licked out o' their boots," as Si Klegg puts it.[115]

As for slaves and slavery, Hinman shows the racism common in many white Union veterans. Shortly after the Emancipation Proclamation is issued, Klegg complains when his regiment goes to work digging defensive works. "I tell ye what, I ain't goin' ter make a nigger o' myself 's long's my name's Si Klegg," he grumbles. "Talkin' 'bout niggers, there's thousands on em lyin' 'round doin' nothin'; why don't the Guvyment make them do the diggin'? I ain't no statesman, but it looks ter me's though 'f anybody's goin' ter have any good out o' this war the niggers'll git the most on it. Ef I had my way I'd make 'em help some way er ruther!" Hinman never mentions the nearly two hundred thousand African American soldiers who bore arms in Union blue. When asked by a Confederate soldier across the picket line why the Union army is "tryin' ter steal our niggers" and "what good'll they do ye when ye git 'em," Klegg replies, "Now, pard, ye can't git me inter no argyment 'bout that, 'cause I ain't no politician," avoiding any discussion of the morality of slavery. Instead, in a stroke of "patri'tism," Klegg declares, "You rebels's fightin' agin the flag o' yer country, 'n' anybody 't does that's goin' ter git walloped mighty bad."[116]

Hinman's book definitely resonated with those Northern veterans desirous of reconciliation with the South. In several passages in the latter part of the book, Hinman compliments the Confederate soldiers and blankets them with respect. Of the Union soldiers he writes, "Bravely, patiently and without complaint they faced the enemy's guns day after day, through weeks and months, and willingly made the awful sacrifice that was demanded." He then adds, "Surely no less can be said of the men of the Confederate armies, in their gallant and yet hopeless struggle. The pages of history bear no record of grander heroism and fortitude than were shown by American soldiers, North and South, during the last year of our civil war." Later, he confides, "Generally speaking, there was no feeling of personal enmity between the soldiers of the Union and Confederate armies. They learned thoroughly to respect one another for their courage and fighting qualities, and war did not make them savages or wild beasts." Still, there's more: "Personally these men were not foes, and they were alike brave in defense of what they believed to be the right."[117] Whatever sentiments Hinman expressed through Si Klegg about the Confederates deserving to be "walloped mighty bad," he was now ready to let bygones be bygones.

In writing the book, chapters of which first appeared in the Union veterans' newspaper the *National Tribune*, Wilber Hinman drew on his own wartime experiences. Hinman enlisted in the 65th Ohio Volunteer Infantry during the summer of 1861 as a corporal, then rose in the ranks to sergeant then captain, major, and lieutenant colonel before finally being mustered out in November 1865. As part of the Sherman Brigade, named for its sponsor John Sherman, a senator and brother of Willian Tecumseh, Hinman saw action at Stones River, Chickamauga, and Chattanooga, then participated in the Atlanta Campaign. Although the brigade did not make the March to the Sea, it did fight in the battles of Spring Hill, Franklin, and Nashville. While *Corporal Si Klegg* is short on details in terms of the names of battles and the other activities that Company Q engaged in, enough evidence appears to show that Hinman modeled the book's narrative on his own. Why Hinman designated Klegg's unit as he did is unclear, but Allen Millett explains, "Many Union infantry regiments referred to those soldiers who were sick, lame, lazy, under punishment, absent without leave, detached, or generally invisible as 'Company Q,'" similar to the soldiers Bill Fletcher describes as the wagon dogs.[118]

A decade after publishing *Corporal Si Klegg*, Hinman produced a nonfiction history based on his experience titled *The Story of the Sherman Brigade*, which Millett calls "a cleaned up, repackaged version of *Corporal Si Klegg and His 'Pard*.'"[119] That same year, John McElroy, co-owner and editor of the *National Tribune*, published *Si Klegg: His Transformation from a Raw Recruit to a Veteran*. McElroy's version is much more detail-specific about real events, places, and historic people. His Si Klegg was not a teenager, but rather twenty-two years old and more mature and heroic than Hinman's Si. And McElroy did not employ eye dialect in his narrative, like Hinman. But McElroy related some of the same stories Hinman told in his book, or variations thereof. McElroy went on to publish several more Si Klegg books over the next decade, so evidently his version of Klegg met with a modicum of popularity. Nevertheless, in 1910 when he was nominated to run for Commander-in-Chief of the Grand Army of the Republic at its national encampment, McElroy faced accusations of plagiarism from within the ranks. While denying the charge, he withdrew his name from consideration.[120]

Hinman died in 1905, so his voice was not heard at the 1910 GAR meeting, and he never filed suit against McElroy in the matter before his death. But here are the facts: Chapters of Hinman's *Corporal Si Klegg* first appeared in print under Hinman's name in the *National Tribune*. *Corporal Si Klegg* sold out its first edition and then was reprinted in 1889, 1890, and again in 1898, all without a peep of complaint from McElroy. Hinman's *Corporal Si Klegg* parallels Hinman's own experiences in the army during the war. Judging from what transpired at the 1910 GAR national encampment, Hinman's *Corporal Si Klegg* remained quite popular with the rank-and-file veterans.¹²¹ McElroy's *Si Klegg* is pretty much forgotten, while Hinman's *Corporal Si Klegg* lives on in the hearts and minds and haversacks of hardcore Civil War reenactors everywhere. Besides, if McElroy was the author of the original book, which proved to be quite successful, why would he write the book again? I'm sure that today in a court of law, some cunning linguist could parse through the different versions of the Si Klegg tales and identify who is the original author of the story. For my money, the credit belongs to Wilbur Hinman.

Uncle Remus Was White!

In *Life on the Mississippi*, Mark Twain recorded that on a visit to New Orleans, he had the opportunity to meet another author of recent renown, Joel Chandler Harris, known for his "Uncle Remus" stories. Word had spread that Harris was in town, and children gathered to get a glimpse of their favorite author. The kids expected to see Uncle Remus, the wise old African American spinner of yarns about Brer Rabbit, in the flesh. They were disappointed, as Twain related: "Why, he's white!" Not only was he white, as Twain describes, Harris was "red-haired and somewhat freckled," so I suspect that Harris was really pasty white.¹²²

Regardless of his whiteness, Harris, through his Uncle Remus stories and other writings, probably did more to establish the stereotype of the inoffensive, happy-go-lucky Negro who knew his place in the postwar decades than any other author. Too young to fight in the war, Harris spent those years working for a newspaper publisher in Eatonton, Georgia, and then spending his off time at the publisher's plantation outside of town. There he often visited the slave quarters and heard folk tales about weaker animals, a rabbit, for instance, outsmarting stronger ones, a fox for instance. From these he later crafted his Uncle Remus tales.¹²³

Harris wrote other things as well, including *On the Plantation: A Story of a Georgia Boy's Adventures During the War*, an 1892 work of fiction admittedly based on his own experiences. The story's protagonist, Joe Maxwell, is "only twelve years old" at the war's start, as was Harris, and "small for his age." Considering Twain's description of Harris later in life as "undersized," that depiction of him in his youth probably rang true. Joe sees little of the actual war first-hand until late 1864 when Sherman's March sweeps through the region. In Harris's fictional town of Hillsborough, "only the echoes of war were heard." "In spite of the war," the narrator tells readers, "it was a happy time, and Joe Maxwell was as happy as any of the rest," including the slaves. In fact, Harris included an entire chapter on the happy slaves.¹²⁴

But Harris's own narrative belies this happiness. "The war was horrible enough, distant as it was," he acknowledges, "but the people who were left at home—the women and children, the boys, the men who were exempt, the aged and the infirm—had fears of a fate still more terrible. They were fears that grew out of slavery, and they grew until they became a fixed habit of mind. They were the fears of negro insurrection."[125] Still, the book is filled with light-hearted stories about life on the plantation, working at the newspaper, hunting, and happy slaves telling folk tales.

Harris gives no mention one way or another why the South fought. Surprisingly, he presents a generally positive depiction of the Northern soldiers he encounters late in the war. He witnesses Federal soldiers under Sherman foraging, of whom he "found them all, with one exception, to be good-humored." While sitting on a fence, Joe watches a large portion of Sherman's army on the move and finds himself "the subject of many a jest, as the good humored men marched by." Joe, or Harris, does not even aim a harsh word at Sherman himself. Perhaps Harris did not want to alienate his Northern readers. Still, seeing the Yankees seems like a dream to Joe: "That the Federal army should be plunging through that peaceful region, after all he had seen in the newspapers about Confederate victories, seemed to him to be an impossibility."[126]

While saying very little severe about the Northern enemy, Harris harshly censured the wartime Confederate government. His criticisms include government-ordered limits on the amount of cotton that could be grown in order to produce more food and inflation caused by the overprinting of paper money. He attacked the impressment law allowing the military to seize private property, although he did not mention the taking of enslaved people. He denounced conscription and the government's failure to care for the families that poor soldiers left behind. And he condemned speculators getting rich while others suffered. Of course, by the time these judgments appeared in print, the Confederate government had long since failed. The Federal government still existed, however, and Harris definitely favored those seeking reconciliation and reunion. "The great changes that have been wrought—the healing of the wounds of war; the lifting up of a section from ruin and poverty to prosperity; the molding of the beauty, the coverage, the energy, and the strength of the old civilization into the new; the gradual uplifting of a lowly race" all are products of the postwar reconciliation. Harris chose not to elaborate on these issues in the book, but combined with his portrayal of Union soldiers, who were now veteran civilians, he definitely did not openly harbor bitterness.[127]

Harris used the reconciliation theme in other writings as well. His short story "The Comedy of War" (it's not ha-ha funny) tells the tale of a Virginia family divided by the war, literally brother versus brother, only to make up as the war ends. While the whole reunion story plays out, there is also a love story involving a sister and a Confederate lieutenant from Georgia named Clopton, whose family slave named Tuck arrives on the scene looking for the lieutenant with a note from mom and a box filled with clothes and food. The slave traveled all the way from Georgia to carry out this mission and serves no purpose in the story except to represent the loyal slave of Southern myth. Even when given a chance to have his freedom before they learn that the war has ended, Tuck passes. Tuck is loyal to the end. "An Ambuscade" also has a loyal slave in it named Plato. After a battle, Plato carries his wounded owner from the battlefield to the soldier's home some forty miles away. Plato is not only a loyal slave, he is the camp servant to the man who fought to keep him enslaved, the man whom he risks his life to save.[128]

Uncle Remus himself also got the chance to prove his loyalty in "A Story of the War." The story begins in 1870 with Vermont native Theodosia Huntingdon visiting her brother John, a former Union soldier, who settled in Atlanta and married a Georgia girl after the war. At the train station, Theodosia is greeted not by John but by his servant Uncle Remus. A few days into her stay, Remus is prompted to tell the story of when he became "a famous warrior" and "volunteered for one day, and commanded an army of one." Remus had been owned by "Mars Jeems," who lived with his mother, "Ole Miss," and his sister Sally. After the war began, Mars Jeems joined the Confederate army. Eventually, the task of running the plantation fell on the shoulders of the loyal Uncle Remus, who assured Ole Miss she can depend on him. Remus proves to be up to the task. Uncle Remus's loyalty went far beyond that, however. After the fall of Atlanta, Sherman's marching army threatens the plantation, and Remus protects its two white residents from harm, intimidating Union soldiers with his well sharpened and polished axe. Later, he shoots a Union sniper he feared would shoot Mars Jeems. At this point, Theodosia asks Remus, "Do you mean to say ... that you shot the Union soldier, when you knew he was fighting for your freedom?" "W'en I see dat man take aim, en Mars Jeems gwine home ter Ole Miss and Miss Sally, I des disremembered all 'bout freedom en lammed aloose." As a result, the Union soldier, John Huntingdon, lost his arm, but is nursed back to health by Sally, who then marries him. And Uncle Remus, who cost John an arm, as Theodosia points out, now serves the Union army veteran, her brother, as faithfully as he had served Mars Jeems. It all seems so heartwarming, as Uncle Remus continues to prove his loyalty *and* to know his place. It's the truth, it's actch'll. Everything is satisfactch'll.[129]

Other authors depicted loyal wartime slaves, but as slaves, not as soldiers. At the turn of the century, prolific Southern author and poet

Armistead Churchill Gordon wrote "Envion." The title character is an enslaved man owned by Mars' Berkeley of one of the First Families of Virginia. When the war breaks out, Berkeley goes off with the Confederate cavalry, taking Envion with him. One particular day, Berkeley tells Envion that he wants him to ride by his side into battle because he fears he would die that day. If that happened, he wants Envion to retrieve a letter he had written to his wife from his pocket so that Envion can bring it to her. Berkeley and Envion ride into battle with the cavalry charge, pistols a-blazing and saber's a-flying, and sure enough, Berkeley is shot. Dodging bullets, Envion, also wounded in the shoulder, carries the dying soldier from the field. He retrieves the letter, buries his master's body, and returns home without a word to anyone else. If a soldier did that, he would be absent without leave and in deep trouble, but Envion's role was the personal slave of his master. In the end, he relates, "I ain't nothin' but a poor good-for-nothin' nigger; but it does me some good ter remember dat I fit in de battle 'long side o' de braves' man dat was in dat wah." The moral of the story is that loyal camp slaves like Envion did their part for the Confederate cause and should be proud of it and honored for it.[130]

Of course, there were limits to what that part was. In "Captain Isam," Harry Stillwell Edwards relates the tale of a camp slave allowed to organize other camp slaves into a fighting company. For days, Isam drills his men while white soldiers make fun of them, but it does not deter him. Finally ordered with his company into battle at Chickamauga, Isam and his men hesitate, stall, and after moving no more than one hundred yards, retreat. When asked to explain what happened, Isam claims that he realized "dat ev'y nigger dere was worf er thousan' dollars, an' som er deh marsters was po' white men, and could n' 'ford to lose er nigger." He adds, "I reck'n Gen'l Bragg and Mas' Alec [the regiment's colonel] done look after dat little bunch er Yankees out en front, an' I better stay back dere and keep dem niggers an' waggins fum bein' runned off." Despite being laughed at, Isam comforts himself and validates his role as a slave and not a soldier with the knowledge that he was "the man who saved thirty-two thousand dollars worth of negroes and a wagon-train at Chickamauga."[131]

The image of the loyal camp slave created an ideal that postwar Southern whites wanted African Americans to emulate: Be obedient and know your place. During the war, that role was to serve, as it was before the war. It was not to carry out the important task of fighting. That was for the white men of the Confederacy to perform, as it turns out, in a losing cause. Thus, Isam and his men fail miserably in their chance to see the elephant. Envion goes into battle with his master but carries no weapon and does no fighting. He is there to retrieve the letter his master wrote to his wife should his master die. Of course, his master could have just given the letter to Envion before going into battle, but then Armistead Churchill Gordon would not have made the point that slaves were with the army not to fight but to serve their masters. And Uncle Remus takes up arms and shoots a Union sniper not to advance the Southern cause or even because the sniper shot at him but rather to protect and serve his master. Such depictions of African Americans with the Confederate army fly in the face of arguments made by neo-Confederates in the last few decades that scads of Black Confederates fought for the South during the war. As Kevin M. Levin argued in *Searching for Black Confederates*, such an idea would have shocked the men, white men, who had fought for the Confederacy. "Such an interpretation would strike actual Confederates as absurd," he noted.[132] It's the truth, it's actch'll. Everything is satisfactch'll.

And Ambrose Bierce Was "an Equal-Opportunity Hater"

Hands down, the most successful late-nineteenth-century writer of Civil War fiction is Ambrose Bierce. Except for Stephen Crane. Despite the fact that Bierce served in the Union army, saw the elephant up close and personal and lived to tell many tales, Stephen Crane, who was not even alive when the cannons roared and the minié balls flew, takes top honors for his story of war and redemption, *The Red Badge of Courage*, much to Bierce's irritation.[133] Perhaps the annoyance and bitterness caused by being overshadowed by this newcomer is what compelled the seventy-one-year-old asthmatic Bierce to wander off in the direction of Mexico, supposedly to join the rebel Pancho Villa, only to disappear forever.

To be sure, Bierce was not a pleasant man. "An equal-opportunity hater," professor of English Jonathan Elmer wrote, "Bierce spent his adult life mocking, condemning, harassing, and skewering everyone from small-time poets to Oscar Wilde.... He was just as merciless to corrupt local pols as to presidents, generals, and industrialists." "It's perfectly clear," Elmer concludes, "that Ambrose Bierce was an asshole." Certainly, Bierce's distemper influenced the way he saw the world and the way he wrote about it, including the war in which he fought. Instead of patriotic and romanticized stories of heroism, Bierce produced gritty realism punctuated by cynicism, sarcasm, satire, and occasionally the supernatural. "Bierce was out of step with the patriotic ideology of his times," noted Russell Duncan and David L. Klooser. "He sharpened his wit and discovered a real ability for satire and sarcasm—an ability stemming from a deep understanding that in the Civil War men had died for causes they did not understand, died to have their manhood recognized according to history's definition at the time: courage, honor, duty." Elmer agreed. For Bierce, "The Civil War ... was a continuous target of mockery and deflation."[134]

Like Wilbur Hinman, Bierce drew from his experience in uniform. Rising to the rank of first lieutenant, he served in the Ninth Indiana Infantry and saw action at the battles of Philippi, Shiloh, Corinth, Perryville, Stones River, Chickamauga, Chattanooga, Missionary Ridge, and the Atlanta Campaign. During the latter, he received a serious head injury, which eventually led to his discharge.[135]

Bierce certainly saw his share of gruesome carnage during the war. Nowhere is this more evident in his writings than in the disturbingly comical, or comically disturbing, short story "Chickamauga." From it we learn nothing of military maneuvers and tactics, heroism, and failures. Rather, the story focuses on a "boy aged about six" who roams from home in the morning to chase an imaginary enemy through the woods with his homemade wooden sword, gets lost, and then falls asleep. Only as the story progresses do readers learn that the boy cannot hear or speak. While he sleeps, the battle sweeps past him, with Confederates in pursuit of skedaddling Union soldiers. The boy remains undisturbed and unable to hear the violence. In some ways, "Chickamauga" is the opposite of a "sensory history," suggesting to readers the consequences of *not* hearing a battle instead of the impact of hearing the din.[136]

When he awakens, the boy encounters wounded and dying men, left behind and crawling toward a creek for water: "They crept upon their hands and knees. They used their hands only. They used their knees only, their arms hanging idly at their sides.... Occasionally one who had paused did not again go on, but lay motionless. He was dead." Unable to fathom what had happened, the child thinks it some kind of game: "On and ever they crept, these maimed and bleeding men." Their bloody faces remind him of the "painted clown" he had seen at the circus the previous summer. To the boy, it is all "a merry spectacle." Having ridden on the back of his father's slave like a horseman on his mount for entertainment, the boy tries to climb on one of the soldiers, thinking his prone position an invitation to get on. The man throws the boy off, and the boy feels fear for the first time when he sees the man's face, "a face that lacked a lower jaw—from the upper teeth to the throat was a great red gap fringed with hanging shreds of flesh and splinters of bones."[137] Recovering from his fright, the boy moves to the head of the herd and with his sword pretends to lead them, unfazed by the knapsacks and blankets and other accoutrement strewn through the woods by the retreating soldiers.

Surely, the contrast between the boy's reaction to the sight of the crawling army and the ghastly reality those men are experiencing has been the subject of many college term papers, the innocence of lads going off to war versus the reality of what war is like, or something like that. Bierce uses the boy's laughter and the humor he finds in the scene to establish this contrast. Eventually, the boy returns to his home and finds it on fire and his mother dead. The horrors of war, which he cannot even express in words, engulfs him, and no one lives happily ever after.

On a lighter note, Bierce like many other soldiers, had no tolerance for incompetent officers, especially politically appointed ones, as seen in "Jupiter Doke, Brigadier General." In the story, General Doke's only concern is his political future, the success of his party (the Republicans), how he and his family can profit from the circumstances of the war, and most importantly, protecting his own skin. Doke ends up being praised by a Republican-controlled Congress for not only attacking but utterly crushing a Confederate advance on his position in Kentucky carried out by an army ten time the size of Doke's brigade. In actuality, readers learn, the advance was defeated by a stampede of mules, more than two thousand, that Doke had been gathering to be used by his men in their retreat, which he anticipated ordering at the first sign of a Confederate advance. Doke accidentally touched off the stampede in the middle of the night, and the Confederates never knew what hit them. So maybe Doke deserves credit after all.[138]

Bierce wrote numerous Civil War ghost stories, and several of them are humorous for their ironic twist endings. In "A Tough Tussle," the brave but inexperienced Second Lieutenant Brainerd Byring is excited about going into battle, but "the sight of the dead" always disturbed him. One evening while supervising a picket line, he notices in the darkness the body of a felled Confederate. "Its presence annoyed him, though he could hardly have had a quieter neighbor." Unable to relocate because his men expect him to be at that spot, Byring feels that his dead companion is taunting him. As time progresses, he senses that the corpse is moving. Suddenly, shots fire out from the direction of the pickets. The Union soldiers retreat, followed by a wave of Confederate cavalry. Then, the larger body of Union troops repel the Confederate advance, sending it back from whence it came. The next morning Byring's body is found along with that of a Confederate private. The lieutenant has been killed by a "sword-thrust through the heart, but not, apparently, until he had inflicted upon his enemy no fewer than five dreadful wounds." The sword that killed Byring had been his own. The only other weapon found is his revolver, fully loaded and still tucked in his belt. The other body, with its several gashes apparently inflicted by Byring, bore "a faint, sickening odor ... [and] a few maggots."[139]

Bierce wrote other Civil War supernatural tales with surprise twists, the most famous being the short story turned award-winning short film turned *The Twilight Zone* episode. In "An Occurrence at Owl Creek Bridge," a Confederate spy escapes hanging when the rope breaks. He plunges into the titular creek, and then.... I'm not going to spoil the ending. You have to read it or see one of the screen versions yourself.[140]

Bierce is probably best known for his publication of a large body of definitions in various versions called *The Devil's Dictionary*. In it, the author put his wit, sarcasm, satire, and cynicism to good use. Bierce's wartime experience probably influenced several of his entries, although not explicitly, but he avoided Civil War-related terms like secede and secession, Union, states' rights, emancipation, and treason or traitor. He did present his oft-quoted definition of "History," perhaps as a jab against the growing industry of Civil War memoirs and regimental narratives: "An account mostly false, of events mostly unimportant, which are brought about by rulers mostly knaves, and soldiers mostly fools."[141] I suspect with an insult like that, the authors of those memoirs and narratives would agree with Jonathan Elmer.

An Unrenowned Warrior

"Next to Poe," claimed writer and diplomat Thomas Nelson Page, "the most original of all Virginia writers was he whose reputation in his lifetime mainly rested on humorous sketches of a mildly satirical and exceedingly original type: but who was a master of a pathos rarely exceeded by any author and rarely equaled by any American author." George W. Bagby "was not a fictionist but a realist." Bagby as a realist author is debatable, but it comes as no surprise that Page saw him that way. Page followed in Bagby's, and Joel Chandler Harris's, footsteps in not only promoting but perfecting the image of the romantic antebellum plantation that came to dominate depictions of the South for decades to come. (Cue the music from *Gone with the Wind*.) Trained as a medical doctor, Bagby turned to writing, and through most of the Civil War years, he served as the editor of the *Southern Literary Messenger*. Afterwards, he returned to writing and lecturing, rubbing elbows with many of the South's literary figures until his death in 1883.[142]

Bagby's most famous essay, "The Old Virginia Gentleman," is a paean to the antebellum Virginia plantation and its patriarch. He describes the prewar South as superior to the North in numerous ways: "Despite immigration, dense population, and concentrated wealth, despite tariffs and protective laws devised for his ruin, [the gentleman] and his brethren of the South at the outbreak of the late war were richer, far, man for man, than their fellow of the North." But wait, there's more: "Property was more evenly distributed, crime and pauperism were almost unknown, jails were empty, poor-houses empty, beggars were wonders, and social elevation, large areas considered, was incomparably superior." In this and other essays, Bagby sings the praises of the antebellum plantation, especially those in Virginia. In one such essay titled "Bacon and Greens," he boasts about how great Virginians were. And what made a Virginian great? Eating Virginia bacon and Virginia greens! I assume that was funnier if you were a nineteenth-century Virginian.[143]

Of course, when Bagby described Virginians, he meant white Virginians, actually white male Virginians. He had a separate paragraph on the wonderful "wife of the native Virginian." As for Virginia's non-white population, described with terms of endearment like "sable attendants," a "troop of little darkies," and "small Ethiops," they were happy, of course. Any other depiction would not fit Bagby's "realist" narrative.

Bagby enlisted in the Confederate army at the war's outset, but his writing skills combined with a chronic case of dyspepsia got him a position in the headquarters of General Pierre Beauregard, where he remained safely distant from the fighting of the Battle of Bull Run, or Manassas from his perspective. His illness proved too debilitating to remain in the army, however, and he received a discharge. Later, he wrote of his experience in an essay titled "An Unrenowned Warrior. The Record of a Man Who Shivered through the Manassas Campaign." Now here we have some realism, and something mildly satirical. Written about 1883, the essay really is a memoir. Thirty-two years old when the call for Confederate troops went out, Bagby did not have the romanticized view of going to war and the notion of "sojering" that many of the younger recruits did. "Truth is," he admitted, "there was a big disgust upon me, more on account of my 'sojer cloths,' I think, than anything else. Nature had not fitted me for a roundabout," a waist-length military jacket, "with brass buttons." I'm guessing that it was too short on him.[144]

"I had always thought 'sojering' tomfoolery any how," Bagby revealed. He complained about "the mistake constantly made at the beginning of the war, that animal bravery was the main requisite in a soldier. What a mistake! Bullies ever ready for a brawl repeatedly proved arrant cowards on the field, while the cowards, so called, turned out to be the most gallant and skilled of soldiers." Reveille also gave Bagby cause for complaint: "I was three-and-thirty years of age, a born invalid, whose habit had been to rise late, bathe leisurely, and eat breakfast after everybody else was done. To get up at dawn to the sound of fife and drum, to wash my face in a hurry in a tin basin, wipe on a wet towel, and go forth with a suffocated skin and sense of uncleanliness..."—but then it gets worse—"...to be squad-drilled by a fat little cadet, young enough to be my son, of the Virginia Military Institute, that indeed was misery. How I hated that little cadet!"[145]

As for the cheers he and his fellow recruits received from a supportive throng as they left the train station in Richmond for the front lines, Bagby lamented, "Oh! What asses men are! As if that were anything to be jolly about!" Bagby never made it to the front with the other men. On the way he came down with a "decided fever" and was left at the town of Gordonsville to recuperate. There he lodged in a "good hotel," bathed properly, put on a fresh night shirt, and slept in a bed with clean sheets. He stayed there "two or three days, taking as little medicine as possible and getting well as slowly as possible." Still feeling ill, he eventually made his way to the vicinity of Manassas where he was detailed to the staff of General Beauregard.[146]

Being on Beauregard's staff proved quite agreeable to Bagby. He watched the main battle at Manassas safely from a distance and then awaited orders for the pursuit of the retreating Union army. Orders never came: "The next day ... it rained, a steady straight downpour the livelong day. Everybody flocked to headquarters. Not one word was said about a forward movement upon Washington. We had too many generals-in-chief; we were Southerners; we didn't fancy marching in the mud and rain—we threw away a grand opportunity." Bagby wrote with hindsight two decades old, but many would agree that he was right. Soon, Bagby returned to Richmond and received a discharge due to his chronic health issues: "Thus ended the record of an unrenowned warrior."[147]

This was not the end of Bagby's humorous take on the war, however. In 1871, he published a series of articles, or chapters, in what he titled "Histry uv the Waw" in the *Southern Magazine*, a publication devoted to presenting the Southern viewpoint on the war and Reconstruction.[148] Using the phonetic spelling style of a cracker box philosopher, Bagby published the "Histry" under the name "Mozis Addums." Despite its misspellings, eye dialect, and idioms, the opening chapter reminds me of the first chapter of many academic books. Bagby, or Addums, first states why he produced this history. While others had written histories of the war "for posterrity," he wrote "for munny." He even disparages writing "for faim." "Literarry and polittikul faim mostly goes out on whiskey enyway, and is uv littil vally."[149]

Next, Addums describes what others had written on the subject and where his work fit into the literature, including his methodology: "Uther histoarians uv the day ... are (or say they are) writin a true and imparchul acount uv what ukurd enduringe uv the waw." Noting how futile such an effort is, Addums rejects that: "I mought as well stait frankly that I do not intend to write a imparchul Histry." Instead, he admits, "I make out my kase in my oan mind befo startin, and then wuk the facts up to it. In this way aloan, I fansy, kin a truly filosophikul Histry be construcktid." His "shell be strickly a parshul Histry, not for the resin that my auntysedants fubbid any other or becaws I billeeve fumlu the South was rite in the matter, but becaws I chews it soe to bee." Therefore, he announces, "I shall not hesitate, whenever it suit my puppus, to tell the most infunnul lies that ever issued frum mortul man." Thus, in writing his history, he divulges, "I shell bring toe my task a mind prejudished to the last degree in favor uv my oan apinyuns, and a heart filled with malice and all uncharrytubbleness for thoas who dar to diffur with me in anyway whatsumeer." In the process, he intends to bring to light *what was not done*—in other wirds, uv what mought have bin done, what ought to have bin done, and yet it was neglecktid to be did." He calls this "the Addumsian Methud."[150]

Addums next explains the causes of the war. All wars, he posits, are caused by two things: "the devlishness uv human nacher, and seckinly, the want uv kommun sense." It is "the devlishness in Gnu-Inglun (I carnt call is human) nacher," providing a list of specifics. The South is not blameless, however: "On the part uv the South the cozzes was difrunt, and ariz from the absinthe uv kommun sence, in billeevin, fust, that cottun was king; seckin, that the just cause always prevales; thudly, that 'twant gwin to larst long; and 4thle [sic], in not knowin that (whist battils meens fitin and pluk will tell) war, in a lerdge sense, meens bizniss, and rekwires bizniss men futto carry it on proper." On this last point, the Yankees are much better suited. As for the anticipated brevity of the war, he asserts, "Evryboddy on both sides wantid the thing to be wound up in a jiffy, so they mought git to makin money agin. They found, howevver, that waw was like going to Kollitch—it requide 4 yeer—Freshmun, Soffmo, Junyer and Seenyer, and was a ixpensiv eddicashon."[151] Good thing they didn't go to grad school.

The last two chapters focus on the war itself, and I've had my fill of eye dialect. I'm sure you have, too. As for the war's outcome, Addums makes a point about the Confederate loss: "The tiem had come for Stait Rites to go up the spout. Thar can't be two senters to one sirkle; leest uv all kin thar be 40 odd sovrin and independunt serkles outside uv and abuv one commun senter." Thus, like Charles Henry Smith's Bill Arp, the "realist" George Bagby's Mozis Addums presaged Frank Lawrence Owlsey's observation that the Confederacy "DIED OF STATE RIGHTS."[152]

Postmodernism? We Haven't Even Done Modernism Yet!

In "An Unrenowned Warrior," George Bagby tells a story about his friend Virginius Dabney, with whom he enlisted in April 1861. Dabney, a man with a "huge bulky figure," a "jolly good nature," and a "fund of wit," was a native of Mississippi and accustomed to extravagant living. "Boys," he announced while in training camp outside of Richmond, "I want you distinctly to understand—this is my last war! This is my first, and I am going to see it through to the bitter end, but after this no more war, no more sleeping on straw for V.D. No Sir!" While Bagby had his military career cut short due to his dyspepsia, Dabney went on to serve as a lieutenant in the 48th Virginia Infantry and then as a captain on the staff of Confederate General John B. Gordon.[153]

Dabney also authored *The Story of Don Miff, as Told by His Friend John Bouche Whacker. A Symphony of Life*. Writing in 2004, literary critic Paul Collins posited, "*Don Miff* may be the greatest Confederate novel ever written, except that greatness is not a condition allowed of Confederate novels." The first sentiment is surely debatable. Dabney admits in the book's preface, "Our author,"—the book identifies Dabney as its editor and its author and narrator as John Bouche Whacker—"has not seen fit to make any reply to the incessant and still increasing onslaughts from pen and pencil alike, to which the South has submitted, and still submits, twenty-one years after Appomattox." That certainly does not sound overly pro–Confederate. But Dabney goes on, "It seems to me best to say, once and for all, that whenever the necessities of the narrative compel him to show his sympathies on one side or the other (as happens two or three times in the course of the story), they will be found to be with those people among whom he was born, by whose side he fought, and with whom he suffered." Dabney punctuates his defense of his fictional author by adding, "I feel sure that no man who knows me, in the South, and equally sure that no man who knows me, in the North, would deem me capable of printing this book, had it been otherwise."[154]

Dabney clearly placed himself with the growing voice of Lost Cause defenders, but he made it clear that defending the Lost Cause was not his purpose in writing the book. In fact, the Civil War actually only takes up a few chapters at its end. Dabney supposedly opposed slavery, but he sounded an awful lot like George Bagby when he described the prewar slave-owning South: "We lived in a land in which no one was hungry; no man was a criminal; no woman fell—from necessity; where no one asked for bread, and all, even slaves, could give it; where Charity was unknown, and in her stead stood Hospitality, with open doors." He acknowledged that slavery was wrong, but argued that "had [Virginians] been let alone, not many years would have passed before we should have freed ourselves from the weight that oppressed us." That was the weight of maintaining slavery. So, it was the slave owners that needed to be emancipated. Slaves themselves were fine with the institution and their relationship with their masters. In fact, readers learn, "Nothing so much delighted our slaves, in those days, as any jolity on the part of their masters," of course, when their masters were not suffering from the oppression of being the owners of other human beings, "Happy and careless themselves, when [slaves] saw their betters unbend they realized more clearly, perhaps, that they were men and brothers."[155]

Dabney projected the sentiment in the book that the war, at least on the part of the South, was not about slavery, but if it were, the abolitionists, "a handful of men with a mission,—a mission to keep other people's consciences," started it. The questions of whether one can debate the greatness of a Confederate novel I will leave to those who still seek greatness in the Confederacy. I doubt that *Don Miff* would rise to whatever standard they establish. Instead, the book has all the trappings of a typical nineteenth-century romance novel. There are love interests, a mystery and a secret identity, a family reunion and reconciliation, and a cute little girl who plays in the streets and talks to strange men set against a circle of well-to-do families living in Richmond who also spend considerable time in the country visiting their relations. Yet Paul Collins also claimed that *Don Miff* is "the American South's great postmodern novel," referring to the literary genre that flowered in the 1960s and after. Except Dabney wrote the book in the 1880s![156]

The titular character, Don Miff, is actually John Smith, a mysterious and intriguing man with hidden talents who comes into the lives of a circle of Virginia families shortly before the outbreak of the Civil War, although readers are unaware of the growing political conflict until more than 80 percent of the way through the book when told that Virginia seceded. The character is believed to be named Don Miff because the first person who has any interaction with him, a young girl of almost four years old, either misheard Smith when he said his name or has a bit of a speech impediment. Some of his new friends continue to refer to him as Don Miff because they do not believe his real name is John Smith. Spoiler alert. It turns out that he is Theodoric Poythress, the long lost, or run away, son of one of the older couples in the story. Readers learn that Theodiric's puritanical father had required the boy to stay home on Sundays except to go to church, although Theodoric was occasionally excused from church by claiming to have a headache. On one such occasion, shortly after the youth turned fourteen, his father caught him away from the house, playing a flute while a slave boy danced to the music, secular no doubt. After receiving a harsh beating from his father, Theodoric skedaddled and over the next decade and a half became, literally, an international man of mystery.

As the story develops, a number of possible love connections emerge. Alice is attracted to the Don (how several of the young women referred to John Smith), but the Don appears to be attracted to Lucy, or maybe Mary.

Lucy, however, is firmly involved with the narrator, John Bouche Whacker, who goes by the name Jack, but Mary might have had a thing for the Don. Charley is a confirmed woman hater, but he may have a soft spot for Alice. It's not the love stories or the secrets revealed about John Smith that provide the laughs in *The Story of Don Miff*. It's the asides and expositions that Dabney included that allowed him avenues to make statements, get things off his chest, and sometimes just rant. Plus, these inserts at times allowed him to have fun with the story and with the reader. The book begins with a long, rambling introductory "monologue," chapter 1, penned, we are told, by Jack Whacker for the benefit of his anticipated "great-great-great-great-great-great-great-great-great-grandson," an "almond-eyed and yellow of skin" lad whom he refers to as "Ah Yung Whack," some three hundred years in the future. He calls his descendant by this name, Whacker explains, because in a dream he was visited by a Chinese diplomat who informed Whacker that the wheels were in motion for the Chinese to dominate the United States, no matter how much opposition arose, as "the fittest will survive." Thus, Dabney engages in a critique of the Chinese Exclusion Act of 1882 and comments on Darwinian theory, which have nothing to do with his plot.[157]

The narrator then launches into a long, convoluted, and at times humorous genealogical exploration on the roots of the Whacker family, and the genealogy next leads to a fanciful explanation of the origins of the term bushwhacker. Most humorous is his comment on the disputed authorship of the poem "The Picket Guard," which became better known as the song "All Quiet along the Potomac, Tonight." "Three hundred and eleven people (two hundred and ninety-nine women and twelve men) went before justices of the peace, when it began to make a noise in the world, and made oath that they wrote it. Which shows, among other things, that there is no lack of justices of the peace in this country." Actually, there were only two people, one woman and one man, but who's counting? Again, nothing to do with the plot.[158]

Tangents continue. Dabney takes a poke at cheap wood-pulp novels, the treatment of Native Americans, imperialism, and Social Darwinism among other things. Later, he digresses on things such as the pleasures of drinking "lager bier," and the value of the word "ouch," which he believes has been grossly underused in literature and given short shrift by grammarians. He critiques the ever-evolving notion of the "woman's ideal man" and criticizes French author Victor Hugo, who "[whined] over the fate of John Brown." (Hugo was an easy mark, being dead since 1885.) Sometimes these departures, offered through the voice of Dabney's fictional narrator, are specifically addressed to his fictional descendant, while others are directed to the reader, breaking the proverbial Fourth Wall. Meanwhile,

Dabney as editor also offers his own comments and occasional critiques of his narrator's opinions through footnotes.[159]

Speaking of Victor Hugo, Dabney's criticism exposes an interesting cultural literacy irony of the war. Hugo's opus *Les Misérables* appeared in print in 1862, and within a year, English translations became available in the United States and gained popularity on both sides of the battle lines, especially among soldiers. According to Vanessa Steinroetter, "The novel played a significant role in how [soldiers] perceived, recorded, and interpreted their experience of the Civil War." A version translated for a Richmond publisher made its way onto the hands of Confederates, especially those in the Army of Northern Virginia. In fact, the book inspired them to adopt a new nickname, "Lee's Miserables." However, most Southern readers at the time did not know that Hugo had harshly condemned slavery and actually praised John Brown for his martyrdom. It is highly unlikely that many Confederate soldiers read the attacks on slavery Hugo interspersed in the book unless they read the version translated for and issued by a New York publisher or the original French version, as the Richmond publisher's translator edited them out.[160] I suspect that many Southerners who later learned of Hugo's censure of slavery said, "Wait…. He wrote what?!?"

Back to *Don Miff*. About a third of the way through the book, Whacker announces "This is not a love story!" After "five or six pages of Able-Analysis" about the Don and Mary, "showing just what these two young people felt, and why they felt it," narrator Jack declares, "I passed a pen across the whole." He explains, "What is the use of all this microscopic anatomy in tracking the progress of heart-affairs? It seems to me that falling in love is as elementary a process as sitting down on an ice-pond. The rub is *how not* to do it."[161]

Then at times other characters in the book intrude into the narration, not to further the storyline being told by Jack Whacker, but to redirect it as they see fit. Charley and Alice often jump in, disagreeing with Jack and with each other over what really happened and how it happened. In fact, Jack admits that the two of them "are the real authors of this book. They have furnished most of the facts; I am to pocket the glory." In fact, it is Alice, about a hundred pages later, who convinces Jack to return, reluctantly, to the love story, or at least to "a single pair of loves." "Alice, woman-like, declared that she would have nothing to do with my book unless I put some love in it…. I have made allusions here and there, in the course of these pages, to such signings and oglings and bosom-heavings and heart-flutterings, accompanied by such meaning starts and deep ineffable glances, that I am willing to admit what Alice claims; that it would be almost an actual breach of faith not to tell people what it all meant."[162]

Thus, Alice agrees to "edit the love-passages of the book," becoming its "LOVE EDITOR." In fact, Alice receives credit for writing an entire chapter, a chapter preceded by a three page "NOTICE TO THE PUBLIC" explaining how Alice came to write the chapter, in which the Don and Mary succumb to their passions. This is followed by another chapter in which Jack and Charley critique Alice's work.[163] By the way, Mary and the Don never hook up because she cannot deal with the fact that he is an agnostic, turned off to religion because of his father.

Readers might expect to find many of the conventions Dabney uses in a novel written decades, even a century, later. How unique these devices were in their time is hard to tell. American writer and editor David Eggers recently noted, "Readers are an amnesiac species, and so, every few decades, we wake up to believe that an author addressing the reader directly, or playing with form, or including references to the author or the book within that book, is new and should be labelled post or meta or whatever unfortunate and confining term will come yet."[164] Enough late nineteenth-century readers must have liked the book; it went through at least seven printings by 1890. Newspapers gave *The Story of Don Miff* ambivalent reviews. The *Hartford Courant* wrote, "In his method the author is as whimsical as the author of 'Tristram Shandy.' It is a dangerous experiment, but it must be said that the author's wit and vivacity vindicate his willfulness." The *Christian Union* noted that the book "contains unmistakable evidence of genuine story-telling ability; there are bits here and there which can be praised almost without qualification; there are glimpses of whimsical humor of a quite unusual sort; and there are pictures of old time Virginia, which have almost a historical value." Bits here and there? Glimpses? Almost a historical value? These were blurbs that the book's publisher, the J.B. Lippincott Company, used to promote *Don Miff* in the front matter of Dabney's second and last book, *Gold that Did Not Glitter*. One thing the papers agreed on was that the book was funny, finding its humor, "whimsical," "fanciful," and/or "sarcastic."[165] They do not use the term "postmodern."

As for *The Story of Don Miff*, Virginius Dabney devotes only about seventy of his nearly five hundred pages to the Civil War, and much of that does not focus on the war itself. But he is sure to let readers know why he thought the Confederacy lost: "Had any one of the Southern leaders read one page of history, not to know that money means men? means cannons, rifles, sabres? means ships, and commissariat, and clothing? means rallying from reverses, and victory in the end?" In short, "it was finances that we blundered fatally."[166] It was all about the Benjamins. Jack, Charley, and the Don all serve in Confederate gray as officers, and the Don dies a lingering death, but not before he forgives Mary, and Mary forgives him, and everyone finds out who he really is. And Charley and Alice, married during the war, later have a son that they name after Charley's childhood friend and Alice's brother, Theodoric Poythress, also known as John Smith, also known as Don Miff.

Girls Will Be Boys and Boys Will Be Girls

The Story of Don Miff was ahead of its time in style if not in story line, with Virginius Dabney employing postmodern conventions as humorous asides to his narrative. Another Civil War book ahead of its time more in substance rather than style is *A Dual Role: A Romance of the Civil War* by William Isaac Yopp.[167] While Yopp had no intention of writing a comedy, a twenty-first-century reader might not help but laugh at the transitioning of his plot.

The story begins like many Disney classics, with tragic parental deaths. The young hero, Hal Claybrooke, is orphaned after a group of Unionist guerrillas raids his parents' Tennessee plantation. The late-pubescent teen is taken in by his family's doctor, Dr. Neile, who soon after raises a company for the Confederate army, which Hal joins. Known by the other soldiers as "the Kid," Hal soon distinguishes himself, especially against the guerrillas that caused his parents' deaths. Because of his bravery, General Nathan Bedford Forrest calls on Hal, now seventeen, to go on a secret mission to Union-occupied Memphis to gather intelligence as a prelude to a raid on the city.

Here's where things start to get interesting. To get into the city and gather the desired intel, Hal comes up with a ploy that would enable him to complete his mission without raising suspicions. He would go to Memphis disguised as a female. He realizes that this transgender transformation would be easy: "The 'Kid' was small and beardless, his features resembling those of a girl yet in her teens, far more than those of a well-tried soldier. Hal naturally enough determined to go disguised as a girl." Such gender fluidity might not be so startling for the twenty-first century, but for 1864 when the scene is set, or 1902 when the novel was published, it would have been quite scandalous. Yopp treats the decision rather glibly. Hal decides "naturally enough" to do it, and "General Forrest fully approved his plans, furnished him with ample funds with which to carry out the project." Thus, Hal Claybrooke becomes Hallie Clay.[168]

Hal "appeared a handsome girl, with laughing blue eyes, delicate smooth transparent skin, adorned by jet black wavy hair," which "all contributed to make him a pretty counterpart." Posing as a music teacher seeking students, Hal/Hallie seeks lodging at the Gayoso Hotel, where the Union army in that district has its headquarters and many officers reside.

He quickly meets Miss Catherine Deboe, who goes by Kate, "a tall, willowy blonde, who looked to be about seventeen," Hal/Hallie's age. She is the daughter of a colonel staying in the hotel. The two girls quickly bond, so much so that Kate invites Hallie to share her hotel room rather than get one of her own. Indeed, Kate insists, breaking down into tears and throwing her arms around Hal/Hallie and begging him/her to agree. "This was more than the boy-girl had bargained for," Yopp confides, "and he knew not how to answer, for if he should untwine Kate's slender arms, from about his neck and fling her from him, she would doubtless feel hurt and perhaps get angry with him." What a horrible moment for the teen soldier, for he knew that a falling out with Kate might interfere with his mission: "With the charming woman's arms about his neck, her soft cheek resting against his own, and her warm breath fanning his glowing cheek, the boy stood transfixed, not knowing how to act." What a dilemma! Succumbing to his duty to the cause, his loyalty to General Forrest, and his desire to avenge his parent's death, Hal/Hallie decides to take one for the team. "Now Kate," Hal/Hallie told her, "I will accept your offer, and assure you I will be very pleased to occupy the room with your own dear self."[169] What a patriot! Before you know it, Hal/Hallie falls in love with Kate.

Sharing a room creates some awkward moments for Hal/Hallie, which Yopp treats rather innocently and family friendly-like, but a modern retelling of the story could have some real fun presenting these events for a more mature audience. Over the next few days, spending time together, Kate seems to fall in love with Hal/Hallie, at times wishing out loud that she was a man. Privately, "Kate knew that the very touch of Hallie's hand thrilled every fiber of her being in such a way as she had never known or experienced before."[170] If only Kate knew. Likewise, one can imagine how potentially embarrassing a situation like this could be for a teenage boy, especially come bedtime, but Yopp does not explore any of that, perhaps for fear of violating the anti-obscenity Comstock Act. Hal/Hallie is a gentleman ... er ... lady?

Hal/Hallie and Kate grow emotionally closer, platonically of course, but soon Forrest launches his attack on Memphis, at which time our hero rejoins his comrades in arms and reassumes his male identity. Thus ends the short life of Hallie Clay. During the raid, the Confederates capture Kate's father, Colonel Deboe. Now back in male persona, Hal sees to it that Colonel Deboe receives good treatment from his captors and then arranges for the colonel's release on his oath of parole. When Deboe, who is none the wiser about Hal/Hallie, returns to Memphis, he finds that Kate has vanished. Confused and fretful about the unexplained disappearance of her dear friend, Kate decided to search for Hal/Hallie. She sets out from Memphis, but knowing the dangers posed to a young woman travelling alone—now it gets even more interesting—she disguises herself as a teenage boy.

Kate adopts the name—get this—Hal Deboe and starts "roaming through the villages and towns contiguous to Memphis, in quest of the one she loved more than ever." As time progresses, autumn into winter of 1864, Kate/Hal comes to believe that she IS a male and becomes convinced that she/he WILL win the heart of Hallie Clay, if only Hallie can be found. Unfortunately, Kate/Hal's pursuit is halted when she/he falls deliriously ill and is discovered as a female. Reunited with her father, she still believes herself to be a male and remains committed to finding her love. "I know I will find Hallie," she explains, "and when I find her, I mean to marry her at once, because I just know she will love me when she finds that I am now a man instead of the girl she left me."[171]

The war ends, and Hal hits puberty, hard, becoming a real manly man. He decides to find Kate, but in the process learns through a third party that Kate has gone "hopelessly insane," without any of the details, and is now in an asylum. Hal takes his inheritance and heads west for Texas, buys half interest in a cattle ranch and becomes rich. Yet he still pines for Kate. Meanwhile, Kate's father continues to seek treatment for his daughter. She improves but has reoccurring "fits of monomania," occasionally believing she is a he. Colonel Deboe takes her to a new asylum in Tennessee for more treatment. The asylum, it turns out, is run by Hal's old guardian Dr. Neile and sits on the land once owned by Hal Claybrooke's family. Dr. Neile puts two and two together and realizes that the person Kate longs for is Hal. Meanwhile, Kate has a major relapse.[172]

Dr. Neile locates Hal and without giving an explanation, asks him to return to Tennessee. He obeys. Despite all his growing up, Hal's voice has not changed, so Dr. Neile hatches a plan. He tells Colonel Deboe:

> I think all we have to do will be to convince your daughter that the voice [she hears from another room] is that of a real man, and not that of a girl, as she believes Hallie Clay to be, and in this way, I think, I can bring about your daughter's permanent cure, for she seems to have but the one hallucination, which is, that the person whom she learned to love so well, as a female music teacher, was a girl, while I assume that her love, or strange infatuation for the girl-boy, was the result of intuitive affinity, which being stronger than reason or the environment of disguise, naturally engendered a love, which, though it appeared to be abnormal in the intensity and nature of the passion, was in reality true sexual love.[173]

That's a mouthful. Long story short, it works. Kate hears Hal's voice, realizes it was coming from a man, and snaps out of it. Kate and Hal marry, and they all live happily ever after.

I can imagine this story being adapted into a movie version, although its appearance differs depending on when it was made. A 1940s version could be a light-hearted romantic comedy co-starring Judy Garland and Mickey Rooney. It pretty much would stick to Yopp's story line. An offering from the 1970s or 1980s would be aimed at a much more mature audience, with definite sexual tension between the main characters and numerous sexual innuendos, maybe even brief nudity. Or maybe it could be directed by John Waters with a role for Divine. A twenty-first-century remake would be much darker with a lot of brooding and long angst-filled inner monologs, a couple of scenes that make no sense, and a very different ending. It would win prizes at the Cannes Film festival.

Yopp was not a professional writer. Rather, he was involved in the manufacturing and marketing of cotton seed products and was considered by one source "one of the great leaders in the field." He did write a resource book for people in his profession titled *Yopp's Cipher Code*, but I suspect this book did not involve cross dressing. Born in 1855 and raised in Tennessee about sixty miles east of Memphis, the setting for *A Dual Role*, Yopp was too young to serve in the war himself. His father, brother, and some other relatives served in the Confederate army, first in the 7th Mississippi Cavalry and then in the 14th Tennessee Cavalry, which later was merged into the 15th Tennessee Cavalry Consolidated. Stories the younger Yopp heard from his veteran kin may have informed his novel about the Civil War.

In fact, there may have been a soldier in one of the regiments that became part of the 15th Cavalry Consolidated who was sent on a spying and smuggling mission to Memphis by Nathan Bedford Forrest, and he may have gone on the mission disguised as a women named Mollie Hayes, and this Mollie Hayes may have gone on several errands for Forrest. Despite the fact that very few people supposedly knew about these secret missions carried out by the spy cloaked as a woman, one can imagine rumors running rife in camp if some hint about a fellow soldier donning a dress to carry out an errand started to circulate. Perhaps Yopp gained inspiration for his Hal/Hallie transformation from bits of old gossip he learned from his kinfolk. Only in this case, the gossipers did not know that the soldier disguised as a woman actually was a woman!

Her name was Mary Ann Pitman, captured dressed in women's garb near Fort Pillow in Tennessee shortly before Forrest's cavalry attacked and committed arguably the war's worst atrocity there. Sent to St. Louis as a prisoner, Pitman, who also went by the name Mollie Hayes, claimed that she had joined the Confederate army disguised as a man, served in the 15th Tennessee Cavalry, and eventually was recruited by Nathan Bedford Forrest to go on a mission to Memphis, an undertaking she accepted. Before saying anything to Forrest, however, the distaff soldier decided that the most effective way to carry out the task was as a woman, so off came the uniform and on went a dress. Pitman then went to Forrest and asked him to identify her. When he could not, she revealed who she was and whom he had known her as; with the general's blessing, off she went to Memphis as Mollie Hayes. While there are glimmers of evidence to back up Pitman's tale and much that cannot be corroborated, the story she told and Yopp's are remarkably similar, except for Hal actually not being a woman disguised as a man who "disguised" himself as a woman.

Hal eventually settled down with his one true love and presumably spent the rest of his life in wedded bliss. As for Mary Ann Pitman, having soured on her support for the Confederacy, after her capture, she became an important informant in a large investigation of organized disloyal activities in the Midwest. She won the trust of the provost marshal general of the Department of the Missouri and, as a woman, ended up becoming a spy for the Union army, first reporting on information she learned as a prisoner and then going on undercover missions in Missouri and elsewhere. At the end of the war, her contributions to the Union cause earned her a five-thousand-dollar payment from the War Department. Pitman received her money and then disappeared from the record.[174] Yopp's *A Dual Role* is a clever tale, but Pitman's story, even if much of her gender-bending activities cannot be proven, might uphold the old saying that the truth is stranger than fiction. And both stories might confirm the notion that when it comes to Civil War writing, as in many of the works discussed here, the line between fact and fiction often blurs.

PART III

"Those who still fight the last romantic war"
The Next Generations

The United States entered the twentieth century as a growing industrial economic dynamo and confirmed colony-possessing world power. Yet while the nation moved forward, many Americans continued to look backward to find meaning in the Civil War. The war generation churned out more memoirs and fiction, but as time progressed, that cohort grew smaller and smaller. The internecine clash was becoming a memory. For many Southerners of this new generation, the war's memory did not fade. Rather it became sharply focused on the clearly defined Lost Cause myth, which justified and rationalized the war as a defense of Southerners' rights, white Southerners' rights, that is, and as a literal defense of Southern homes and families from an invading horde of Yankees. Missing from the interpretation is any mention of the defense of slavery, although sometimes there is discussion of the defense of the slaves from the terrible things the Yankees planned to do to them—especially giving them their freedom. Such an interpretation allowed Southerners to blame the North for the heavy economic and social toll the war took on the South and the continued impact of the war. In 1930, for instance, writer, editor, literary influencer, and all-around consummate curmudgeon H.L. Mencken, a native of Baltimore, published "The Calamity of Appomattox" in which he argued that had the South been victorious, it still would be controlled politically by "gentlemen," not the "vermin" found in Washington, and it would be thriving economically. There would be no Ku Klux Klan, which had had a rebirth in the decade before the article appeared, and the victorious Confederates probably would have abolished slavery by the mid-1880s. Furthermore, according to the Marylander, the two American republics probably would be getting along, maybe even cooperating during times of external threat like the recent world war. In short,

Mencken concluded, if the Union "had been broken in 1865, life would be far pleasanter today for every American of any noticeable decency."[1] Like many others of a Southern bent, Mencken was still fighting the war, only now it had become a war of words.

Northerners also did not forget the war, but the war had been won already. Why keep fighting it? Remember the old adage about winners going about their business? Northerners had no compelling reason to develop an elaborate justification for the war and rationalization of its outcome, instead sticking with the themes of putting down the rebellion, saving the Union, and sometimes, but not always, freeing the slaves. Furthermore, rather than look to the past, Northerners had plenty of new trends to examine—industrialization, urbanization, immigration, imperialism, and Progressivism—in order to make sense of their early-twentieth-century world.[2] Nevertheless, Americans still found reason to retell the tales of the Civil War. When they did, sometimes they found humor in the war, and sometimes they found the war humorous.

The Blue and Gray in Black and White, Then in Technicolor

The twentieth century introduced new and revolutionary inventions and technologies into American culture. In particular, motion pictures provided people with a new way of entertaining and telling stories, and it did not take too long for the Civil War to become popular fodder for this new American film industry. By 1929, the end of the silent era, at least 424 films on the conflict hit the big screen, especially during the war's golden anniversary years 1911 to 1915.[3]

Undoubtedly, the most significant of these early war films, the magnum opus, was D.W. Griffith's *Birth of a Nation*. Based on Thomas Dixon's 1905 novel *The Clansman*, this 1915 feature film depicts a noble South that goes to war to protect its rights against a malevolent North. In the wake of its loss, the South suffers at the hands of immoral Yankee carpetbaggers and unfettered former slaves, now free to run amok (i.e., rape white women) and be manipulated by said Yankees. Only the rise of the glorious Ku Klux Klan saves the South, giving it a new birth. Employing many innovative cinematographic effects and longer than any film produced before, *Birth of a Nation* met with a huge box office turnout and two thumbs up from President Woodrow Wilson. It also encountered a great deal of controversy and protests from African Americans led by the still fairly new NAACP and from at least some members of the Grand Army of the Republic.[4]

Some of the comedic films of the silent era, and at least through the 1960s, reflected the same Lost Cause mentality found in *Birth of a Nation*, although usually in a less malicious version. Many did not, however. Film historian Hal Erickson noted that the film industry found it most prudent not to dwell on the causes of the war: "So far as these comedies were concerned, once upon a time there was a four-year period of unpleasantness in which Americans wearing blue uniforms fought Americans wearing gray uniforms, and that's all we care to say on the subject."[5]

The first comedic Civil War film, *The Battle of Who Run*, told the tale of two officers, one Confederate and one Union, vying for the love of the same woman, played by Mabel Normand, against the backdrop of a fictional battle, Who Run, which sounds an awful lot like Bull Run if it took place in a Dr. Seuss story. Director Mack Sennett saved money on the thirteen-minute short by surreptitiously filming battle scenes that were part of another Civil War movie's production. Months later Sennett released *Cohen Saves the Flag*, in which two Union soldiers vie for the love of the same woman, played by Mabel Normand (sound familiar?), this time against the backdrop of the Battle of Gettysburg. Sennett again saved money by filming scenes being staged for another of Civil War film. The year before, Sennett made another short with a Civil War connection, *Stolen Glory*, in which a Union army veteran vies with an old farmer for the love of an elderly woman, under the backdrop of a Grand Army of the Republic reunion. To save money, Sennett used shots of an actual GAR convention's parade so he did not have to stage one. The woman was not played by Mabel Normand.[6]

While American film producers preferred dramatic depictions of the war or melodramatic romances involving divided families and conflicted lovers, a few more Civil War comedies hit the silver screen during the silent era. The 1914 offering *The Deadly Battle of Hicksville* poked fun at the romanticized dramas with a story about two friends fighting in the opposing armies and reunited on the battlefield. Unfortunately, information available about this "rib tickler" film as it was promoted is pretty much bare bones, and the film, like so many others of this era, appears to be lost. Lost, too, is Mack Sennett's 1919 popular comedy *Salome vs. Shenandoah*, in which an inept theatrical troupe stages two productions, one of the popular play *Salome*, based on the biblical story, and the other based on the Civil War drama *Shenandoah*. The film stars Ben Turpin, the most famous skew-eyed film star to grace the big screen until the arrival of Marty "What hump?" Feldman. Turpin plays a general in the Civil War stage production and Moses in the other.[7]

After the fifty-year anniversary, the number of films focusing on the Civil War diminished. Still, a few more funny silent films did appear, including one of the first feature-length comedies. In 1922, slap-stick stunt specialist Harold Lloyd starred in *Grandma's Boy*. While not a Civil War story, per se, the plot line does have a significant flashback to the war. Lloyd plays a coward vying for the affections of a young lass with a bully that has hounded him since grade school. Called on to be part of a posse to capture a "tramp" who killed a local businessman, Lloyd instead cowers under his bed. Then his grandmother, who raised him, tells him of his grandfather—cue the flashback—also a coward, called upon in the 1860s not only to serve in the Confederate army, but to go on a special mission behind the lines to capture a special code from a Union general. The grandfather nearly fails in his quest due to his lack of bravery, but then he encounters a haggish-looking woman who gives him a special "charm," a small statue of an almost equally haggish-looking woman, and tells him that no one can hurt whoever possesses the charm. To make a long story short, the grandfather retrieves the code and captures four generals in blue to boot. Fortified with this knowledge and carrying the alleged charm from his grandmother (it all turns out to be a made-up story), Grandma's boy catches the tramp, beats up the bully, and wins the girl.[8]

Another full-length comedy titled *Hands Up!* arrived in 1926. A delightful send-up of Civil War melodramas, the film begins with Abraham Lincoln's plan to obtain gold from a loyal mine owner in Nevada. Learning of the scheme, Robert E. Lee sends a Confederate spy named Jack to Nevada either to steal the gold or to stop it from shipping. Jack arrives at the Union outpost close to the mine dressed just like Dudley Doo-Right's nemesis Snidely Whiplash, only to be arrested immediately as a spy and ordered to be executed. After the firing squad tries but fails to shoot Jack several times, he escapes. Travelling to the mine on the same stagecoach with the mine owner and his two daughters, Jack and his fellow travelers are captured by Native Americans led by Sitting Bull, but Jack saves the day by showing Sitting Bull how to shoot dice and teaching the rest of the captors a dance resembling the Charleston. The mine owner then makes Jack foreman of the mine, and both daughters fall in love with him. Nevertheless, Jack is captured and preparations are made to string him up, but before that happens, both daughters try to save Jack by claiming to be his wife. Then word arrives that the war is over. Jack is now torn between the two sisters, but just then an old friend of the mine owner arrives and introduces Jack to his six wives. The old friend, Brigham Young, gives Jack an idea, and off the three lovebirds go to Utah.[9]

The best-known Civil War comedy, silent or otherwise, came out the same year as *Hands Up!* Buster Keaton's *The General* met with little popular enthusiasm and a harsh response from critics upon its release, but years later came to be seen as a film classic. *The General* begins at the war's outset with Keaton's character, Johnnie Gray, unable to enlist in the Confederate army because he is too valuable as the engineer of his train, the General. Many people assume Johnnie is a coward, including his fiancée, Annabelle Lee. Thus, estranged from one of his loves, Annabelle, Johnnie focuses on his other, his train and his work. When Union spies steal the General, and inadvertently kidnap Annabelle, Johnnie pursues using a variety of methods—on foot, on a hand car, on another train—and encounters much resistance, which leads to great slapstick visual humor. He manages to free Anabelle, retake the General, and flee south, pursued by two trains. He also learns of an impending Union assault on his neck of the woods. After more slapstick, he makes his way back to his own lines. With Annabelle and the train safe, he warns the Confederates of the looming attack. Johnnie becomes a hero and gets a commission as a lieutenant. Plus, he gets the girl. This was not Keaton's last foray into the Civil War. In 1939 he starred in a short film titled *Mooching through Georgia*, a brother-against-brother story set in Kentucky. While Keaton performs many sight gags in the film, unlike *The General*, *Mooching* is a talkie. Personally, I think Keaton is much funnier when he keeps his mouth shut.[10]

In discussing *The General*, which he produced and directed, Keaton explained that he told the story from the perspective of the Confederates because people like underdogs, and the Confederacy lost. As the film industry shifted to talking films, however, the demand for Civil War films declined, and a decade passed before another full-length Civil War comedy appeared, perhaps the only one of the 1930s. In 1936 producer Hal Roach tried to see if his *Our Gang* franchise of cinematic shorts could be stretched out to feature length with *General Spanky*. Along with George "Spanky" McFarland, the film features *Our Gang* favorites Carl "Alfalfa" Switzer and Billie "Buckwheat" Thomas. Like *The General*, *General Spanky* definitely leans to the South. Spanky, a six-year-old bootblack working on a Mississippi River steamboat with no apparent parental supervision, and his new friend, the young slave Buckwheat, jump off the boat after they run into some trouble. On shore Buckwheat aligns himself with Spanky because he does not want to be considered a runaway. The two end up being taken in by Marshall Vallent, a nice man they met on the steamboat. The war begins, and Marshall goes off to join the Southern army while Spanky stays at the Vallent homestead with orders to take care of Marshall's sweetheart, Louella. To do this, Spanky creates a home guard with Buckwheat and another new friend, Alfalfa. They call it the Royal Protection of Women and Children Regimental Club of the World and Mississippi River, or the R.P.W.C.R.C.W.M.R. for short. I guess that the boys aren't ready for the He-Man Women-Haters Club yet. Spanky and his gang protect the girl, save Marshall from execution, and in the end, everything is O-Tay![11]

I noted that *General Spanky* was perhaps the only feature-length Civil War comedy of the 1930s because some might include Shirley Temple's 1935 vehicle *The Littlest Rebel* on the list. Temple plays Virginia "Virgie" Cary, whose father joins the Confederate army, and as a scout, is captured as a spy and sentenced to death. With the help of a loyal enslaved man named Uncle Billy, played by Bill "Bojangles" Robinson, Virgie seeks out the only person who can save her father: Abraham Lincoln. Touched by the little girl's story, the president issues a pardon, but not before Shirley Temple wears blackface, sings "Polly Wolly Doodle-All-A-Day," and tap dances with Bill Robinson. The same year *The Littlest Rebel* came out, Temple starred in another film that might sound like a sequel but it is not. Released before *Rebel*, *The Little Colonel* is set after the war. Temple plays Lloyd Sherman, whose mother, a Southerner, married a Yankee after the war, causing a falling out with her unreconstructed father, Colonel Lloyd. Before the movie is over, Lloyd helps mom and granddad reconcile, saves the family fortune, and tap dances with Bill Robinson. It is painful to watch the demeaning characterizations used to depict enslaved people in both these films, especially *The Littlest Rebel*. Much of what passed for humor in 1936 comes at their expense, especially the characters named James Henry, played by Willie Best in *Rebel*, and Mom Beck, played by Hattie McDaniel in *Colonel*.[12]

More than a dozen years passed before the next Civil War comedic feature hit the big screen. In *A Southern Yankee*, Red Skelton plays Aubrey Filmore, a bell boy working in a St. Louis hotel in early 1865, who becomes embroiled in an espionage scheme. Almost put to death by the Confederates, Aubrey is saved by the bell, or actually, the war coming to an end. There seems to be a lot of that in these movies. And he gets the girl, to boot. In the film, Skelton employed a number of sight gags reminiscent of Buster Keaton's performance in *The General*, and rightly so. Keaton consulted on the film and designed many of the stunts.[13]

Through the 1950s and 1960s, Civil War comedies continued to be a rare commodity in Hollywood. One worth mentioning is *Advance to the Rear* (1964), starring Glen Ford and Stella Stevens. A group of misfit soldiers who, through no fault of their own, appear to be cowards in battle get court martialed, demoted, and sent west, where they can do no harm. Dubbed Company Q, and we've heard what that means already, the unit includes a kleptomaniac, an arsonist, a bare-knuckles fighter who punches whoever is near him when he hears a bell, a soldier with perpetual hiccups, another who accidentally blew up a latrine, and one who for some inexplicable reason is a horse magnet. The Confederates learn of this odd group and think that it must be an elite force, so they send a spy in the form of Stella Stevens to gather information. She travels with a group of prostitutes heading west on the same paddle boat carrying Company Q up the Missouri River. Once arrived, Company Q learns that it must protect a shipment of gold that will be sent back east. The film was supposedly based on a 1957 novel, *Company of Cowards* by Jack Shaefer, which in turn was inspired by a 1956 *Saturday Evening Post* article by William Chamberlain, neither of which was comedic. The whole thing about getting gold from the West, a Confederate spy trying to thwart the plan, and a love story sounds an awful lot like *Hands Up!* to me. Both also have stereotypical Native Americans. What *Advance to the Rear* has that none of these other works has is its own song, or at least Company Q does, about a "company of cowards" who have "come to save the day." It was sung by The New Christy Minstrels.[14] In the end, Company Q saves the gold, but only after a frenetic clash with the Confederates who come to steal it in a scene that very easily could have been accompanied by the song "Yakety Sax." And Glenn Ford gets the girl.

Advance to the Rear went to theaters in 1964, during the height of the Civil War's centennial celebration. Three years later, Roy Orbison's *The Fastest Guitar Alive* arrived. The popular country-pop singer played a Confederate agent intent on stealing gold from the San Francisco mint. The film bears many of the tropes of *Hands Up!* and *Advance to the Rear*, with the exception of Orbison's unique guitar, which doubles as a shotgun.[15] After that, Civil War comedies were a rare thing. Even then, according to one reliable source, of the nearly five hundred Civil War films produced between 1897 and 1961, only nineteen, about four percent, were comedies.[16] While a few war-themed, dark comedies became quite popular in the 1970s, films like *M*A*S*H* and *Catch-22*, for instance, people had lost interest in the war of the 1860s. And besides, because of the impact of the Civil Rights movement, Vietnam, and other factors, the common habit of ignoring the causes of the war, especially slavery, and of portraying enslaved people as dim-witted, obedient servants, or worse, would have made it very difficult to create a humorous film about the war like those that came before this period. If film makers wanted to find a way to laugh at the Civil War while side-stepping these serious issues, they needed to find a novel way to frame the story. More on this later.

What If Lincoln's Doctor's Dog Wrote a Biography?

While film offered a new dimension for portraying the Civil War in the twentieth century, depictions of the war still found their way into print. In fact, in 1932, humorist James Thurber wrote a parody piece for the *New Yorker* predicting that within a decade, Congress would pass a law placing fines on the authors of biographies and requiring permits to do so, with Civil War biographies being the biggest offenders. Written in the first person and set shortly after the passage of the imagined law, the piece tells of a meeting between the author and Director Rumsonby of the newly-created Bureau of Publishing Statistics and Biographers' Permits. The director tells the narrator, "The fine for Grant is five thousand dollars, for [Jeb] Stuart thirty-two hundred and fifty, and for Jackson four thousand.... Lincoln carries the maximum fine of fifty thousand dollars and two years' imprisonment or both. Everybody wants to do Lincoln." Rumsonby reveals that authors had found a way around the law by writing books that were not "biography in the technical sense of the word," but rather "fictive and suppositional." In other words, they were "what if stories." Civil War buffs and even academics have long engaged in the practice of speculating on what if this or what if that, often in ways that might have turned the war for the South. What if the Confederates had pursued the Union army after the victory at Manassas? What if the British had given diplomatic recognition to the South? What if Stonewall Jackson had not been killed? What if things had gone differently for the Confederates at Gettysburg? And of course, what if Stonewall Jackson had not been killed and had been at Gettysburg? By the 1930s, if not earlier, the "what if" game had become a thing, and Thurber's fictive bureaucrat relates the tale of the book that made it all the way to the Supreme Court: "If Lincoln Had Shot Booth." The court's ruling in favor of the book's methodology quickly "led to seventy-four other If books on Lincoln, including 'If Lincoln Had Missed Booth,' 'If Booth Had Hit Mrs. Lincoln,' 'If Mrs. Lincoln Had Shot Mrs. Booth,' and so on."[17]

Thurber's inspiration for interjecting the "what if" genre into his tale no doubt came from an actual series of articles that ran in *Scribner's Magazine* starting in 1930, the first being "If Booth Had Missed Lincoln" (ring a bell?) by Milton Waldman. It was followed by the doubly fictive and suppositional "If Lee Had Not Won the Battle of Gettysburg," in which British statesman, historian, and future prime minister Winston Churchill presupposes that the Confederates won the battle. He offers a series of ersatz counterfactuals that were actually factuals, "ifs" if you will, that strongly resemble what actually happened. But the more important chain of events resulting from Churchill's world turned upside down is what he posits happened after the Confederate victory. Lee occupied Washington two days later, then singlehandedly ordered an end to slavery in the Confederacy, which led to British recognition of the new nation and, more importantly, undercut the moral imperative Northerners felt for continuing the war, leading to the Treaty of Harper's Ferry ending the war with the Confederacy independent.[18] H.L. Mencken definitely would have liked this outcome. Also, no doubt, *Scribner's* what-if Civil War articles inspired Thurber to write his own speculative what-if essay, the aforementioned "If Grant Had Been Drinking at Appomattox," which appeared in the *New Yorker* a month after *Scribner's* first installment.

The popularity of Lincoln as the focus of biographical books as suggested by Thurber was confirmed by George Stevens in his 1938 release *Lincoln's Doctor's Dog and Other Famous Best Sellers*, a non-fiction work having nothing to do with the Civil War and everything to do with the world of publishing and the making of a best seller circa the 1930s. "There are ... new lives of Lincoln in constant succession every year," he notes. In fact, he reveals about half way through his brief book, "There's one of those stories that run around the trade to the effect that all books on Lincoln sell, all books about dogs sell, and all books by doctors sell—so the man who writes a book about Lincoln's doctor's dog is going to clean up." Thus, Stevens's title. It took nearly two decades, but someone finally heeded Stevens's suggestion, although not in book form. In 1955 the prolific writer Christopher Morley published an article in *The Saturday Review* titled, you guessed it, "Lincoln's Doctor's Dog." In this warm and fuzzy tale, Morley tells of a doctor's struggle in treating his difficult patient for "extreme and mental fatigue." Lincoln is not getting better and the doctor becomes more and more frustrated because the president will not rest. With other treatments failing, the doctor sends over to the president's mansion a month-old puppy from his own dog's litter with instructions for Lincoln to spend the day with the little critter away from his work. The ploy works. Frolicking with the pup cures the president of his infirmities, much to the relief of the doctor.[19]

Sixty-five years later, a book titled *Lincoln's Doctor's Dog* finally made it into print as a collection of short stories, vignettes, and home spun tales designed to offer some good-natured fun. Written by James O. Long and reminiscent in tone of the crackerbox philosophers, the volume stars a dog named Cooper, a stray that follows the president's doctor around until making himself at home at the president's mansion. There he becomes a behind the scenes witness to the on-goings of the Lincoln administration. In the process, Cooper eats part of the president's hat, the boot of a young lieutenant, and the original Gettysburg Address, which had been much longer than the one Lincoln actually presented. Despite the fact that the stories mention soldiers and generals, readers have little clue that a war is going on, never mind slavery as its cause. I suspect that Long's *Lincoln's Doctor's Dog* put to rest George Stevens's theory about what topics sell.[20]

To be sure, not all American writers had much use for the Civil War, except maybe only as a source of humor. Born in 1862 as the war was hitting its stride, Edith Wharton often wrote about a post-war America where Civil War veterans and their stories ran rife, but not for her, with one notable exception. In 1924 Wharton published a series of novellas set in New York that in some ways stand as a prequel to her 1920 Pulitzer Prize winning *The Age of Innocence*. The third of the series, *The Spark*, focusses on a Civil War veteran turned prominent banker named Hayley Delane with most of the action taking place in the 1890s. A character study more than anything else, *The Spark* also can be seen as an elaborate joke's long set up leading to a one-two punchline. The unnamed narrator, fresh out of college, is drawn to Hayley as a mentor because of Hayley's strong sense of morality. While in awe of Hayley in many ways, the narrator is a bit perplexed that the elder banker has little knowledge of or use for things literary. The narrator traces this back to the years Hayley spent in the army during the Civil War, a revelation in itself that surprises the youth. Hayley ran off at the age of sixteen to join the Union army and received a serious wound at the Battle of Bull Run.[21]

Eventually, the narrator gets Hayley to open up somewhat about his time in the war, and here readers learn that the source of Hayley's sense of right and wrong, his moral compass, stems from his weeks convalescing in a military hospital in Washington, where Hayley relates, he met "a sort of big backwoodsman who was awfully good to me." "I don't think he believed in our lord," Hayley, a regular church goer, explains, "yet he taught me Christian charity." As time wore on, the narrator and Hayley's friendship grows, and then, on a Sunday afternoon social visit to the narrator's apartment, Hayley picks up a book that conveniently is lying out and flipping through it, he exclaims, "By Jove—there he is!" Pointing to an engraving of a man's portrait inside the book, Hayley continues, "I'd know those old clothes of his anywhere." The book, of course, is *Leaves of Grass*, and the "queer fellow," the "heathen" who nursed Hayley back to health while in Washington, was—wait for it—Walt Whitman. Cue the rim shot! Ta-tah, boom!![22]

But wait, there's more. "How on earth did the old boy get his portrait in a book?" our hero asks. "Has somebody been writing something about him?" The narrator explains that the man Hayley knew in Washington wrote the book and that he was a poet. The narrator then reads a few of Whitman's wartime poems, especially focusing on the soldiers the poet encountered. "He was a great chap," Hayley exclaims. "I'll never forget him.—I rather wish, though," Hayley adds, "you hadn't told me that he wrote all that rubbish." Cue the muted trumpet! Wah, waaaaaah!![23] (I'm curious to know what Hayley would have thought of the really bad poetry of the Civil War.)

Frankly, I Do Give a Damn

Writing in the mid-1950s about Civil War fiction, Lawrence S. Thompson argued, "For almost a century the real secret weapon of those who still fight the last romantic war has been the American novel." If true, then no novel has caused more casualties than Margaret Mitchell's *Gone with the Wind*. Representing a new generation of the plantation genre in the lineage of Thomas Nelson Page, Joel Chandler Harris, and George W. Bagby, the book's distortion of history has shaped many people's understanding of the past since it first hit the shelves. It won the Pulitzer Prize for Fiction in 1937, and two years later became one of the most popular films ever produced. More people have read *Gone with the Wind* than any serious scholarly study about the Civil War era. By 2010, over thirty million copies of the book had been sold in at least 185 different editions and numerous translations. It continues to perform well, and according to a 2014 Harris Poll, the massive tome remains the second most popular book in America, beaten out only by the Bible.[24]

Author M. Carmen Gómez-Galisteo has observed, "Because of its popularity, it is not surprising that *Gone with the Wind* has fallen prey to a great variety of parodies of all sorts." For that reason, and knowing that I should address at least some of those parodies, I decided that it was time for me to read *Gone with the Wind* myself. So, in May 2020, I started reading Margaret Mitchell's opus. All of it. Every damned word. The edition I read, and as pointed out, there have been many, ran 1,024 pages.[25] Every. Damned. Word.

Gone with the Wind (hereafter *GWTW*) tells a familiar story. Girl wants guy number 1. Girl doesn't get guy number 1. War breaks out. Girl gets other guy. Other guy dies. Girl flirts with mustached guy. Girl doesn't get guy number 1 again. War doesn't go well. Girl doesn't get guy number 1 yet again. Girl flirts with mustached guy again. Girl gets yet another guy. The other guy dies. Girl gets mustached guy. Again, girl doesn't get guy number 1. Girl doesn't want guy number 1 anymore. Girl loses mustached guy. And tomorrow is another day.

As I read my way through the first chapter, the thought struck me that the book actually might be a spoof or satire of Southern stereotypes, and a nasty one at that. Early in that chapter, readers encounter the Tarleton twins, "outstanding in their notorious inability to learn anything contained between the covers of two books." Indeed, the two "had less grammar than most of their poor Cracker neighbors."[26] Being sons of the planter class, the twins are sent to college, or colleges, despite their ignorance. Their tenures are brief, however, being accepted and then expelled from the University of Virginia, the University of Alabama, the University of South Carolina, and then the University of Georgia. The Tarletons' lack of appreciation for education is matched only by Scarlett O'Hara's disdain for anything intellectual.

A few short pages later, the narrator informs readers that in the South, "no one was permitted to whip a horse or a slave." Of course, slave owners treat their slaves well, and slaves are happy and obedient and know their place. What need would there be to punish them physically? Unless, of course, they step out of their place. Next, readers encounter inbreeding: "The Wilkes and the Hamiltons always marry their own cousins." Everybody knows that, and before long, cousins Ashley Wilkes and Melanie Hamilton marry, much to non-cousin Scarlett's chagrin. And the book's first attack on Northerners, specifically Cade Calvert's "Yankee stepmother," contains a jab at the notion of Southern honor and violence. It seems that the second Mrs. Calvert took exception to Stuart Tarleton shooting Cade in the leg, and she insulted Stuart over it. There was "no excuse for insulting me," Stuart explained. After all, Stuart was all "lickered up" when he did it. But as brother Brent reasons, "She's a Yankee," and because of that, she "ain't got very good manners."[27]

Was Mitchell critiquing the fabled Southern way of life? Soon, any notion that Mitchell meant her book to be a satire disappeared, although intentionally or not, she continued to cast a humorous light on other Southern customs and practices. Particularly amusing is Mitchell's description of Southerners visiting:

> When a Southerner took the trouble to pack a trunk and travel twenty miles for a visit, the visit was seldom of shorter duration than a month, usually much longer. Southerners were as enthusiastic visitors as they were hosts, and there was nothing unusual in relatives coming to spend the Christmas holidays and remaining until July. Often when newly married couples went on the usual round of honeymoon visits, they lingered in some pleasant home until the birth of their second child. Frequently elderly aunts and uncles came to Sunday dinner and remained until they were buried years later.[28]

Putting aside the moments of humorous description, I found the book's prose incredibly well written and its narrative compelling. Having finished the book, two big things struck me. First, *GWTW* projects a rather ambivalent view of the war the Confederacy waged against the North and the Federal government. While the book has many characters who are Southern patriots to the bitter end and beyond, its two main characters, Scarlett and Rhett Butler, certainly are not. Scarlett not only cares little about the Southern cause, she resents the war for disrupting her romantic plans and her privileged lifestyle. Rhett, on the other hand, doesn't give a damn about the Confederate cause, predicting accurately that the South will go down to defeat at the hands of the Yankees. He uses the situation to amass a fortune blockade-running smuggled goods, not always goods that will help the South win the war but nonetheless worth a tidy profit. Only later do the two espouse the Confederate cause, now lost, and only when it suits their personal interests. (This is surprising because Rhett shares a unique trait with the Confederacy's greatest hero, Robert E. Lee. Like the general, Captain Butler had "absurdly small feet.") Late in the book, Mitchell describes the "unwritten code" of the Lost Cause: "Reverence for the Confederacy, honor to the veterans, loyalty to old forms, pride in poverty, open hands to friends and undying hatred to Yankees." She then asserts that "between them, Scarlett and Rhett had outraged every tenet of this code."[29]

The second thing that struck me was the book's staggering racism. *GWTW* is a book about racist people who own slaves, fight to keep slaves, and then not only resent losing slavery but strive to keep their former slaves in their place. Naturally, characters if portrayed effectively would embody racist traits. But it struck me as more than that. Mitchell used a language of racism that is more than a reflection of the attitudes of her characters of the 1860s. This language asserted these racist ideas as universal truths, recognizable to the typical white reader of the 1930s. She did not describe white characters who believe that African Americans are inherently inferior. She described African Americans as inherently inferior. Only those who are trained properly—Mammy, Prissy, Pork, Uncle Peter—know their place. After the war they continue to carry on in their role as someone else's property. Formerly enslaved people who embrace emancipation—"free issue negroes," or a harsher term—cause serious problems while being manipulated by Yankee carpetbaggers and Southern scalawags. And it becomes acceptable to murder any African American man suspected of insulting or assaulting a white woman. Even Rhett agrees with this practice. Black Lives didn't Matter.

The timing of my tackling *GWTW* could not have been more ironic. As I was reading this racist book about racist people, African American George Floyd was killed by a Minneapolis police officer, and the nation exploded in protest that lasted for months. My intention is not to analyze this 2020 occurrence. Rather, I think back to 1936 and after and wonder how many people had their views on race relations shaped, or confirmed, by reading *GWTW*. In the decades before and just after Mitchell's publication, racially motivated lynchings had been a common occurrence. Just two decades later, fourteen-year-old Emmitt Till was accused of assaulting a white women and brutally murdered. And I wonder what residual influence, direct or indirect, the book and subsequent movie continue to have on racial attitudes.

Which makes it difficult to return to my main focus, humor. Three years after *GWTW* appeared in print, the epic film version hit the theaters and was greeted by huge audiences and an Academy Award for Best Picture. The film clocks in at over three and a half hours, even though it cuts out huge sections of the book and deletes two of Scarlett's three children. Nevertheless, the story on screen does present several comical moments: Rhett Butler popping up from the sofa and asking "Has the war started yet?" after a dejected Scarlett shatters a figurine against the wall above him; the widowed Scarlett Hamilton dancing from the waist down, hidden by the booth she is tending and her large hoopskirt at the "Monster Bazaar for the Benefit of Atlanta's Own Military Hospital"; Aunt Pittypat fainting when Scarlett actually does dance with Rhett at the Bazaar, violating all sorts of widowhood protocols; and, of course, with Atlanta under invasion by the Yankees and burning, and Melanie Wilkes in painful labor, the slave Prissy proclaiming, "I don't know nothin' 'bout birthin' babies!" It is hard not to laugh in the moment, but in reality, the African American characters in *GWTW*—Mammy, Pork, Sam, and Prissy—are often portrayed in a rather clownishly comical way, which differs little from the book.[30]

Mammy and her peers are loyal slaves before and during the war, and they still know their place after it. Nevertheless, the movie is sanitized of the book's strongest racist depictions. To be sure, the movie is still pretty racist, but unlike the book, it does not harp on how awful the "free issue Negroes" are. While mob violence against African Americans appears, there is no direct mention or glorification of the Ku Klux Klan. And while Rhett is briefly arrested after the war, movie viewers never learn that in Mitchell's book the charge had been murdering a black man, which Rhett admits to Scarlett. He killed in order to defend the honor of a white woman. The movie version of *GWTW* reached even more people than the book did. The movie "became the primary medium through which [Americans] learned about slavery," according to historian Ibram X. Kendi, while Matthew Christopher Hulbert has observed that realistic depictions of slavery on film could not compete with images presented in *GWTW*, *Birth of a Nation*, *The Littlest Rebel*, and the Disney version of the Uncle Remus stories, *Song of the South*.[31]

With that said, it did not take long for *GWTW* to become the subject of parody. In February 1937, *The New Yorker*, always in the vanguard of literary matters, ran a two-page cartoon strip predicting how a movie version of *GWTW* would look, complete with a Hollywood ending. A few years later, cartoonist Al Capp appropriated the *GWTW* storyline to create his own comic arc in his popular cartoon *Lil' Abner*, which ran for three weeks in many newspapers in the fall of 1942 before Margaret Mitchell threatened legal action for copyright infringement. Nearly half a century later, *Mad* magazine took a swipe at *GWTW* with a parody titled "Groan with the Wind." Written by Stan Hart and illustrated by Jack Davis of *Beauregard!* (lack of) fame, "Groan" portrays comical scenes depicting the antics of Harlott, Rhetch, Ashtray Wilts, and Miss Melonhead as they maneuver through the Civil War and Reconstruction.[32]

No parody of *GWTW* has gained as much attention or fame as the one done by television's *The Carol Burnett Show* in November 1976, appearing shortly after *GWTW* ran for the first time on network television. "Went with the Wind!" clocked in at almost twenty minutes of the extremely popular hour-long prime-time show and starred Carol Burnett as Starlett O'Hara and Harvey Korman as Ratt Butler, with Tim Conway playing Brashley Wiles and guest star Dinah Shore as Melodie Wilkes. The skit spoofs many of the memorable moments of the movie, but it is Vicky Lawrence who often steals the scene playing Sissy, especially when she delivers the skit's "Frankly, Miss Starlett, I don't give a damn" final line. Fortunately, Lawrence does not appear in blackface. The skit makes no mention of Sissy being enslaved; in fact, it does not mention slavery at all. It is most memorable for the green dress Starlett makes from the curtains, however, which still has the long curtain rod attached and running across her shoulders when she puts it on. Burnett's costume, complete with curtain rod, is now housed at the Smithsonian Institution.[33]

Neither *Mad* magazine nor *The Carol Burnett Show* encountered any litigation for their versions of *GWTW*. That would not be true for Alice Randall's *The Wind Done Gone*, published in 2001.[34] Randall, an African American writer, set out to tell the story untold in Mitchell's *GWTW*, the story of race relations at Tara and within the O'Hara family. Using (mostly) different but obvious names for the main characters, Randall does not necessarily retell the story related by Mitchell but rather fills in the narrative before the barbeque at Twelve Oaks in April 1861 and what happens after Rhett doesn't give a damn. Readers learn of many of the familiar events of *GWTW* through a different lens. The main character, Cynera, is the daughter of "Mammy" (Mammy) and "Planter" (Gerald O'Hara), which makes her the half-sister of "Other" (Scarlett). Cynera is sold off from Tara by Planter to a friend in South Carolina because she has become a distraction to Mammy and her mammying responsibilities for Other and because of the growing bond between Cynera and Other's actual mother, "Lady," who was left out of the mothering business because Other had a mammy. Sold once again to satisfy debts, Cynera comes into the possession of "Beauty," an Atlanta brothel owner. There, Cynera, who has grown to be quite beautiful herself, meets "R" (Rhett), who falls in love with her. Besides Other having a mulatto enslaved half-sister, Randall's version informs readers that Other is, herself, biracial. In a long-since covered up scandal, a great-grandmother of Other's on Lady's side of the family was Black.

Without going through the whole story line, other revelations include the fact that Cynera orchestrated the meeting between R and Other. "Garlic" (Pork), Planter's personal valet, is the guiding force behind the often-intoxicated Planter's personal success and pulled the strings to make the plantation, called "Tata," a success before the war. Mammy, on the other hand, grooms Other from a young age to torment white men as a form of revenge. Thus, Other becomes the flirtatious, amoral manipulator she is by the age of sixteen. Randall's version of Prissy, "Miss Priss," is not the addle-brained, immature servant of the original story. Rather, she harbors a strong hatred for "Mealy Mouth" (Melanie), whom she blames for the deaths of two brothers back when Mealy's family owned Priss and her mother. One brother starved to death when Priss's mother wet nursed Mealy's son. More scandalous, the other was whipped to death when Mealy learned that he was having a relationship with her husband, the "Dreamy Gentleman" (Ashley). Some slaves believe that Priss killed Mealy Mouth. Priss is not the only character involved in homicide. Mammy and/or Garlic also killed Other's three brothers as babies to eliminate any future competition to Garlic's control of Planter and Tata. And a drunken Other dies at Tata after contracting small pox and then falling down the stairs after catching a glimpse of what she looked like in a mirror. In *GWTW*, Margaret Mitchell comments numerous times and rather disdainfully that the enslaved people see and hear everything. The story told by Randall bears that out.

Literary scholar Henry Louis Gates, Jr., testified in defense of Randall's book in the lawsuit brought by the Mitchell Estate. He pointed out that ridicule is often the objective of parody, asserting, "Scholars have long established that parody is at the heart of African American expression, because it is a creative mechanism for the exercise of political speech, sentiment, and commentary on the part of people who feel themselves oppressed or maligned and wish to protest that condition of oppression or misrepresentation." Highlighting irony has been an effective way to ridicule through parody, which is definitely true in *The Wind Done Gone*.[35] For the Mitchell Estate, an illegitimate mulatto child of Gerald O'Hara, the killing of white (well, mostly white) babies by slaves who supposedly knew their place, a homosexual Ashley Wilkes, and a Scarlett O'Hara who was legally black was too much. Thus, the estate initiated a lawsuit against the publisher of *The Wind Done Gone*, Houghton Mifflin, to try to stop the book's release. The suit claimed copyright infringement against the book because it appropriated the characters from *GWTW* without authorization.

Okay, *Mad*'s parody suggests that Ashtray is gay, too, and "Groan" does have a couple of quips about slavery, but nothing very biting. Perhaps the Mitchell Estate realized a lawsuit against the well-established *Mad* magazine with its long history of parody would look foolish. Unlike *The Wind Done Gone*, which Houghton Mifflin publicized well in advance, *Mad*'s "Groan" probably appeared with little fanfare. The Mitchell Estate probably learned of the parody only after it went on sale. Whatever the case, I suspect that if the Mitchell Estate had sued, *Mad*'s publisher would have said, "What, me worry?"

In the end, Randall, Houghton Mifflin, the first amendment, and parody won out, as the court ruled against the Mitchell Estate. *The Wind Done Gone* hit the market, billing itself as "The Unauthorized Parody" and asserting on its copyright page: "This novel is the author's critique of and reaction to the world described in Margaret Mitchell's *Gone with the Wind*. It is not authorized by the Stephens Mitchell Trusts and no sponsorship or endorsement of the Mitchell Trust is implied." It went on to have a respectable six-week run on the *New York Times* Best Sellers List.[36] I doubt that most people would find *The Wind Done Gone* laugh-out-loud funny, but humor can be found in its subversive use of ridicule and irony.

Randall's *The Wind Done Gone* is grounded in that subversive tradition of African American humor. Writing in 1965, with the ink in Lyndon Johnson's signature on the Civil Rights Act of 1964 and the Voting Rights Act of 1965 still wet, Philip Sterling observed that African American humor "is not always an escape into laughter by means of the comic.... American Negro humor is often an escape into pride and dignity; into a sense of that human equality the substance of which was (and is) too often denied; and into a spirit of a triumph that chronic adversity contradicts." Such humor can be found in Jordan Anderson's letter to his former master and in Elizabeth Keckley's memoir. It permeates a tradition of African American folklore that depicts an underdog, a rabbit for instance, outsmarting and defeating an apparently superior foe, a fox for instance, and can be seen as a form of parody. But before the Civil War, when slavery was the norm in the South, and for a century or more after, when segregation and Jim Crow were the law and lynching was all too commonplace, African Americans had to be cautious about how they used humor for fear of violent retribution.[37] Laugh-out-loud humor that poked fun at whites directly could be dangerous, indeed life threatening. Even now, it's next to impossible to separate the African American wartime experience from slavery, and slavery is just one of those things that can't be made funny.

Humor in the form of parody, if subtle, can be found in other Civil War–related writings by African Americans. For example, Paul Laurence Dunbar's 1902 sentimental novel *The Fanatics* focuses largely on the white population of a southern Ohio town and some of its families divided by the war. When I first read *The Fanatics*, I missed the humor, although one sentence jumped out at me, enough so that I made a note of it. After an early scene focusing on one of the story's main families and their emotional discussion of a son going off to fight for the Union, Dunbar writes, "It was strange talk and a strange scene for these self-contained people who thought so little of their emotions; but their very fervor gave a melodramatic touch to all they did that at another time must have appeared ridiculous." I found the sentence odd, but not funny. Perhaps Dunbar was ridiculing Northerners and their 1861 emotional outpouring to fight the Confederacy in a war that will end slavery, framing the scene in contrast to their decades of apathy about the institution. In a 2007 article, scholar Jennifer A. Hughes argued that in *The Fanatics*, Dunbar employs a form of parody called ironic incongruity to ridicule Northern whites for their bad treatment of African Americans, especially those freed by the very war that Northern whites waged against the slave-owning South. Hughes concluded, "To miss the emphasis that Dunbar puts on incongruity in *The Fanatics*," which she asserted has eluded readers for a century, "is to miss the artistic risk that Dunbar took in figuring the great American joke—that is, the existence of slavery (and its racist aftermath) in the democratic United States—into narrative form."[38] Hughes's observation suggests that there is more humor in various forms to be found in writings about the Civil War by African Americans. So, if you're looking for a literary dissertation topic, there it is. Just cite me in your acknowledgments.

Another work that fits Hughes's paradigm is Ishmael Reed's postmodern *Flight to Canada*, a novel set in the last days of the Civil War but taking place in the 1970s, with appearances by Abraham Lincoln, Harriet Beecher Stowe, John Wilkes Booth, Edgar Allan Poe, Barbara Walters, and, of course, Walt Whitman. The story focuses on the people enslaved by Arthur Swille, a despicably powerful, outrageously rich tycoon known as "the uncrowned king of America" who is believed to be behind the Lincoln assassination. Three are runaways pursued by the henchmen of their master while the others are part of Swille's household but by no means as obedient as he thinks. Reed deals with issues of race, power, slavery, and freedom, with the line between slavery and freedom often blurred. He tells the story from the perspective of the enslaved people and usually in an irreverent and off-beat way. Reed's finished product is a rather contorted, but no less humorous, portrayal of history. The book is more a statement about the 1970s than the 1860s, but it still has relevance to issues of race today.[39]

By the late twentieth century, creating a laugh-out-loud comedy in any format dealing with the Civil War had become incredibly perilous without potentially cheapening slavery, stereotyping enslaved people, or ignoring slavery and slaves altogether. The now-defunct UPN network tried its hand at a Civil War sitcom in 1998, meeting with immense failure. Set in the early years of the war, *The Secret Diary of Desmond Pfeiffer* depicted a black British nobleman who flees England due to gambling debts and gets hired as Abraham Lincoln's buffoonish personal butler. Even before the show aired, it came under fire from multiple sources for making light of slavery, but *Desmond Pfeiffer* deserved to be criticized because it was just plain bad. In its short run on TV, *Desmond Pfeiffer* established itself as one of the worst programs ever to appear. In 2010, the magazine *Entertainment Weekly* ranked it at number five of "TV's 50 Biggest Bombs and Blunders," and two books that appeared in 2004 recognized *Desmond Pfeiffer*, one calling it one of the "dumbest events" in television history and the other one of the "dumbest moments in business history."[40]

As I write this, the consequences of the killing of George Floyd along with a long history of racial injustices are still playing out. It has contributed to the removal of numerous statues celebrating the Confederacy and Confederate leaders, succeeding where many years of protest have failed. It proved to be the final push to force the Mississippi state legislature to redesign the state's flag, removing the Confederate battle flag that had been part of the state banner's design since 1894. Finally, the streaming service HBO Max decided to remove from its catalog the film *Gone with the Wind*, at least until it could be presented in conjunction with a discussion of its historical context.[41] These consequences are still developing, and it's yet to be seen who will have the last laugh.

Happy Birthday, Gray and Blue

As the Civil War approached its one hundredth birthday, the topic still remained one of great popular interest. However, the appeal of the Civil War on the big screen dwindled in the 1940s and 1950s, overshadowed by a new American war with new heroes. While Hollywood churned out myriad films about World War II, during those decades it produced forty-two Civil War films, down from fifty-seven in the 1920s and 1930s and a whopping 349 in the 1910s.[42] Of them, I'm aware of only one that was meant to be funny (intentionally, that is): *The Southern Yankee*.

The lack of comedic Civil War films released in the 1950s might serve as evidence of Pulitzer Prize-winning historian Arthur M. Schlesinger, Jr.'s claim that the decade was "the most humorless period in American history."[43] Yet funny Civil War stuff did make its way into print in the decade that brought us the Korean War, McCarthyism, the war on comic books, and Vice President Richard Nixon. Besides the essay "Lincoln's Doctor's Dog," two noteworthy books appeared. In 1953, James Street released *The Civil War: An Unvarnished Account of the Late but Still Lively Hostilities*. A prolific author and native Southerner, Street aimed his short, often irreverent book at a popular audience. In it he proclaimed, "Almost a hundred years after the first shot was fired, we Americans cannot even agree on a name for our Civil War Between the States, much less on what caused it or exactly what happened." The war, he continued, "was a lapse into national schizophrenia, a monstrous metamorphous during which Dr. Jekyll, a pretty good sort, changed himself into two Mr. Hydes who promptly tried to beat each other to death and who really never have forgiven each other although they have shaken hands and smiled for history's photographers." Containing echoes of the crackerbox philosophers without the misspellings, the book challenges many of the Civil War sacred cows people cherished in his day: "The South still talks about it and the folks know a lot about the Confederacy's battles but almost nothing about its Constitution, its Congress and its courts. The North still devours scads of books about it and has swallowed some of the weirdest myths since King Arthur."[44]

Despite his Southern heritage, Street was not a huge fan of the Lost Cause explanation for the war, although he still held to some stereotypes that have since been dispelled. I doubt that his book got the stamp of approval of the United Daughters of the Confederacy. "This holocaust," Street explained, "has been blamed on slavery, States' Rights, the protective tariff, free soil, Yankee mendacity, Southern treason, sun spots, the dictates of God and the Revelation of Saint John. For many years the wise men accepted it as a dog-eat-dog carnage between northern capitalism and southern agrarianism. More and more, however, historians are swinging to the idea that a moral issue was paramount, and the moral issue was slavery."[45] Street definitely acknowledged slavery in complex ways as the cause of the war, an admission one might not expect from a Southerner writing in the 1950s, although his discussion, like the whole book, is brief.

As for the war's outcome, Street blamed that squarely on the South rather than embracing the Lost Cause canard that noble Southern men fought bravely and valiantly but were defeated by a North that dared to have more men, more industry, more food production, better transportation, and a whole lot more liquid capital and, those cheaters, used those advantages to win. "In the field of finance," he divulged, "the Confederate government was as naïve as a southern backwoods preacher at Monte Carlo's roulette tables." The South "couldn't even support herself in peace and had to buy everything from locofocos [a nineteenth-century friction match] to locomotives." In short, he concluded, "the South cut her own throat." In a backhanded way, Street defended Abraham Lincoln. Street asserted that Lincoln "became a despot," but he did so "to save democracy from itself and to ensure its survival." As Street saw it, Lincoln "was fifty years ahead of his country in civil and human rights, maybe a hundred years. So he grabbed all the reins and handled the horses himself, determined to save the wagon even if a lot of folks got run over." This, to Street, was the war's "most fascinating paradox of all."[46]

Street also commented on the origins and sound of the famous rebel yell, or yells as he suggests: "As a reporter in my youth I covered several Confederate reunions and regretfully do I report that most of the veterans had to be rehearsed in the yell. I got the impression that during the Civil War there were probably as many Rebel Yells as there were Rebels." He did add, "After a few toddies the veterans would shift their tobacco chaws and cut loose on what seemed to me a spontaneous yell." Whether their yells sounded uniform is left unsaid.[47]

A native Mississippian, Street's Southern credentials were pretty solid. Furthermore, he stood by what he wrote, even those things that he thought might upset his fellow Southerners. For instance, he admired William T. Sherman, a rather heretical position. As a final "Note to the Reader," Street asserted,

> I will not answer acrimonious letters. I will not answer the challenges of my sources unless the complainants list their sources for challenging me. I will ignore Southerners who call me a renegade, Southerners and Yankees who call me a biased hillbilly, a Jim-Crowing poll-taxer, a reactionary, a fascist, a Communist or an egghead. Don't write me that line that you learned your Civil War history at your grandma's knee. Grandma's knee is a rightly nice place to pray, but it's a poor place to learn history.[48]

Street did not directly challenge the state of race relations in his day, but some of the things he wrote about slavery as the cause of the war and Abraham Lincoln's advancing civil and human rights certainly must have made many Southerners uncomfortable.

As for the glorification of the war, which he anticipated would escalate with the centennial, Street declared, "Romanticists can moon and mouth from here to eternity about the glories of the Civil War, but 'the last war between gentlemen' was a nasty mess," adding, "Even most of the songs were pretty dreary."[49] I wonder what he thought about the war's poetry.

A year after Street's little Civil War book came out, H. Allen Smith published another little volume titled *The Rebel Yell: Being a Carpetbagger's Attempt to Establish the Truth Concerning the Screech of the Confederate Soldier Plus Lesser Matters Appertaining to the Peculiar Habits of the South*. A native Northerner and popular writer, Smith didn't appreciate that others often "classified him as a humorist." He preferred to think of himself, and to have others think of him, as "a reporter with a humorous slant. I am funny," he noted, "only because the world is funny." In the book, Smith right away identified his inspiration, describing a new book he had just read by economist William J. Baxter, *Today's Revolution in Weather*, which presciently described what today we call global warming and climate change. Baxter argued that "the hot zones of the earth are moving steadily and inexorably northward." This drove Smith to the troublesome conclusion that for the United States, "*the North was going to become the South.*" "It is axiomatic that climate molds and fashions people," he explained. "It follows that if the weather of the Confederate states is moving up to the Northern portion of the United States, then the people of the North will become drawling duplicates of today's Southerners." Yet there was so much the Northern people did not know about the "ennobling traditions" of the Southern people. Therefore, enlightening the North on one of those traditions, the rebel yell, would be Smith's contribution to the learning curve. By understanding the yell, Smith believed, Northerners "will have taken a major step toward becoming passable Southerners."[50]

In his quest to identify the actual sound of the rebel yell, Smith first stopped at Chapel Hill, North Carolina, home of the University of North Carolina and also home of none other than his pal James Street. Street's book *The Civil War*, in which he suggested there were several rebel yells, probably had not come out yet at the time of the visit. In fact, he still may have been writing it. Nevertheless, meeting with Street proved fruitful for Smith, at least at first. Smith asked Street if he could do the yell, and Street obliged. "He arose from his chair," Smith described, "faced north, appeared to suck fifteen cubic feet of air into his lungs, and then uttered the rebel yell. The lapels on my jacket flapped and fluttered, a picture standing on the piano fell over, and I felt certain that the big tube in Mr. Street's television set was gone." Smith tried to write out the sound of the yell Street let out, but I'll spare you. "'That,' said Mr. Street, dabbing at the tear in his eyes, 'is the rebel yell. I heard it from my grandfather and from my grandfather's compatriots. I also heard it in my newspapering days while covering reunions of the Confederate heroes.'"[51]

Smith's search did not end there. Not everyone agreed that Street had it right. Smith's quest brought him to various locations and social gatherings: a hog-calling contest; the Gettysburg battlefield; a theater showing a Robin Hood film; a tobacco auction; the office of a denture-wearing lawyer from Charleston, South Carolina; and the home of the famous historian of the War Between the States, Douglas Southall Freeman. During his odyssey, folks treated Smith to nearly a dozen versions of the rebel yell. And then, to complicate matters more, a North Carolina newspaper quoted

Smith's friend James Street that there may have been as many rebel yells as there were rebels, a sentiment Street put in his book. In the end, *The Rebel Yell* leaves the whole matter unresolved.

The book ends rather abruptly, first with an editor's note explaining that Smith determined not to give up on his quest, so he disappeared into the swamps of the Florida Everglades looking for a man he had heard knew the sought-after screech. The editor then included a bit of writing brought out of the swamps believed to be what could be the last writing of H. Allen Smith, titled "REVOLT OF A DAMN YANKEE." Its author defended the people of the North against beliefs held and accusations made by Southerners that the former were "a decadent people" who are "drenched in frustration and shame because of the humiliation we suffered at the hands of the South." Northerners, he affirmed were "sick and tired of being pushed around and abused by Southerners.... Why, in the name of John Brown, can't they leave us alone?" Okay. I'm sure that many Southerners of the 1950s would reverse the roles in this statement and believe it to be true. The author used several issues in his defense, but the most oddly interesting has to do with women. He proclaimed that Southerners "act, sometimes, as if we were not aware of the fact that we have a Woman problem.... Let them understand, once and for all, that we'll handle the problem the way the Lord ... meant it to be handled." Criticisms, the author continued, arose "because we choose to segregate our men from our women, maintaining separate washrooms for them in public; compelling the women to go to one side of the shoe store and the men to the other side; even sending them to separate colleges." He added, "I was raised from the cradle by a faithful old Woman ... bless 'er big whole heart." Southerners "suffer the delusion that we could end our Woman problem with a snap of the fingers, when any sensible person knows that it is going to take generations," perhaps "seven or eight or thirty-five."[52] Reverse the roles again, so that Northerners criticize Southerners, and exchange the word "woman" for the word "Negroes," and this sounds an awful lot like an attack on the 1950s Jim Crow segregated South. It's hard to believe that *that* was not Smith's intentions, although veiling it as he did gave him plausible deniability. Perhaps here, Smith was being a reporter with a humorous slant taking on a very serious subject.

At least one Civil War historian saw fit to poke fun at the centennial. In 1963 Thomas Connelly, who had just earned his doctorate from Rice University, published *Will Success Spoil Jeff Davis? The Last Book about the Civil War*, using the pen name T. Lawrence Connelly. In it he spoofed the centennial, as well as the Southern obsession with the war, its heroes, and other related aspects in general. He also took an occasional subtle jab at the South's opposition to the Civil Rights movement, and ended the book with the assertion, "The war will never be over. Let minié balls corrode, Confederate money crumble, the imitation battle flags rot. As long as there is a tear-jerking poem to be read, a droll statue to be unveiled, a cannonball to be unearthed, a fast buck to be made—then there will always be a Confederacy." Five years later, as Thomas Connelly, he published an abbreviated and modified version in essay form in *The Journal of Mississippi History* titled "That Was the War that Was." Written as the war centennial was winding down, it continued to parody the passion for the war reignited among Southerners by this anniversary, proclaiming, "The Civil War did not end in 1865, nor will the fighting end as the centennial draws to a close in 1966."[53]

People outside of the United States also took note of the centennial. In January 1961, the British humor magazine *Punch* published "The American Civil War Made Easy," a guide to enable "Englishmen" to "know enough to hold their own in conversation with any celebrating Americans they happen to meet." The piece is an olio of names, facts, and events presented in a jumbled narrative that might have been told by Amelia Bedelia. (If you've had kids or have been a kid in the last sixty years, you probably know who she is.) Appearances are made by Abraham Lincoln and his stove pipe hat (the hat appears first); William Tecumseh Sherman; Robert E. Lee and a drinking Ulysses S. Grant; John Brown; Clark Gable; Buster Keaton; and more. I doubt that the real war got into the essay, but at least Walt Whitman made it.[54]

Two novels using the Civil War anniversary as a backdrop hit the bookstores while the celebration was in full swing. In *An End to Bugling*, Edmund G. Love provides a fantasy in which God, or "the Supreme Commander," decides to "join into the commemoration of the centennial of the Civil War" by ordering a reenactment of Jeb Stuart's Cavalry's activities during the Gettysburg Campaign in order to "demonstrate what the Civil War was really like." So, the cavalry of the Army of Northern Virginia led by Jeb Stuart, some 3,000 horsemen, leave their celestial abode and are transported to Poolesville, Maryland, arriving on June 28, 1963, exactly where they were one hundred years earlier. The warriors are unaware of the fact that it is a century later, while the public remains oblivious to the fact that the troops are the real deal, or at least a ghostly version of them. People first think they are some sort of planned reenactment or parade. Early on, the general and his staff are hosted by a local chapter of the United Daughters of the Confederacy, although the soldiers can't understand why these "daughters" look like grandmothers. Soon Stuart and company outstay their welcome. Over the next few days, the cavalry encounters befuddled local and state police from two states; 125 semi trucks that can go sixty miles per hour and are operated by good "union" men; frozen TV dinners; a raucous party thrown and attended by jet-setters, complete with belly dancers and bag pipers; civilians who think that the Confederates might be communists; and an ineffective National Guard equipped with tanks. The cavalry excursion is slowed down by the diesel-powered "wagons" they captured but occasionally aided by information found on historic markers along the road. Just as Stuart's Cavalry miraculously appears in Poolesville, the general and his men disappear as they reach Gettysburg on the morning of July 2, 1963, ten decades after their original arrival and in both cases too late to be of any help to Robert E. Lee.[55]

In Jacob Hay's *The Mindleberg Papers*, narrator Nicholas Bentley "Bent" Saltire is hired to write a history of Mindleberg Mills' contribution to the Civil War. By the 1960s, Mindleberg had evolved into a "far-flung Mindleberg textile empire," with its center in Textilia, North Carolina. When I first sat down to read this book, I expected the narrating hero to discover in his research a deeply hidden secret exposing that the Mindleberg company had been less than loyal to the Confederacy in one or more ways. I was surprised when I read that J. Sydney Cheek, the personal assistant to company owner Pierre Mindleberg, tells Bent very candidly that the wartime president of the operation was believed by many to be "the greatest sonofabitch produced by the late Confederate States of America." Colonel Marius Mindleberg, it appeared, had been a "war profiteer, cotton speculator, blockade runner" and perhaps worse. "Nobody's sure how he got his colonelcy—God knows he didn't get it fighting." Company founder Solomon Mindleberg allowed Marius to run the business after the lad had graduated from Harvard. When the war broke out, Marius denounced it as "sheer stupidity" and refused to enlist, as one might expect a young man in his early twenties to do. Then rumors started to circulate in Textilia that Marius was speculating in cotton, selling shoddy materials to the Confederate government for a big profit, trading with the enemy, and so forth. It didn't help when he disappeared from town for long stretches of time, until he left for good, eventually spending the rest of his life abroad, according to Cheek, "living it up like a Russian grand duke on his ill-gotten gains until he died in the arms of his mistress, a prima ballerina of the Paris Opéra, at his villa at Nice … at the ripe old age of forty-one."[56]

While combing through unprocessed Mindleberg material stashed away in the attic of the local historical society, Bent discovers a metal box containing bundles of letters written in code. Then he finds three uncoded letters to Marius thanking him for his service: one from Confederate president Jefferson Davis, one from Confederate secretary of state Judah P. Benjamin, and one from the adjutant to the commander of the Army of Northern Virginia, Robert E. Lee. It takes some doing for Bent to crack the code, but when he does, he discovers that Marius was not the scoundrel people thought him to be. Instead, "Marius Mindleberg had been the Confederacy's master spy in the North." When this news becomes public, "All hell broke loose when Dixie discovered her brand-new hero," especially in North Carolina and especially in Textilia.[57]

The plot thickens even further when it's discovered that Marius was, in fact, a double agent, working for the United States government to hinder the Confederacy. Furthermore, Marius's father Solomon was also a secret Unionist, sending information to Marius about Confederate industrial output and shortages. To make a long story short, when this new turn of events is revealed, there is an awful lot of anger, a near riot, accusations of a "Yankee Communist trick," wailing and gnashing of teeth, and so forth. But in the end, it's decided that instead of having a new hero for the South to celebrate, the best thing to do will be to celebrate Marius Mindleberg as a national hero, thus fostering unity and sectional reconciliation. People accept this, except for the unreconstructed rebel president of the local Civil War Roundtable and the United Daughters of the Confederacy. They don't buy in.

It's surprising that Hollywood did not turn either of these books into a film. *An End to Bugling* would have made for an entertaining romp with an all-star cast similar to films like *It's a Mad, Mad, Mad, Mad World*. *The Mindleberg Papers* would have been a very different film, a romantic comedy (Bent has a romance with his assistant). If Cary Grant had been younger, he would have made a great Bent. As for Bent's love interest, Doris Day definitely would fit the bill. Both stories are a bit dated, however, especially *The Mindleberg Papers*. It is quite sexist in a 1960s *Mad Men* with a touch of *Austin Powers* sort of way. Add to that some occasional antisemitism and a bit of homophobia, the book—no defense—was a product of its time.

What's not in either book is a defense of the Lost Cause. Despite following the adventures of a band of angelic Confederate brothers, Edmund Love did not celebrate them as noble defenders of home and family or anything else. It's just a lot of good clean fun, made easier by the total absence of any mention of slavery. *The Mindleberg Papers* is more critical of the Lost Cause myth, despite having several characters who vigorously embrace it. "The Southern myth," Mindleberg Mills' president Pierre Mindleberg admits, "the Southern cavalier fighting for the honor of Southern womanhood against hopeless odds, all that eyewash, all that nonsense has done more harm to the South than the war ever did." In pondering the turn of events in light of the centennial festivities, Bent asks himself, "What, finally, was this whole Civil War hysteria all about? Wasn't it, really, as Pierre had put is, a sentimental orgy celebrating a hideous war that never should have happened? A War that hadn't succeeded in settling most of the major issues over which it was fought. That left both sides as hypocritical as ever?" He adds, "What high comedy even the concept of a centennial celebration must be to the Negroes." Unfortunately, we never hear what they think. The only African Americans mentioned in the book are servants, janitors, porters on trains, and purchasers of bootleg liquor with little or nothing to say.[58]

Appearing at the tail end of the centennial but not promoting the Lost Cause despite its title is Richard Brautigan's *A Confederate General from Big Sur*.[59] Set in 1957, this short, postmodern novel introduces Lee Mellon through the eyes of his friend, narrator Jesse. Mellon, a narcissistic, boozing, violent, homophobic drifter, claims to have a grandfather named Augustus Mellon who served as a general in the Confederate army and distinguished himself during the Battle of the Wilderness. Upon consulting Ezra J. Warner's reference work *Generals in Gray: Lives of the Confederate Commanders*,[60] Lee and Jesse find no such general. Nevertheless, Lee has Jesse swear to agree that his grandfather was, in fact, a Confederate general. This has nothing to do with the rest of the narrative, nor do the numerous Civil War-related references Brautigan occasionally drops, such as Mellon's homemade bread having the consistency of hardtack; a pick-up truck that looks like a Civil War truck if there had been trucks back then; a ditty sung by Lee about a general being sent to Gettysburg; a random reference to Ulysses S. Grant and the Army of the Potomac; and Walt Whitman making it into the book along with his poem "Bivouac on a Mountain Side." Instead, we get an account of booze and drugs; annoying frogs; abandoned cabins in Big Sur, the setting of most of the story; two alligators; a part-time, high-priced call girl; an insane insurance salesman hiding from his family; a pomegranate; and more.

Meanwhile, a third-person narrator claims that the Big Sur region of California had seceded from the Union during the Civil War and contributed to the Confederate army the 8th Big Sur Volunteer Heavy Root Eaters, a small regiment made up of Digger Indians. Upon arriving on the scene of the Battle of the Wilderness in 1864, members "began dancing in a circle, the general [Robert E. Lee] and his horse in the middle, while all around them waged the American Civil War, the last good time this country ever had." This second narrator also reveals that a private named Augustus Mellon, a "thirty-seven-year-old former slave trader," skedaddled from the Confederate army during the same battle.[61] So much for the heroic Confederate general from Big Sur. How much the Civil War centennial influenced Brautigan's writing of *The Confederate General* is unknown, and the purpose of the use of the Civil War references is debatable, probably providing a thesis for scores of college term papers for years to come. Nevertheless, the book definitely reflected shifts going on not only in literature but also in American society in general.

The Civil War centennial came at the end of an old era and the beginning of a new one. Humor related to the centennial's celebration mirrored that found in the literature of the previous century. But the times, they were a-changin'. The Civil Rights Act of 1964 and the Voting Rights Act of 1965 improved African Americans' lives, but the assassinations of Malcolm X and Martin Luther King, Jr., and continued unrest signaled that much had been left unresolved. Add that and the assassinations of two Kennedys, Vietnam War protests, the Watergate scandal, and a growing youth counterculture that questioned authority to a shift in historians' understanding of the causes of the Civil War, the consequences of Reconstruction, and the realities of slavery, and many of the ways that the Civil War had been understood and explained since it broke out would need to be reevaluated. In light of this reevaluation, artistic folks would have to figure out new ways to have fun with, or make fun of, the Civil War. Or maybe they could find an approach that did not necessarily have to deal with these new understandings of reality by turning to a genre that by its very nature presented an unreal understanding of reality.

The last year of the Civil War centennial brought to the silver screen *Two Thousand Maniacs!* In April of 1965, six Northerners travelling through the South—two married couples and one pair who will be brought closer together during the film—are redirected by fake detour signs into the tiny hamlet of Pleasant Valley. The town's inhabitants, including the mayor, warmly greet them and inform them that they will be the guests of honor for their "centennial celebration." Although no one ever tells the visitors what they are celebrating, one might assume that it has something to do with the Civil War, especially since many of the residents are waving Confederate flags throughout the festivities. Later, one of the couples find a plaque on the edge of town cluing them in on the occasion. It reads: "In April, 1865, a group of renegade Union soldiers laid waste the village of Pleasant Valley and killed and mutilated many of its citizens. This marker is a memorial to the gallant citizens who gave their lives and testament to their vengeance pledged in their memory." The centennial is about revenge against Yankees!

The discovery comes too late, at least for the other four guests. While the two who found the sign manage to escape the town (while falling in love and deciding to get married), the others suffer gruesome deaths at the hands of their hosts involving dismemberment or other forms of bloodletting, with some cannibalism thrown in for good measure. The couple that escapes makes its way to a neighboring town and its sheriff, and the three return to Pleasant Valley, except there's nothing there. Only then does the sheriff tell the two that Pleasant Valley had stood there one hundred years earlier. Local folks tell a tale of a horrible thing that happened right at the end of the Civil War involving murderous Yankee soldiers, and that the area now is supposedly haunted by the ghosts of the two thousand dead that once called Pleasant Valley home. In the last scene, viewers see two of the mayor's ghostly cronies talking about how good this centennial had been and looking forward to the next in another one hundred years.

If one can get past the violent deaths, *Two Thousand Maniacs!* is a cornball comedy. Despite their homicidal tendencies, the residents of Pleasant Valley are depicted as Southern redneck nitwits, a caricature of Southern whites that became more and more common in film and television during the Civil Rights movement. While the spectral inhabitants of Pleasant Valley are buffoons, they also are all white. There is not a Black person in sight, but there is a black cat that appears to be lynched by a psychopathic pre-adolescent boy.[62] *Two Thousand Maniacs!* paved the way for a genre of supernatural-themed, Civil War-related films that did not necessarily have to deal with the newly developing understanding of the real war emerging since the 1950s and 1960s because of their unreal focus. Some of these films were funny, some intentionally so, and others not.

States' Rights of the Living Dead

Two Thousand Maniacs! was not the last Civil War–related film framed in the supernatural or horror genre. In fact, in 2005 *Two Thousand Maniacs!* was remade as *2001 Maniacs*, starring Robert Englund, best known for portraying Freddy Krueger in the *Nightmare on Elm Street* films. Updated for the twenty-first century but still using the same plot premise, the remake portrays eight Northerners detoured to Pleasant Valley for what appears to be a regular occurrence rather than a once every hundred years event. This version also includes one African American resident, the town's butcher, plus among the Yankee "guests" there is a Black biker dude, his Chinese girlfriend, and a gay guy. The new version is of a much higher quality and is gorier, kinkier, and just as cornball, maybe more so. The flick also has a pair of wandering minstrels walking in and out of scenes singing "The South's Gonna Rise Again," mirroring the 1964 film. And there's more cannibalism. Lots more cannibalism.

While *2001 Maniacs* has a decidedly neo–Confederate Lost Cause tone to it, casting such films in the realm of the supernatural often, but not always, has allowed film makers to avoid the controversial issues that became harder to dodge since the onset of the Civil Rights era. After all, with characters busy trying not to be viciously slaughtered, possessed, or eaten, who has time to deal with slavery? Unfortunately, this approach to storytelling often makes for some pretty bad films. For example, take the

1977 Swedish production *The Shadow of Chikara*, which is also known as *Demon Mountain*, *The Curse of Demon Mountain*, *Thunder Mountain*, *Wishbone Cutter*, *Dead of Night*, and *The Ballad of Virgil Cane*, depending on when, where, and in what format the film was released. The film uses the song "The Night They Drove Old Dixie Down," sung, we are told in the lyrics, by Virgil Kane, but the movie has nothing to do with the classic ditty first recorded by The Band. The film stars several B-list movie actors of the 1960s and 1970s, including Joe Don Baker, Sondra Locke, Ted Neely, and character actor Slim Pickens. After the last battle of the war, a dying Confederate soldier named Virgil Cane (not Kane), played by Pickens, reveals to some of his comrades the location of a stash of diamonds he hid in a cave on a far-away mountain in Arkansas. He warns them to "watch themselves up there on that mountain. It's spooky up there." And so it is. The diamonds are guarded by a spirit named Chikara, and you guessed it, spooky things happen.

The Shadow of Chikara is set immediately after the Civil War. The 1986 release *The Supernaturals* takes place one hundred and twenty years later. A small unit of United States soldiers out on maneuvers in an Alabama forest encounter flesh-eating Confederate soldiers brought back to life to avenge their deaths at the hands of murderous Yankees. The depiction of the modern soldiers might have been reminiscent of the film *Stripes* if Bill Murray, Harold Ramis, and company had not been funny. Rather than its plot or humor, *The Supernaturals* is memorable for its star (trek) studded cast. Nichelle Nichols, Lt. Uhura from the original *Star Trek* series, plays the unit's commander, and Levar Burton, soon to be featured in the franchise's second television incarnation, *The Next Generation*, is one of the G.I.s. Originally, Maurice Gibb of the Bee Gees had been tapped to write the musical score for *The Supernaturals*, but the music he produced (perhaps a follow up to "Staying Alive"?) was not used. As a consolation prize, he appeared in the film as a Union soldier.[63] The cast of *Grey Knight*—Corbin Bernsen, Martin Sheen, and Billy Bob Thornton—could not save that 1993 film from its own pretensions. In fact, the presence of these established actors might actually explain why this not very good film takes itself way too seriously. The plot revolves around Union and Confederate soldiers doing battle with undead, blood drinking Union and Confederate soldiers. The dead are not really vampires, but they're not really zombies, either.

While some viewers might find these films funny because of how bad they are, in my opinion, the funniest Civil War-related films are the zombie films. (I know that zombie humor is not for everyone, so if it's not your thing, just skip ahead to the next section. The book is almost done.) There is something inherently funny about zombie movies, even when they are not intended to be funny. Perhaps it is the absurd nature of the premise of the dead rising back to some form of life (un-life?) to eat the flesh of those still living. Or perhaps it is the over-the-top makeup employed to convey the notion that these walking creatures are actually dead. Or it could be the herky-jerky movements performed by the actors to portray a reanimated dead human. Then again, it could be the single-minded efforts of these movie zombies to chase down a living person to eat his or her brains, only to be stymied by something as mundane as a ladder or a doorknob.

In the first decade of the twenty-first century, zombies became a cultural phenomenon, with films like *Zombieland* (2009), books like Max Brooks' *World War Z*, and Seth Grahame-Smith's recasting of Jane Austen's *Pride and Prejudice and Zombies*, and a whole new Marvel graphic novel universe made up of walking dead superheroes leading the way. Writing for *Time* magazine in 2009, journalist Lev Grossman noted, "The walking dead are staging a pop-culture coup." Referencing the earlier splash made by Stephenie Meyer's *Twilight* book series and the film adaptations that had begun to appear, Grossman proclaimed, "Zombies Are the New Vampires."[64] And that was two years before AMC launched its *The Walking Dead* franchise.

Much of this new wave of zombie stories is cast in a humorous light, especially the movies. Along with *Zombieland*, there are the "zom coms" *Shaun of the Dead* (2004), *Ah! Zombies!!* (2007), the joint Spanish-Cuban production *Juan of the Dead* (2011), *Cockneys vs. Zombies* (2012), the musical *Anna and the Apocalypse* (2017), *The Dead Don't Die* (2019), and the 2019 sequel *Zombieland: Double Tap*. The Civil War, with all the dead that it generated, lends itself to stories of the dead reawakening. As with the supernatural films already discussed, the Civil War zombie genre rarely addresses issues related to slavery and the war. On the other hand, it has served as a metaphor for the neo–Confederate notion that the South will rise again.

A notable short Civil War zom com came out on the cusp of this zombie renaissance, written and directed by Devi Snively. *Confederate Zombie Massacre!*, viewers are told, is based on a little known battle of the Civil War. Union soldiers engaged in the clash with Confederates are almost all killed, when one of them, against the orders of their now dead commander, Captain Stephens, unleashes a chemical weapon, a green gas that wipes out their opponents, including the buxom Nurse Mona. Later, the accidental release of more gas brings the dead back to life as zombies. When the Union soldiers discover that Stephens is still alive, one says, "Captain Stephens is dead," prompting another to respond, "Yeah, but does he know that?" Stephens eventually delivers one of the film's more memorable, if not familiar, lines: "I love the smell of brains in the evening."

It smells like victory." Soon the zombified Confederates and the captain attack the Federals, leading to a dramatic, and funny, fight scene, complete with graphic sound effects *à la* the 1960s *Batman* television show (Thwack! Doink! Thwonk! Splat!) and a reanimated Confederate drummer girl providing some rhythm while killing two soldiers with her drum sticks, to boot. Safe from all this, and eventually the only one alive, is a Union soldier named Jensen, who for most of the story has been off tap dancing or doing "a little soft shoe" in a nearby cabin. He is confronted by Nurse Mona, but Mona is more interested in dancing with him than eating his brains. Snively's film was shown at the 2008–2009 Viscera Film festival, which features works directed and/or produced by women. Her low budget story works as humor because it does not take itself seriously, although like other supernatural Civil War films, it avoids slavery. And viewers are left with a moral at the end of the production: the little zombie drummer girl holds up a sign that reads "Make love not war."

If *Confederate Zombie Massacre!* is low budget, *The South Will Rise Again* (2006) is extremely low budget. Written, produced, directed by, and starring (as zombie Confederate Colonel Zack Daniels) Charles E. Cullen, this short film is set in 2006 and also has a message. Besides the South rising again, the DVD case (it went straight to DVD) tells us, "Political correctness causes cannibalism!" The DVD case (which offers much more information than the film itself) states that the "proud southern corpses of the Confederate army dead arose" and "began eating their way to Washington, hell bent on changing the opinions of cowtowing [sic] political elites." An Uncle Remus–like narrator tells a different story. When asked what the zombies did when they rose, the narrator replies, "Well, they commenced to eating people, mainly Yankees." But the zombies also look for three things: "Cheap beer, cigarettes, sour mash whiskey, and redneck women." Evidently the narrator cannot count.

A feature film that interjects zombies into the Civil War is the deadpan but rather silly *Abraham Lincoln vs. Zombies* (2012), definitely a "so bad it's good" example. As a boy, Abraham Lincoln survives a zombie attack, although as a result he is forced to kill his zombified mother. He then dedicates his life to killing zombies. Flash forward to November 1863, just before President Lincoln is scheduled to give an address at the dedication of the cemetery at Gettysburg. Before he dies, the lone survivor of an expedition to capture Fort Pulaski at Savannah, Georgia, returns to Washington with a tale of horrific bloodshed at the hands of flesh-eating people. When the soldier dies, he turns zombie. Learning of this, Lincoln decides to take matters into his own hands. With his trusty folding scythe he keeps ready for such action, the president leads a select group of secret service men to take possession of the fort and kill the zombies. One of the secret service members, John Wilkinson, turns out to be an actor moonlighting as a Federal agent, John Wilkes Booth. At the fort, the expedition finds some surviving Confederate defenders, including the fort's commander, General Thomas "Stonewall" Jackson, who lost an arm but evidently not his life at Chancellorsville. Lincoln also reunites with an old sweetheart, Mary Owens, who is now a prostitute but somehow ends up fostering a boy named Theodore Roosevelt (yes, THAT Roosevelt). The boy eventually says something about speaking softly and carrying a stick. To make a long story short, Lincoln and his scythe and a lot of gunpowder save the day, although only a few survive the chain of events. A year and a half later, Lincoln is infected by a zombie, actually Mary Owens. He sends a message to John Wilkinson, who has returned to the stage, to set in motion his own pre-arranged assassination to deter another zombie outbreak. *Abraham Lincoln vs. Zombies* was produced and distributed by The Asylum film company, known for its "mockbuster" films, low budget films that mimic more popular productions to feed off their popularity, and I assume in the process have a little fun doing it. In this case the source is *Abraham Lincoln: Vampire Hunter*, to be discussed shortly.[65]

If *Abraham Lincoln vs. Zombies* is so bad it's good, *Curse of the Cannibal Confederates*, also known as *Curse of the Screaming Dead* (1982), is just bad. Produced by Troma Entertainment and directed by Tony Malanowski, the film depicts a group of twenty-somethings who go camping and hunting in the woods, only to inadvertently resurrect a group of dead Confederates who were tortured and killed by Union soldiers during the last days of the Civil War. Once again, the South rises again. Long-time president of Troma Lloyd Kaufman considers *Curse of the Cannibal Confederates* one of the worst films Troma ever released, and there were some real stinkers. According to journalist Jamie Russell, *Curse* is considered by many to be one of the worst zombie flicks ever made.[66]

On the other hand, 2011's *Exit Humanity* is a much higher quality film with good production values, a plot that makes sense, quality acting, and a lot of untapped potential for dark humor: a mysterious deadly plague; a veteran forced to kill his beloved wife, his son, and then his horse; a megalomaniac former Confederate general and his band of merry men; a witch; a woman who is immune to the disease; and gory zombies galore. Alas, instead of absurdity, it goes for artistry. Perhaps too much so. It's not a bad movie; it's just not funny.

The twenty-first-century flowering of zombie stories also made its way into print, and leading the charge was Seth Grahame-Smith's rewrite of the Jane Austen classic *Pride and Prejudice and Zombies*.[67] The 2009 publication splices together Austen's story concerning early nineteenth-century British landed gentry with Grahame-Smith's introduction of a zombie pandemic and many of the main characters trained in the deadly arts of killing the undead. The resulting mash-up is a rather humorous tale that retains Austen's sentimental romanticism. The collaboration inspired several other similar supernatural rewrites of classic works, including a couple set in the Civil War era. In 2010, Porter Grand took liberties with a well-known Louisa May Alcott novel to produce *Little Women and Werewolves*. If *Little Women* provides insight into the lives of girls growing into womanhood in a Northern town during the 1860s, *Little Women and Werewolves* provides insight into the lives of girls growing into womanhood in a Northern town during the 1860s while in the midst of a century-old werewolf epidemic. The biggest take away of the book is that werewolves are nice people, except for once a month when the moon is full. Then they would sooner eat you.[68]

While the *Little Women* mash-up provides only a glimmer into the Civil War, Steven A. Thompson's reworking of Stephen Crane's Civil War masterwork takes the war head on. The finished product is *The Dead Badge of Courage*, a story of the war that pits the living against the living dead. *Dead Badge* portrays Henry Fleming's struggle to prove his manhood, his courage, in the face of the enemy but ditches the whole North vs. South story to relate a conflict that started when the dead began to rise, creating a war of brother against dead brother. As I read the book, I had to wonder if somewhere out there the spirit of Ambrose Bierce, still jealous over that upstart kid Crane, who wasn't even alive during the war, resented that Crane's book was turned into a zombie story instead of one of his tales.[69]

In the wake of the mash-up mania touched off by *Pride and Prejudice and Zombies*, Seth Grahame-Smith turned his attention to rewriting history, resulting in another *New York Times* best seller, *Abraham Lincoln: Vampire Hunter*. We already know that Lincoln books sell, and in 2010 vampires were still a trending commodity, so why not. In *Vampire Hunter*, a young Abraham Lincoln witnesses his mother killed by vampires. This and other events lead him to become a vampire hunter. The narrative follows Lincoln through various stages of his life, including when he meets a good-hearted vampire named Henry Sturgis who mentors him in the arts of slaying blood suckers. Unlike most other supernatural Civil War stories, *Vampire Hunter* confronts the slavery issue head on, presenting the political and economic leaders of the slave-owning South as a cabal of vampires using enslaved people to feed their need for blood, eventually causing the Civil War, and almost winning it because of the use of hard-to-kill vampires on the battlefield. Eventually, Lincoln saves the day, helped by Sturgis, Mary Todd Lincoln, an African American friend named Will Johnson, longtime friend and political ally Joshua Speed, and Underground Railroad conductor Harriet Tubman. Two years after the book appeared, *Vampire Hunter* hit the big screen in a film directed by Tim Burton. Books about Lincoln sell, but movies? Not always, and thus the film version of *Vampire Hunter* bombed big time, I think, because the movie, like the book, took itself too seriously.[70]

While the vampire and zombie genres flourished in the first decade of the twenty-first century, a new wave of dystopian tales led by *The Hunger Games* trilogy took its place among the nation's best sellers, especially among teen readers. In 2018 Justina Ireland added her voice and a compelling Civil War-related zombie story to the mix with her best seller, *Dread Nation*. Ireland's book provides an intelligent account of what might have happened had the dead begun to rise starting on the Gettysburg battlefield. The United States we are introduced to is still beset by this plague of zombies, especially in the South, where the dead are completely out of control. The uprising of the dead in the middle of the war forced Jefferson Davis to agree to surrender the South in exchange for aid from the Union army to help confront the overwhelming number of zombies besetting the Confederate States. Part of the agreement brought slavery to an end, leading to a postwar apartheid-like racial system where African Americans had few rights and many were trained to kill zombies. After all, they were expendable. Jane McKeene, the story's seventeen-year-old protagonist, was born two days before the dead began to rise. She gets sent off to an elite school—Mrs. Preston's School of Combat for Negro Girls—and becomes an incredibly well-skilled killer of "shamblers," as she calls the zombies. She also stumbles upon a scheme hatched by corrupt white officials to build a zombie-free haven in the Great Plains and finds herself banished to the site, which is far from zombie-free. Ireland's narrative is fast moving, intelligent, and absorbing, and her characters, specifically her African American characters, provide just the right level of sarcasm, snide remarks, and sass to interject a healthy dose of humor into this disturbing tale.[71]

A second post–Civil War fantasy story complicated by zombies also appeared in 2018. St. Wishnevsky's *Were-Zombies of the Old Dominion* is set almost half a decade after the end of the Civil War, terminated by an armistice with the Confederates having the upper hand because they learned to bring the dead back to life as zombies and to use them in battle. Only the Union Army's discovery that silver in bullets killed zombies led the South to seek the truce. Flash to 1913 with the war precariously still on hold, and we meet the story's main character, Beast, a zombie who works burying bodies in Richmond's Hollywood Cemetery. Beast is bitten by a werewolf he is ordered to bury; the creature is not dead, and actually is an operative with the Northern Military Intelligence Division. The little nip the hairy spy gives Beast before he runs off mysteriously starts a process of reanimation in the zombie. Having spent the last half century as a laboring, mindless drudge with no memory of his past, Beast starts to have thoughts. Slowly. He leaves the cemetery for the first time since he arrived, looking for his only friend, a girl who is actually hundreds of years old and the daughter of a mummy. But wait, the tale is about to get weird. Fast moving, outlandish, and at times hilarious, the story contains elements of several of the narratives previously discussed. The Confederate States, which is maintaining an army of zombies made up of enslaved Blacks and poor whites, is actually controlled by vampires, with a person believed to be Jefferson Davis's grandson at its head, but he turns out to be John C. Calhoun. Then there's the huge demonic vampire leading the Confederate army, Nathan Bedford Forrest. Wishnevsky's self-published book may never be a best seller, but as silly as the premise is, the story has a complicated plot with many twists and turns and subplots, plus some real character depth. One more thing. As Beast begins to remember things, he wonders what he could have done that led to the very poor treatment he received as a ditch digger in the cemetery for half a century. He recalls that his name before his zombification had been Ben, and eventually readers discover why his Confederate keepers called him Beast. He learns that his name is Benjamin. Benjamin Butler. Yes, THAT Benjamin Butler.[72]

And with all this interjection of zombies into history, or history into zombie stories, it was also inevitable that someone, specifically Worm Miller, produced *A Zombie History of the United States*. In a scholarly an deadpan style, Miller splices into the sweep of American history the walking dead, which he argues had been systematically erased from the nation's story by journalists, historians, and politicians. Talk about revisionist history. He traces the existence of zombies in the nation going back before the Revolutionary War. By the time of the Civil War, Southern planters use zombies as slave labor, but only after an effective muzzle had been invented to stop them from biting. During the war, Abraham Lincoln "frees" the slave zombies by ordering that they mercifully be "terminated." A hybrid class of zombies existed, however, and they seek to gain equality by serving in the army, but to no avail.[73]

The Civil War served as a vehicle for numerous zombie stories and other supernatural tales through the late twentieth and into the twenty-first centuries. Many of these films represent platforms for promoting the Lost Cause myth, or portraying the Confederate South as inherently evil, or ignoring any judgment on the causes or consequences of the war just to tell a scary, gory, and maybe funny story. Besides the horror stories, the Civil War has continued to find a place in other twenty-first-century literature with a humorous twist, providing a number of messages for contemporary readers about the causes and consequences of the war.

Everything Old Is New Again

In Steve Hely's *How I Became a Famous Novelist*, narrator Pete Tarslaw tells readers, "Writing a novel about the Civil War is lazy. Brother against brother, battles in peach orchards and wheat fields, all those Biblical names, the poignant geography, Abe Lincoln and slavery hanging over everything. There's so much built in pathos, it writes itself." Tarslaw is jealous of his peer Josh Holt Cready, "the precocious author of *Manassas*, a novel about a precocious author named Josh Holt Cready who retraces the steps of his ancestor who fought for the Union and died at Cold Harbor." "Accompanied by the Ghost of Ulysses Grant," the *New York Times*' writeup of Cready's book tells us, "a young writer goes in search of his ancestor, a gay Civil War soldier." *Manassas* not only earned Cready a spot on the *Times* best sellers list, it also enabled the successful author to purchase a $3.5 million three-story brownstone.[74]

In the last half century, the Civil War has continued to capture the imagination of fiction writers, and some of their works have attained considerable critical and commercial success. While some novelists have presented the war with stark realism, others in this era of postmodernism have employed deconstruction and surrealism to weave their stories, creating quirky characters, preposterous situations, and outlandish plots and subplots. For many recent postmodern books, according to American Studies scholar Wolfgang Hochbruck, "the subject is Civil War just by chance, or as an ironic point of reference."[75]

A case in point is Padgett Powell's *Mrs. Hollingworth's Men*. Powell's main character is a present-day, unsatisfied Southern housewife who believes, "The American Civil War, arguably, [was] as silly a war as they come." In fact, "she was virtually ignorant of" the conflict. Nevertheless, the war "was beginning to haunt her." While writing a grocery list, Mrs. Hollingworth fantasizes about, among other things, Nathan Bedford Forrest, someone about whom she may or may not know something or some things. Juxtaposing this narrative is a second plot involving Roopit Mogul, a media tycoon who is a cross between Rupert Murdoch and Ted Turner. With the help of two rednecks named Rape Oswald and Hod Bundy and a malfunctioning hologram projector, Mogul tries to manufacture and promote a prototypical macho "New Southerner" based on Nathan Bedford Forrest. The two stories eventually merge to create some outrageous hijinks.[76]

In the first installment of his sweeping and satirical fictionalized take on American history, *The American People, Volume 1: Search for My Heart*, Larry Kramer portrays many of the nation's heroes and villains as gay. This includes Abraham Lincoln, who is killed by John Wilkes Booth after the president spurns the actor's advances in what Lincoln's former lover Joshua Speed had planned as an erotic *ménage à trois* at the Willard Hotel. Kramer also posits that half the soldiers who died from disease in the war actually died from AIDS. And Walt Whitman makes it into Kramer's book.

Derek McCormack has a similar take on the war in *The Well-Dressed Wound*, a play about a play staged at the P.T. Barnum American Museum that "is a fashion show by the dead for the living." "What follows," according to the volume's back cover, "is the most fiendish runway show ever mounted, complete with war dead, deconstructed couture, and gay ghosts infected with all manner of infectious agents, including cozy AIDS."[77] I'm sure that many people find this work to be *avant-garde* and artistic, but frankly it reminded me of something that might have appeared in an old *Saturday Night Live* "Bad Playhouse" skit hosted by Leonard Pinth-Garnell.

Set more firmly in the Civil War era is Stephen Wright's picaresque novel, *The Amalgamation Polka*. Wright introduces Liberty Fish, a boy who grows up in a quirky but ardently abolitionist family in upstate New York. We meet characters like the wise Euclid, a former, perhaps runaway, slave living in the Fish family's root cellar; Arthur Fyfe, a naked hermit claiming to be one hundred and forty-six years old and the captain of the forest; and Liberty's uncle Potter, a man very willing to take a walk on the wild side and wanting to take Liberty with him. Wright also introduces readers to obscure words like "gonfalon," "antifugmatic," "crapulous," "addlepated," "camstuginous," and "bantling." Indeed, Wright describes the main character as a "dew-eared" bantling. At age sixteen, this dew-eared bantling enlists in the Union army and goes off to war, but eventually he deserts the army to find and meet his maternal grandfather, a cruel, slave-owning South Carolinian whom Liberty blames for his mother's psychological problems. And then there are the dancing bearded ladies.[78]

Shifting between the Civil War era and the afterworld is George Saunders' *New York Times* best seller *Lincoln in the Bardo*, a story of personal loss focusing on the 1862 death of son Willie and its impact on the Lincoln family, with Willie's ghost trapped in "the bardo," a Hindu version of Catholicism's purgatory. Specifically, Willie's spirit is in the cemetery where he is interred, and he can see when his father comes to visit his resting place. In the bardo, Willie interacts with others who died with unresolved issues and had not experienced the "matterlightblooming phenomenon," similar to going "into the light." For example, there is a middle-aged man named Hans Vollman who expired before he could consummate his marriage to a virginal lass much younger than him, and thus he walks around naked with a perpetual large, and regularly growing larger, erection. No one in the bardo seems to care. Then there is Roger Bevins, who has an ever-changing number of eyes, noses, cheeks, hands, and who knows what else. The story is not specifically about the Civil War, but the war can't help but crawl into it every now and then. Rather than writing his own war-related narrative, Saunders borrows passages from other published and unpublished writings in a cut and paste manner. He properly cites all his quotes, so it's not plagiarism. The method works for a postmodern novel, but it should get a high school or college student a failing grade on a research paper.[79]

Despite the trend toward postmodern deconstruction and reconstruction, there's an awful lot in the humor literature of the early twenty-first century that resembles, intentionally or not, works that have already appeared in terms of the themes and tropes they employ, the genres they fit into, and the characters they use. One of the best recent works with a humorous flavor set in the Civil War era is James McBride's National Book Award winning *The Good Lord Bird*. McBride retells the story of John Brown through the eyes of an enslaved boy that Brown unintentionally frees and simultaneously orphans named Henry Shackleford, only Brown believes that the prepubescent Henry is a girl. Deciding it best not to try to correct the unpredictable and volatile old man, Onion goes with it. Oh, yeah, Brown decides that he is going to call Henry Onion because the boy, er, girl, eats a lint-covered and putrid onion that Brown had been toting around in his pocket as a good luck charm. The story begins in Kansas during the "Bleeding" days and follows Onion's adventures, mostly but not always with Brown, through the raid on Harpers Ferry. Providing laughs in what is fundamentally a serious slice of American history is Onion's gender bending, the youth's reactions to the events around him, the survival methods he utilizes, and McBride's capture of John Brown's quirky personality.[80]

This is not the first time that an author employed a boy cross dressing as a literary device. See the discussion of *A Dual Role*. And it is not the first time that an author has placed a fictional character in the company of John Brown and obtained chuckles. In 1994 George MacDonald Fraser added *Flashman and the Angel of the Lord* to his series of books presenting memoirs of the adventuresome antihero Sir Harry Flashman of the British army, winner of the Victoria Cross and all-round scoundrel, imposter, lecher, and racist and a cheating, lying, thieving, cowardly cad. In *Angel of the Lord*, through a series of unfortunate events and missteps mixed with the past coming back to haunt him, Flashman finds himself shanghaied off to the United States and forced by three different secretive organizations to infiltrate John Brown's gang to make sure that Brown fails.

Or succeeds. The three groups aren't all on the same page about that. Like *The Good Lord Bird*, *Angel of the Lord* follows the story through the Harpers Ferry raid.[81]

Fraser never completed a volume that interjected Flashman into the Civil War, but he appears to have planned it. As early as the series' first installment, the memoir's editor and annotator Fraser notes that Flashman had served as a major in the United States army in 1862 and then a colonel in the Confederate army in 1863. In *Angel of the Lord*, he adds in a footnote, "Flashman ... served on both sides in the Civil War, as a Confederate staff colonel and as a major in the Union forces, with whom he won the Congressional Medal of Honor." Editor Fraser promises that all this would eventually be explained as he made his way through the disorganized Flashman papers. Fraser does present Flashman's, and presumably his, British view on the sectional conflict that led to war: "The fact is that America rubbed along with slavery comfortably enough while the country was still young and growing." But really the United States was not one country but two:

> It was only when the free North and the slave South discovered that they had quite different views about *what kind of country the U.S.A. ought to be* on that distant day when all the blank spaces on the map had been filled in, that all the trouble started. Each saw the future in its own image; the North wanted a free society of farms and factories devoted to money and Yankee 'know how' and all the hot air in their ghastly Constitution, while the South dreamed, foolishly, of a massa paradise where they could make comfortable profits from inefficient cultivation, drinking juleps and lashing Sambo while the Yankees did what they dam' well pleased north of the 36' 30" [sic] line.

The road to the Civil War, he continued, began with the Revolution and the Declaration of Independence. If Americans "had the wit to stay in the empire," Flashman insisted, "instead of getting drunk on humbug about 'freedom' and letting a pack of firebrands (who had a fine eye to their own advantage) drag 'em into pointless rebellion, there never would have been an American Civil War and that's as sure as any 'if' can be."[82]

A "fan fiction" imitation, *Flashman and the War Between the States*, briefly went on the market in 2012. Written by Barry Tighe, it quickly ran into copyright issues and disappeared, however, only to resurface with the title *Sir Thomas "British Tommy" Armstrong and the War Between the States* a year later.[83] My inclination is to leave Flashman to George MacDonald Fraser.

Besides Stephen Wright and James McBride, other authors have employed young people in their Civil War tales. Performance artist, author, and "gender outlaw" Kate Bornstein relates what Tom Sawyer's pal had been up to in her short story "Dixie Belle: The Further Adventures of

Huckleberry Finn." Through a letter sent to Tom, Huck explains that after being stranded in New Orleans because of the war, and having no ambition to fight, he found work in a brothel as a transvestite prostitute. (This is not Huck's first time cross dressing.) Huck also tells Tom that at the brothel he has encountered Mark Twain, whom he encouraged "to write new stories about this new life of mine the way he done before."[84] Evidently, Huck's efforts to prompt Twain to write about his new transvestite career is another private history of a campaign that failed.

Another child main character, a tomboy rather than a transvestite, graces the pages of Terry Kroenung's award winning *Brimstone and Lily*. She is twelve-year-old Verity Sauveur, who learns that she has supernatural powers and is destined to save humanity, or die trying. Verity is aided by a magical talking sword; various animals and a tree, also able to speak; soldiers that at one time had been part of Napoleon's cavalry; flying horses; and pirates. Working against her are white-haired henchmen called Bullies; a street-walking woman turned monstrous demon named Venoma; homicidal crows; recently killed soldiers brought back from the dead (not exactly zombies); a weapon that shoots "Pluto's Bane," which liquefies its victims from the inside out; manure monsters and more. Billed as "a wacky fantasy novel of the Civil War," *Brimstone and Lily* definitely found inspiration in the Harry Potter series. Throughout the book, Kroenung also drops direct and indirect references to literature ranging from Shakespeare to *The Hitchhiker's Guide to the Galaxy*, plus films like *Village of the Damned*, *The Princess Bride*, *The Birds*, *Beauty and the Beast*, *Aladdin*, *Moby Dick*, *Monty Python and the Holy Grail*, and an ending hinting at a plot twist worthy of the *Star Wars* saga. Some might assume that such a book would fall into the category of kiddie or YA lit, but despite the twelve-year-old main character, there are definitely things in the book that would earn it a PG-13 rating, mostly for some bawdy language.[85]

Children also play a central role in David Lee's *Country in Ruin, 1865*. Time traveler Sir Wesley Chamberlain's trip back to 1865 to make the world a better place leads to the invention of a plasma weapon that incinerates its victims (perhaps Pluto's Bane?) and the unleashing of a virus that turns people into flesh eating zombies, or "Loons," because the afflicted act like lunatics. So, Sir Wesley returns to 1865 to escort a dying Abraham Lincoln to the future to save his life, turning him into a "bionic" man with an artificial arm as well as other bionic parts, so that Lincoln can unite the nation back in 1865 and lead the counterassault against the army of Loons now threatening the North, the South, and the world. *Country in Ruin* probably has appeal for young adult readers, but it too would get a PG-13 rating for its graphic violence.[86]

As suggested by the bionic Abraham Lincoln, the time travel, the futuristic plasma weapon, and other things in the book, *Country in Ruin* falls into the genre of Steampunk fiction. Author Lee defines Steampunk as "fusing science fiction with our romanticized notion of Victorian-era life." I'd also throw in a blending of futuristic technology and industrial revolution-era inventions. And lots of goggles. Steampunk also visited the Civil War era in *The Amazing Screw-On Head*, appearing first as a graphic story by Mike Mignola and then as a short, animated film, with Paul Giamatti, David Hyde Pierce, Molly Shannon, and Patton Oswald lending their voices. The title character is a—you guessed it—head that can be screwed on to a number of devices to carry out secret missions for Abraham Lincoln. Really the head is part robot, part computer with a lot of sarcasm. Then there is David Erik Nelson's *Tucker Teaches the Clockies to Copulate*. The North defeats the South using robots, or clockies. After the war, many of the unwanted and unneeded clockies flee to the West to live out their humdrum lives. Then along comes an unbathed, maimed, alcoholic, pot-smoking Confederate veteran who decides to teach a community of clockies living in Utah what really matters in life. Now that's reconciliation! *Tucker Teaches the Clockies to Copulate* does not get a PG-13 rating.[87]

Brimstone and Lily and *Country in Ruin*, like several other works discussed earlier, interject the supernatural into the Civil War story to ask that age-old question, "What if?" In the graphic novel *Rebel Dead Revenge: Stonewall's Arm*, Gary Kwapisz put his own spin on the ever popular "What if?" question, "What if Stonewall Jackson had been at Gettysburg?" tweaking the question a bit to ask, "What if Stonewall Jackson had been at Gettysburg, and had been a zombie?"[88] I'm sure that this new variation of the question will keep Civil War Round Tables across the country abuzz for years to come.

Other "What if?" stories without demons, ghouls, or zombies have continued to appear. Andrew J. Heller offered a double "What if?" alternative or speculative history with *If the North Had Won the Civil War*.[89] As the title suggests, the book begins with the premise that the South had won the war. While set in modern times, the book divulges what happened after victory in bits and pieces. The Confederate States of America becomes the world's richest nation because of the invention of cottoline, a fuel much like gasoline. In great demand, cottoline allowed for machines to replace field hands, and so in 1912 the Confederacy abolished slavery. But it did not abolish racism. To replace slavery and its racial controls, the Confederacy created an apartheid system where persons of African descent have to live on a Negro Preserve. Despite its economic prowess, the Confederate States is an international pariah. It's a pretty dismal vision of what the Confederacy might have looked like had it won. Heller drops other clues of an unpromising future for a victorious South, such as the apparent nonexistence of airplanes and rural electrification becoming a reality only in the 1950s, but not on the Negro Reserves. And forget about freedom of speech, especially if it has anything to do with slavery, the war, or race relations. When an historian wrote an alternative account proposing that the North won the war, its publication not only faced potential backlash but it would also probably have violated the Seditious Publications Act, a law that allowed the Confederate government to throw an author into jail indefinitely while authorities conducted an investigation of what would probably have been an unlimited amount of time.

Heller's book definitely is not an apologetic for the lost cause, nor is *C.S.A.: The Confederate States of America*, a "mockumentary" film also positing the idea of a victorious South. Writer and director Kevin Wilmott crafted a faux history in which the Confederacy, with the military aid of the British and the French, defeats the Union army and captures Washington, driving Abraham Lincoln into permanent exile after a two year imprisonment. The whole United States becomes the Confederate States of American, and its new government succeeds in spreading slavery into the North rather easily, forcing other non-white ethnicities into bondage and conquering the rest of the Western Hemisphere, save Canada, to create a new, slave-based empire. Wilmott designed his film to appear as a controversial British documentary being shown for the first time in the Confederate States. The film within the film comes complete with commercial breaks and sham advertisements for products relating to slavery. Some of the products, which use Jim Crow–like caricatures in their logos and ads, are actual products once on the market in the United States. And Walt Whitman makes an appearance.

Wendy Jo Cohen offers another Civil War mockumentary, this one fabricating a forgotten turning point in the war, *The Battle of Pussy Willow Creek*. A misfit regiment, the 13th Rhode Island Infantry, led by Georgia-born, West Point graduate, morphine-addicted, and very gay Major Jonathan Franklin Hale, becomes detached from the main body of the Union army as the clash at Gettysburg nears. In the wrong place at the right time while the Army of the Potomac is distracted by Robert E. Lee's invasion, Hale and an unlikely cast of characters thwart a secret plan to capture Washington by a joint force of Confederate and British soldiers under the command of Hale's former lover, with whom he had a bad breakup. In Ken Burns style, the mockumentary employs bogus historian commentators, and its soundtrack includes a song about the battle and a hauntingly sad tune about a soldier pining for home, "I Dream of Annie's Biscuits."

Several other works of fiction employ historians as characters to tell Civil War stories. In J. Clayton Rodgers' *Close Before Striking*, Hank

Cheatham, an American history professor at a university in Virginia, comes to believe that the Confederates won the Battle of Gettysburg, among other fallacies. Hank's problems stemming from a hypnotism session he does not remember having gone awry is predictable, but several humorous plot twists are not. Despite the laughs, it's hard to sympathize with the protagonist, who at heart is a bit of a Lost Causer. In fact, it's hard to sympathize with any of Rodgers' characters, but maybe Rodgers was not looking for that. In fact, he takes a swipe at many things in the book, including academia, political correctness, political incorrectness, parenthood, old age, mental illness, Ritalin-taking children, hoarders, racists, anti-racists, G-string-wearing opossums, the French, Civil War reenactors, and body odor. More likeable historians star in the comical romance *Pride, Prejudice and Cheese Grits* by Mary Jane Hathaway. Two rival historians square off at a small Southern college, with their competition evolving into a romance *à la* that of Jane Austen's Elizabeth Bennet and Mr. Darcy.[90]

Joining Jane Austen, Mark Twain, and J.K Rowling in providing inspiration for Civil War-related stories is Miguel de Cervantes. In *Colonel Quicksot*, author Heironymus Poe borrows the Don Quixote story to tell the modern-day tale of Jubal Bushrod Quicksot, a middle-aged man hopelessly lost in the Lost Cause who after suffering economic setbacks, unrequited love, and a lightning strike to his noggin comes to believe that he is his Confederate hero ancestor, the war is still in progress, and he must travel from his crumbling plantation near Charleston to Atlanta on a secret mission to defeat that villainous Yankee, William Tecumseh Sherman, and turn the tide of the war. This pastiche is filled with many zany situations and numerous oddball characters, and I definitely laughed when I briefly encountered the curator of the Quicksot Archives of the Charleston Library Society, a Mr. Scurf, because thanks to Nathaniel Hawthorne, I know what scurf means.[91]

And Walt Whitman continues to get into the books, although not always the real Walt Whitman. In the anonymously published book *Wild Walt and the Rock Creek Gang*, a demoralized, depressed, burned out from his time tending to wounded soldiers and his stalled poetry career Whitman goes to Rock Creek in the District of Columbia for one last visit before his planned skedaddle home to New York. There he meets two poetry-loving nonconformists engaged in a forbidden tryst, Ezra and June, who recognize the broken-down poet. The two rejuvenate him in a secret mystical and erotic ceremony that channels the Muses and the spirit of John Keats. Whitman, in turn, performs the ceremony on a Confederate soldier who has fled the army after witnessing too much carnage. The spirit of the ceremony, including the story, or "tell" that goes with it, is passed on to others through a select group of people sworn to secrecy. Along the way, a few other writers are brought into the pantheon of the so-called Rock Creek Canon, including Edna St. Vincent Millay and Richard Brautigan of *The Confederate General from Big Sur* fame. In fact, we are told, Brautigan's story of the general is based on the one told by the rebel on French leave saved by Walt Whitman, with a few details changed.[92]

Finally, in this present-day age of fake news, alternative facts, cancel culture, and conspiracy theories come two tales of the Civil War deniers. In Jacob M. Appel's *Surrendering Appomattox*, high school history teacher Horace Edgecome confronts the charismatic Roland G. Royster and his daughter Sally who believe that the Civil War is a hoax and that Edgecome in teaching the war should give equal time to "the other side." It all seems like a bunch of silliness until the Treasury Department's secretive Division for the Analysis and Assessment of Fraudulent Historical Enterprises, better known among the few people aware of its existence as the Historical Denial Cults division, gets involved investigating Royster's nefarious motives.[93]

Then there is even more silliness in the mockumentary *The Civil War Hoax: Civil War Deniers* (2018). Directed by Jon Silver and written by Silver and Joseph Gartner, *The Civil War Hoax* introduces a group of people who are certain for a variety of reasons that the war did not happen. One theory posits that the war was staged by a collective of white men that has ruled the world since the dawn of time to create the illusion that the war had been fought for freedom. Another denier claims that the conflict was not between North and South but rather between Americans and space aliens, and the brother against brother image was a coverup. Still, a feminist historian argues that the war was actually a four-year frat party and the story of there being a war was created to explain to participants' wives why the guys were gone for so long. And so on. If the deniers are correct, then there was, in fact, no real war to get into the books, in which case, Walt Whitman was correct, sort of.

Conclusion

Word on the street has it that an in-depth sweeping study of the use of humor in the telling and retelling of the Civil War will hit the market soon, so keep an eye out at your favorite local book dealer. That author then plans to allow his Great American Civil War Novel, with all its brother against brother, battles in peach orchards and wheat fields, all those Biblical names, the poignant geography, Abe Lincoln and slavery hanging over everything, so much built in pathos, and of course, lots of laughs, to write itself so that he can retire on the profits.

From the crackerbox philosophers to the bad poets and Biblical satirists, the well-known authors and the forgotten, the memoirists and novelists, the movie makers and illustrators, the zombie stories of gore and glory, and of course, Walt Whitman, too, humor has been used in many ways to explain the Civil War, and the Civil War has likewise been used to generate humor. Not having a groundbreaking thesis to prove or a revolutionary paradigm to shift, I find little compelling need for an elaborate conclusion beyond that. I hope you enjoyed reading this book as much as I did writing it, had a few laughs, and maybe even learned some things. I did. And so, for now, That's All Folks!

Chapter Notes

Preface

1. The quote appears in Whitman's book of prose *Specimen Days* (1882), which can be found in various published print and electronic forms. Ed Folsom briefly traces the origins of the quote in "An Unpublished Whitman Manuscript about Writing the 'History of the Secession War,'" 48–49.
2. Ohler, *Blitzed*, 191.
3. Kennedy, "Where's the Humor in History?" 27–28, quote on 27.
4. Nickels, *Civil War Humor*.
5. Wilson, *Patriotic Gore*.
6. Madden, "What Is Civil War Humor?," 121–28, quote on 121.
7. White, "Preface," in *A Subtreasury of American Humor*, xvii; Martin, "Introduction to the Modern Library Humor and Wit Series," xi. Martin is the series editor.
8. Nickels, *Civil War Humor*, 17.
9. See for instance the discussion of Elizabeth Keckley's *Behind the Scenes* and its parody *Behind the Seams* in Part II.
10. See for instance McPherson, *For Cause and Comrades*.

Part I

1. Kaufman, "The American Civil War," 151–52; Nickels, *Civil War Humor*, 17; Grinspan, "'Sorrowfully Amusing,'" 313–338.
2. Tandy, *Crackerbox Philosophers in American Humor and Satire*, [ix]–xi; 25.
3. Quoted in McArthur, *The Oxford Companion to the English Language*, 395.
4. Landon, "A Biographical Sketch," 13–26.
5. Browne, *The Complete Works of Artemus Ward*, 56, 166–67, 169–70.
6. Browne, *The Complete Works of Artemus Ward*, 186, 188, 192.
7. Locke, *The Nasby Papers*, 6.
8. Locke, *The Nasby Papers*, 35.
9. Blair, *Native American Humor*, 39, 41, 44.
10. Blair, *Native American Humor*, 41. The Civil War letters were published in book form in 1864 as *Letters of Major Jack Downing of the Downingville Militia*, quotes on 118, 208, 240.
11. Blair, *Native American Humor*, 47, 53; Ketcham, "Biographical Sketch," xi–xii; Perry, *Radical Abolitionism*, 177; Lowell, *The Biglow Papers* [1st Series], 3–16; Lowell, *The Biglow Papers*. 2nd, v–lxxx.
12. Blair, *Native American Humor*, 102, 105; Fahs, *The Imagined Civil War*, 202, 205. The letters were published as *The Orpheus C. Kerr Papers* in 1862, 1863, and 1865.
13. Newell, *The Orpheus C. Kerr Papers* [1862], 29–30.
14. Newell, *The Orpheus C. Kerr Papers* [1862], 283, 284–85.
15. Solomon, *The Complete Three Stooges*, 62–64, 274–75.
16. Fahs, *The Imagined Civil War*, 204–11; Thomas, "Lincoln's Humor," 14.
17. Hanchett, *Irish*, 1–35 passim.
18. Hanchett, *Irish*, xiii, 65–67, 79–80; Halpine, *The Life and Adventures, Songs, Services, and Speeches of Private Miles O'Reilly*, 25–29.
19. Halpine, *The Life and Adventures, Songs, Services, and Speeches of Private Miles O'Reilly*, 42–45, 52–53.
20. Hanchett, *Irish*, 83–84; Halpine, *The Life and Adventures, Songs, Services,*

and Speeches of Private Miles O'Reilly, 54–56; Jimerson, *The Private Civil War*, 99–100.

21. Halpine, *Baked Meats for the Funeral*; Kaser, *The New Orleans of Fiction*, 109, 270; Hills, *MacPherson, the Great Confederate Philosopher and Southern Blower*.

22. Fahs, *The Imagined Civil War*, 220. Smith republished the letters in 1866 in a volume titled *Bill Arp, So Called. A Side Show of the Southern Side of the War* and then in 1873 as *Bill Arp's Peace Papers*.

23. Smith, *Bill Arp's Peace Papers*, 50, 106.

24. Smith, *Bill Arp's Peace Papers*, 53, 56–57.

25. Smith, *Bill Arp's Peace Papers*, 58–59, 99; Owsley, *State Rights in the Confederacy*, 1.

26. Smith, *Bill Arp's Peace Papers*, xiii; Cronin, *High Private*.

27. Cronin, *High Private*, 97–98.

28. Blair, *Native American Humor*, 138; Harris, *The Life and Letters of Joel Chandler Harris*, 46; Day, "The Life of George Washington Harris," 33–68.

29. Eskridge, *Rube Tube*; Isenberg, *White Trash*, 233–36; Graham, *Framing the South*, 168–69.

30. White and White, *A Subtreasury of American Humor*, xiv; Lynn, *The Comic Tradition in America*, xiii; Baker, *Russell Baker's Book of American Humor*, 21; Carlisle Jr., *American Satire in Prose and Verse*, xiii. FYI: Josh Billings was the pen name of Henry Wheeler Shaw, who was popular after the Civil War.

31. Blair, *Native American Humor*, 49; Walker and Dresner, *Redressing the Balance*, 25–130; Morris, *Women Vernacular Humorists in Nineteenth-Century America*; Camfield, *Necessary Madness*; Kreger, "The Nineteenth-Century Female Humorist as 'Iconoclast in the Temple,'" 5–38; Fahs, "The Feminized Civil War," 1461–94; Young, *Disarming the Nation*; Habegger, "Nineteenth-Century American Humor," 884–99, quote on 887; Sanborn, *Memories and Anecdotes*.

32. Whitcher, *The Widow Bedott Papers*.

33. Knight, *Writers of the American Renaissance*, 394; Diffley, *To Live and Die*, 381.

34. *Harper's Weekly*, November 8, 1862.

35. *Harper's Weekly*, January 31, March 13 and May 16, 1863; Butler, *Butler's Book*, 547; *Southern Literary Messenger* (March 1863).

36. Sanborn, *Memories and Anecdotes*, 158–60; *Lowell [Massachusetts] Daily Citizen and News*, April 22, 1864.

37. Greenwood, *Records of Five Years*, 159–60.

38. Greenwood, *Records of Five Years*, 159.

39. White, *Poetry*.

40. *National Cyclopaedia of American Biography*, vol. 1: 197; *Dictionary of American Biography*, vol. 10: 113–14; *The New Gospel of Peace: According to St. Benjamin* was first released as four separate pamphlets published anonymously between 1863 and 1866, and then in one volume in 1866. Quotes are from that volume.

41. *The New Gospel of Peace*, 1, 2–3, 4, 8, 10.

42. *The New Gospel of Peace*, 13, 15, 16, 17–18, 22–28, 30, 35, 41, 42, 49, 52, 53, 60–61, 64.

43. *The New Gospel of Peace*, 82, 83; Curran, *Soldiers of Peace*, 77–90.

44. On the debate over the authorship of the work and its impact, see the "Publisher's Advertisement" in *The New Gospel of Peace*, v–xxvi; *Frank Leslie's Illustrated Newspaper*, September 12, 1863; *New York Illustrated News*, October 31, 1863; *Harper's Weekly*, November 14, 1863 and November 21, 1863; *The Liberator*, September 16, 1864 and September 22, 1865; *New York Times*, May 12, 1884; and White's obituary in the *New York Times*, April 9, 1885.

45. *Revelations*; *Book of the Prophet Stephen, Son of Douglas*; Wood, *Black Scare*, 37–38.

46. *Boston Daily Advertiser*, September 17, 1863; *The Round Table*, May 12, 1866, cited in the "Publisher's Advertisement" of *The New Gospel of Peace*, xvi; "Mr. Bright's Platform," *The Index*, February 24, 1864.

47. Roosevelt, "Expansion and Peace," 21–33, quote on 24–25.

48. Kadmus [Nathan Brown], *De Históri ov Magnus Mahárba end de Blak Dragun*, 5.

49. Dunne, *Calvinist Humor in American Literature*, 1–2.

50. The essay appeared in the July 1862 issue. Citations are from the version ap-

Notes—Part I

pearing in Lathrop, *The Complete Works of Nathaniel Hawthorne*, vol. 12: 299-345.

51. Stewart, "Hawthorne and the Civil War," 91, 96-98, quote on 97; Fuller, "Hawthorne and War," 665.

52. "Chiefly About War Matters," 299-300.

53. "Chiefly About War Matters," 314-15.

54. The magazine published the section a decade later under the title "Our Whispering Gallery," *The Atlantic* (April 1871): 510-12.

55. "Chiefly About War Matters," 309-10.

56. "Chiefly About War Matters," 304-05; Curran, "Quaker Guns," 1581-82.

57. "Chiefly About War Matters," 322, 324.

58. "Chiefly About War Matters," 320.

59. "Chiefly About War Matters," 333, 334.

60. "Chiefly About War Matters," 329-30, 330-31; Fuller, "Hawthorne and War," 671.

61. See Bense, "Nathaniel Hawthorne's Intention in 'Chiefly About War Matters,'" 200-214; "Chiefly About War Matters," 305; Cynthia Wachtell, "Nathaniel Hawthorne's Funny Civil War," *New York Times*, May 17, 2013.

62. Balcerski, "'A Work of Friendship,'" 655-79; Stewart, "Hawthorne and the Civil War," 98-106.

63. Wilson, *Patriotic Gore*, 466; Tandy, *Crackerbox Philosophers*, 121; Trapp, "Sentimental Poetry of the American Civil War," 1; *New York Times*, November 19, 1865; Keiley, *In Vinculis*, 201; Bagby quoted in Rubin, *The History of Southern Literature*, 182.

64. See Douglas Adams's *The Hitchhiker's Guide to the Galaxy*, first published in 1978 and since appearing in many versions combined with its sequels.

65. Brown, *This War*.

66. Brown, *This War*, 7-8, 8-9, 10, 11, 18, 24, 59, 65.

67. Brown, *This War*, 70, 71.

68. *New Haven Daily Palladium*, September 23, 1863.

69. Lloyd, *The Devil in Dixie*; http://www.hymntime.com/tch/bio/l/l/o/lloyd_gw.htm (accessed December 31, 2021).

70. Lloyd, *The Devil in Dixie*, 8-9, 18, 20, 25, 27, 28, 29.

71. Lloyd, *The Devil in Dixie*, 42, 43, 48, 61, 62, 63, 64.

72. Lloyd, *The Devil in Dixie*, 66-67, 69, 73-74.

73. Beck and Friedwald, *Looney Tunes and Merrie Melodies*, 100-01, 248, 332-33.

74. Silsbee, *D.D.D.*, 3; "Operation for Club Foot," 95; "Old Woodward," 275.

75. Smith, *The Royal Ape*; Fish, *Lincoln Literature*, 80.

76. Smith, *The Royal Ape*, 4, 8, 33.

77. Smith, *The Royal Ape*, 9, 66, 83.

78. Whitney, "Lincoln's Life as Dramatic Art," 335; Lowry, *The Stories the Soldiers Wouldn't Tell*, 48-60; Giesberg, *Sex and the Civil War*, 1-2, 59-108.

79. Southwood, *Beauty and Booty*; Fletcher, *Rebel Private*.

80. Kendrick, *She Wouldn't Surrender*, [1], [5], 8.

81. Charyn, *I Am Abraham*, 454.

82. Waugh, *Abraham Lincoln Spanked Me*; Sharp, *From the Case Files of Abraham Lincoln's Penis, Private Eye, Part 1*; Steward, *The Lincoln Diddle*.

83. Miller, *Ahab Lincoln*; Irelan, "Goon, Warrior, Communitarian, and Mythos" 50-52.

84. Rebelle, *Abram*, 53. *The Southern Literary Messenger* (March 1863), cited in Ellinger, "The Southern Poetry of the Civil War," 51. For *A Pickle for the Knowing Ones*, see http://en.wikipedia.org/wiki/Timothy_Dexter (accessed December 31, 2021).

85. Rebelle, *Abram*, 53, 54, 60.

86. Rebelle, *Abram*, 62.

87. White, *Poetry*, iii.

88. White, *Poetry*, viii-ix, 66, 179-80, 182-83.

89. White, *Poetry*, viii, 66; McWhirter, *Battle Hymns*, 41-50.

90. White, *Poetry*, 254-55; McWhirter, *Battle Hymns*, 17, 146-47. McWhirter includes a slightly different version of the lyrics, but White's version is used here. White, however, does not credit Work as the lyric's author.

91. White, *Poetry*, 255; McWhirter, *Battle Hymns*, 146-47.

92. McWhirter, *Battle Hymns*, 95, 164, 169, 186.

93. White, *Poetry*, 45.

94. White, *Poetry*, viii, 291, 297.

95. Simms, *War Poetry of the South*, v; Clark Sutherland Northup, "The

Novelists," 149; Simms, *The Sword and the Distaff*.

96. Simms, *War Poetry of the South*, vi.

97. I base this on the publication of newspaper advertisements for White's book that appeared as early as April 1866 and the date Simms included at the end of his introduction, September 8, 1866.

98. Simms, *A City Laid Waste*.

99. De Leon, *South Songs*; http://en.wikipedia.org/wiki/Thomas_Cooper_de_Leon (accessed December 31, 2021); Moore, *Rebel Rhymes and Rhapsodies*; Moore, *Songs of the Soldiers*.

100. Ellinger, "The Southern War Poetry of the Civil War"; Moss, *Confederate Broadside Poems*; Hayes, *Civil War Limericks*.

101. Fremantle, *Three Months in the Southern States*. Quotes from Gallagher's "Introduction" to this edition, pp. xiv and xxii–xxiii.

102. Fremantle, *Three Months in the Southern States*, 60, 69.

103. Fremantle, *Three Months in the Southern States*, 173. The version of the Fremantle diary edited by Walter Lord and published in 1954 as *The Fremantle Diary: A Journey of the Confederacy* identifies her as Velazquez.

104. Fremantle, *Three Months in the Southern States*, 192, 258.

105. Fremantle, *Three Months in the Southern States*, 14.

106. Fremantle, *Three Months in the Southern States*, 138–39.

107. Fremantle, *Three Months in the Southern States*, 129.

108. Fremantle, *Three Months in the Southern States*, 265.

109. Fremantle, *The Moonshine Mule*.

110. Shaara, *The Killer Angels*; Fremantle, *The Moonshine Mule*, 5.

111. Fremantle, *The Moonshine Mule*, 305.

112. Fremantle, *The Moonshine Mule*, 110, 111–12, 140.

113. Ferguson, *Land of Lincoln*.

114. Vowell, *Assassination Vacation*.

115. Horwitz, *Confederates in the Attic*, 18.

116. Horwitz, *Confederates in the Attic*, 209–81, quote on 275.

117. Horwitz, *Confederates in the Attic*, 277–78.

118. Horwitz, *Confederates in the Attic*, 279–80.

119. Horwitz, *Confederates in the Attic*, 199–200; "Attention Gynaecologists!," 233–34; Breeden, "The Case of the Miraculous Bullet," 23–26.

120. "Miscellaneous," 263–64; Breeden, "The Case of the Miraculous Bullet," 23, 26.

121. Linderman, *Embattled Courage*, 266–71; Blight, *Race and Reunion*, 140–50.

122. Luebke, "'To Transmit and Perpetuate the Fruits of Victory,'" 65–66; Janney, *Remembering the Civil War*, 104–05; Jordan, "'Our Work Is Not Yet Finished,'" 484–503; Maxwell, "Sketch of the Author," 14–15.

123. Hill reproduced the poem woven into a fictionalized account of an 1811 murder he first published in 1866. See *The White Rocks*, 255–56.

124. Hill, *Our Boys*.

125. See Eberly, *Bouquets from the Cannon's Mouth*.

126. Hill, *Our Boys*, v.

127. Hill, *Our Boys*, 75, 329, 400.

128. Hill, *Our Boys*, 172–73.

129. Hill, *Our Boys*, 333.

130. Hill, *Our Boys*, 75, 241, 312, 329.

131. Hill, *Our Boys*, 76; Prokopowicz, *Did Lincoln Own Slaves?*, 132.

132. Hill, *Our Boys*, 118–20; 163–65; 242; 243; Hill, *John Smith's Funny Adventure on a Crutch*.

133. Hill, *John Smith's Funny Adventure*, 13, 14.

134. Waugh, *Reelecting Lincoln*, 354–55.

135. Maxwell, "Sketch of the Author," 14–16; Jordan and Haddon, *Genealogical and Personal History of Fayette County, Pennsylvania*, vol. 2: 487; Blight, *Race and Reunion*, 172–98.

136. Reprinted in Mitchell, *The Autobiography of a Quack and The Case of George Dedlow*, 113–149.

137. Carroll, *Spiritualism in Antebellum America*.

138. Mitchell, *The Autobiography of a Quack*, 141–44.

139. Mitchell, *The Autobiography of a Quack*, 148.

140. Goler, "Loss and the Persistence of Memory, 160–83; Mitchell, "Phantom Limbs," 563–69, quote on 564; Faust, *This Republic of Suffering*, 180–85.

141. The short story is reprinted in Jones, *New Confederate Short Stories*, 146–62.

142. Moody, "The Ghost of General Jackson," 146, 147, 149, 151, 153.
143. Kaufman, "The American Civil War," 152.
144. See Gallman, *Defining Duty in the Civil War*, esp. 18–20, 65–66, 82–86, 91–93, 102, 115–16, 202; and Walsh, "'Cowardice Weakness or Infirmity,'" 492–526.
145. *Catalogue of Miscellaneous Books of the Pennsylvania State Library*, 35; Steiner, *Descriptions of Maryland*, 67; Robertson, "Morford, Henry 1823–1881," 133; *The Chronology of American Literature*, 227.
146. Robertson, "Morford, Henry 1823–1881," 133.
147. Armstrong, *Red Tape and Pigeon Hole Generals* [1864]. This study will use a version published in 1999 as *Red-Tape and Pigeon-Hole Generals: Andrew A. Humphrey in the Army of the Potomac*.
148. Armstrong, *Red-Tape and Pigeon-Hole Generals*, ix, x, xiv, 256, 359; Gallman, *Defining Duty in the Civil War*, 19.
149. Armstrong, *Red-Tape and Pigeon-Hole Generals*, 17, 21.
150. Armstrong, *Red-Tape and Pigeon-Hole Generals*, 138–39, 146 (emphasis added), 147.
151. Stowe, "Humphreys, Andrew Atkinson (1810–1883)," 1016–17.
152. Armstrong, *Red-Tape and Pigeon-Hole Generals*, 44, 45, 46.
153. Armstrong, *Red-Tape and Pigeon-Hole Generals*, 46, 47, 48, 82; Stowe, "Humphreys, Andrew Atkinson (1810–1883)," 1016.
154. Armstrong, *Red-Tape and Pigeon-Hole Generals*, 48.
155. Armstrong, *Red-Tape and Pigeon-Hole Generals*, 50, 51, 52, 209.
156. Armstrong, *Red-Tape and Pigeon-Hole Generals*, 51.
157. Armstrong, *Red-Tape and Pigeon-Hole Generals*, 168–69.
158. Keiley, *A Rebel in Two Federal Pens*, 7–13; Keiley, *In Vinculis*; O'Grady, "Anthony M. Keiley (1832–1905)," 613–35.
159. Keiley, *A Rebel in Two Federal Pens*, 6; *"In Vinculis,"* 387; Blight, *Race and Reunion*, 152.
160. *War of the Rebellion*, I, 15: 426.
161. Keiley, *A Rebel in Two Federal Pens*, 21.
162. Keiley, *In Vinculis*, 54–55.
163. Keiley, *In Vinculis*, 55.
164. Keiley, *In Vinculis*, 78–79.
165. Keiley, *A Rebel in Two Federal Pens*, 57.
166. Keiley, *A Rebel in Two Federal Pens*, 28, 116.
167. Keiley, *A Rebel in Two Federal Pens*, 104, 114.
168. Grinspan, "'Sorrowfully Amusing,'" 313–38. Grinspan takes the phrase from Mark Grimsley's observation of the "hardening" of the war as it progressed by the Union army. See *The Hard Hand of War*.

Part II

1. "Chiefly about War Matters," 303.
2. Jordan and Rothera, *The War Went On*, 4; Blight, *Race and Reunion*, 189–90.
3. Davis, "'A Matter of Sensational Interest,'" 338–49; Caron, "'How Changeable Are the Events of War,'" 151–71; "Topics of the Time," 943.
4. Peck, *How Private Geo. W. Peck Put Down the Rebellion*, 11–12.
5. Wiley, "A Time of Greatness," 3, 5.
6. Peck, *How Private Geo. W. Peck Put Down the Rebellion*, 13–14, 56, 219–20.
7. Peck, *How Private Geo. W. Peck Put Down the Rebellion*, iii.
8. Martin, *A History of the 4th Wisconsin Infantry and Cavalry in the Civil War*, 472; Peck, *How Private Geo. W. Peck Put Down the Rebellion*, 15.
9. Peck, *How Private Geo. W. Peck Put Down the Rebellion*, 25–26, 31.
10. Peck, *How Private Geo. W. Peck Put Down the Rebellion*, 226.
11. https://en.wikipedia.org/wiki/Peck%27s_Bad_Boy (accessed January 2, 2021).
12. Aldrich, *The Story of a Bad Boy*; Kidd, *Making American Boys*, 49–85, quote on 57.
13. Twain, "The Private History of a Campaign that Failed," 193–204, quotes on 193, 201.
14. Twain, "The Private History of a Campaign that Failed," 194, 195, 199, 202, 203.
15. Twain, "The Private History of a Campaign that Failed," 203.
16. Twain, "The Private History of a Campaign that Failed," 203, 204.
17. Rachels, *Mark Twain's Civil War*,

29; Twain, *Mark Twain*, 679–82, quotes on 679–80, 682; Twain, *Life on the Mississippi*, 237.

18. Scharnhorst, *Mark Twain*, 214, 259.
19. Rachels, *Mark Twain's Civil War*, 93.
20. Kidd, *Making American Boys*, 57; Twain, "Tom Sawyer's Conspiracy," 136–38.
21. Twain, "Lucretia Smith's Soldier," 108–12; Twain, "A Curious Experience," 35–46; Twain, "A True Story, Repeated Word for Word As I Heard It," 578–82.
22. Watkins, *Company Aytch*, 5; Blount, *Robert E. Lee*, 95.
23. Hunter, *Johnny Reb and Billy Yank*, [6].
24. Swiggett, *The Bright Side of Prison Life*, [3].
25. Watkins, *Company Aytch*, 14, 9.
26. Robson, *How a One-Legged Rebel Lives*, 14–15.
27. Daniel, *Recollections of a Rebel Surgeon*, 37.
28. Fletcher, *Rebel Private*, 4.
29. Daniel, *Recollections of a Rebel Surgeon*, 18–19.
30. Watkins, *Company Aytch*, 8; Bennett, *The Civil War Diary of Freeman Colby*, 17.
31. Goss, *Recollections of a Private*, 3–4; Fletcher, *Rebel Private*, 71.
32. Goss, *Recollections of a Private*, 17; Grigsby, *The Smoked Yank*, 26.
33. Bennett, *The Civil War Diary of Freeman Colby*, 189–91.
34. Wilkeson, *Turned Inside Out*, 172–73.
35. Wilkeson, *Turned Inside Out*, 124.
36. Grigsby, *The Smoked Yank*, 27, 32, 33; Wilkeson, *Turned Inside Out*, 142–43.
37. Bennett, *The Civil War Diary of Freeman Colby, Volume 2: 1863*, 12–16.
38. Grigsby, *The Smoked Yank*, 35.
39. Fletcher, *Rebel Private*, 108–10.
40. Fletcher, *Rebel Private*, 9–11, 110; Daniel, *Recollections of a Rebel Surgeon*, 100–01.
41. Wilkeson, *Turned Inside Out*, 2–3, 14, 188.
42. Wilkeson, *Turned Inside Out*, 26–27.
43. Bennett, *The Civil War Diary of Freeman Colby, Volume 2*, 27–31.
44. Watkins, *Company Aytch*, 168.
45. https://en.wikipedia.org/wiki/Frank_Wilkeson; https://en.wikipedia.org/wiki/Samuel_Wilkeson (both accessed January 2, 2021).
46. Fletcher, *Rebel Private*, 6; Watkins, *Company Aytch*, 37; Bennett, *The Civil War Diary of Freeman Colby*, 157–58.
47. Swiggett, *The Bright Side of Prison Life*, 17, 227; Blight, *Race and Reunion*, 152, 184–85; Cloyd, *Haunted by Atrocity*, 56–82.
48. Frost, *Camp and Prison Journal*.
49. Frost, *Camp and Prison Journal*, 149.
50. Frost, *Camp and Prison Journal*, 145–46, 161.
51. Yacovone, "'Surpassing the Love of Women,'" 195–221.
52. Fletcher, *Rebel Private*, 202–04.
53. Grigsby, *The Smoked Yank*, 60–61.
54. Pickett, *What Happened to Me*, 1–3.
55. Davis, *Ghosts and Shadows of Andersonville*, 50; Hesseltine, "The Propaganda Literature of Confederate Prisons," 56–66; Byrne, "Ralph Orr Bates," 186.
56. Thompson, "The Civil War in Fiction," 84–85.
57. Pierson, *Whipt 'em Everytime*.
58. *Concord Monitor*, March 16, 2019, available at https://www.concordmonitor.com/Henniker-author-writes-new-book-24136621 (accessed February 15, 2020); Bennett, "APPENDIX. ABOUT the DIARY," in *The Civil War Diary of Freeman Colby*, 316.
59. Bennett, *The Civil War Diary of Freeman Colby*, 42–43.
60. Bennett, *The Civil War Diary of Freeman Colby*, 250–51.
61. Bennett, *The Civil War Diary of Freeman Colby, Volume 2*, iii, 398–405.
62. Hajdu, *The Ten-Cent Plague*.
63. Hajdu, *The Ten-Cent Plague*, 196; Harrison, *The Art of Jack Davis!*, 22–27; 141; *Jack Davis*, 194; The Cartoon Daily, August 23, 2011, http://www.dailycartoonist.com/index.php/2011/08/25/check-out-rejected-comic-strip-by-jack-davis/; Potrzebie, February 23, 2008, http://potrzebie.blogspot.com/2008/02/jack-davis-beauregard.html (both accessed February 28, 2020).
64. *Les Tuniques Bleues*, https://en.wikipedia.org/wiki/Les_Tuniques_Bleues (accessed January 27, 2020).
65. Lambil and Cauvin, *The Bluecoats, No. 1*; *The Bluecoats, No. 2*; *The Bluecoats, No. 3*; and *Les Tuniques Bleues: Black Face*.
66. Browne, *Four Years in Secessia*, 59.

67. Browne, *Four Years in Secessia*, 16.
68. Browne, *Four Years in Secessia*, 32–36, 147, 160–61.
69. Browne, *Four Years in Secessia*, 257.
70. Kutzler, *Living by Inches*, 61–82, quote on 63; Zinsser, *Rats, Lice and History*, 152, 168.
71. Mitchell, *The Vacant Chair*, 89–113; Browne, *Four Years in Secessia*, 31, 114.
72. Browne, *Four Years in Secessia*, 382–83.
73. Browne, *Four Years in Secessia*, 333–38.
74. Browne, *Four Years in Secessia*, 380; Carlson, *Junius and Albert's Adventures in the Confederacy*, 13, 249–53.
75. Keckley, *Behind the Scenes*.
76. Keckley, *Behind the Scenes*, 87–88.
77. Keckley, *Behind the Scenes*, 275–76, 279–82.
78. Ottolengui, *Behind the Seams*, 5, 19–20.
79. Neary, *Fugitive Testimony*; Stokes, "Elements of Bile," 115–49; Nelson, "Behind the Seams," 542–58; and Young, *Disarming a Nation*.
80. Litwack, *Been in the Storm So Long*, 335; Jackson, *Ralph Ellison*, 263; Odom, *Saving Black America*, 151; https://www.huffpost.com/entry/in-recently-discovered-le_n_1247288 (accessed December 21, 2019).
81. I thank Roy Finkenbine of the University of Detroit-Mercy for this information.
82. *New York Daily Tribune*, August 22, 1865; *Liberator*, September 1, 1865.
83. *Boston Daily Advertiser*, August 25, 1865; *Lowell Daily Citizen and News*, September 5, 1865.
84. Child, *The Freedmen's Book*, [iv], 265–67; *The Freed-Man: A Monthly Magazine Devoted to the Interests of the Freed Coloured People* (November 1, 1865), 84; *The Anti-Slavery Reporter and Aborigines' Friend* (1865), 274.
85. Gannon, *Americans Remember Their Civil War*, 65–67; Woodson, *The Mind of the Negro*, 511 (quote), 537–39 (letter); "Letters of Negroes," 88–90.
86. "Statement of Policy," 3–4; "A Letter from a Freedman to His Old Master," 72–74. For the Reddick quote see p. 80.
87. "To My Old Master," 15; ["To My Old Master"], 2.
88. Dunbar, "The Wisdom of Silence,"
191–204; Breed and Italie, "How did ex-slave's letter to master come to be?"
89. Martin B. Duberman, *In White America: A Documentary Play* (New York: Samuel French, Inc., 1964); https://www.broadwayworld.com/article/50th-Anniversary-Production-of-IN-WHITE-AMERICA-to-Play-New-Federal-Theatre-1015-1115-20150918 (accessed December 30, 2019); https://www.detroitperforms.org/2013/03/jordan-anderson-writes-a-letter/ (accessed December 21, 2019); Earnest, *Dead Letter Office*.
90. Kelley, *Freedom Dreams*, 111–12; Brophy, *Reparations*, 21–23; Sanders, *Ambiguities of Witnessing*.
91. Starkeeper, *The Un-Promised Generation*, 32, 41, 56, 57 (emphasis in the original), 59.
92. Gannon, *Americans Remember Their Civil War*, 67–76.
93. Sterling, *Laughing on the Outside*, 21, 24.
94. Redding, "Escape into Pride and Dignity," 18.
95. Sterling, *Laughing on the Outside*, 218, 222–23.
96. http://coreyrobin.com/tag/jourdan-anderson/ (accessed December 20, 2019).
97. Wilson, *Patriotic Gore*, 133, 143. The memoir has been republished several times. This work cites *Personal Memoirs of U.S. Grant* (1990).
98. Hindley, "What Drove Ulysses Grant to Write about the Civil War"; Davis, "'A Matter of Sensational Interest,'" 341; Waugh, *U.S. Grant*, 167–213.
99. Perry, *Grant and Twain*; Wilson, *Patriotic Gore*, 142–43.
100. Grant, *Personal Memoirs*, 29, 36.
101. Grant, *Personal Memoirs*, 243.
102. Nick Sacco, "Interpreting the Man," 29.
103. The story first appeared in the December 6, 1930, issue of the *New Yorker* and has been reprinted in other Thurber anthologies. See for instance *The Thurber Carnival*, 140–42.
104. Ellington, *The Trial of U.S. Grant*, 178. See also Brands, *The Man Who Saved the Union*; White, *American Ulysses*; Chernow, *Grant*; and Waugh, *U.S. Grant*, 38–40, 56, 26–63. Waugh spoke at the grand opening of the John Y. Simon Book Collection of the Ulysses S. Grant National Historic Site Library, St. Louis, Missouri,

October 9, 2010. She also comments about the stereotypical drunken Grant in popular culture in *U.S. Grant*, 40.

105. Forehand, *Robert E. Lee's Lighter Side*, 11; Blount, *Robert E. Lee*, 7.

106. Robert Edward Lee, *Recollections and Letters of Robert Edward Lee* (Mineola, NY: Dover Publications, Inc., 2007 [1904]), 9–10.

107. Blount, *Robert E. Lee*, 170–71; Lee, *Recollections and Letters of Robert E. Lee*, 405; Grant, *Personal Memoirs*, 129.

108. Hinman, *Corporal Si Klegg and His "Pard."*

109. Hinman, *Corporal Si Klegg and His "Pard,"* 4, 48.

110. Millett, "Introduction," ix, xii; Webster, "Wilbur F. Hinman's *Corporal Si Klegg* and Stephen Crane's *The Red Badge of Courage*," 285–93; Wertheim, "*The Red Badge of Courage* and Personal Narratives of the Civil War," 61–65.

111. Hinman, *Corporal Si Klegg and His "Pard,"* 3, 43, 234.

112. Hinman, *Corporal Si Klegg and His "Pard,"* 39, 51–52.

113. Hinman, *Corporal Si Klegg and His "Pard,"* 90, 91, 93.

114. Hinman, *Corporal Si Klegg and His "Pard,"* 12, 103.

115. Hinman, *Corporal Si Klegg and His "Pard,"* 356–57, 417–18.

116. Hinman, *Corporal Si Klegg and His "Pard,"* 429, 467–68.

117. Hinman, *Corporal Si Klegg and His "Pard,"* 593, 611, 654.

118. Millett, "Introduction," xiv–xxxi.

119. Hinman, *The Story of the Sherman Brigade*; Millett, "Introduction," xxxii.

120. McElroy, *Si Klegg*; *National Tribune*, September 29, 1910.

121. Millett, "Introduction," xxx; *National Tribune*, September 29, 1910.

122. Twain, *Life on the Mississippi*, 210.

123. Harris, *The Life and Letters of Joel Chandler Harris*, 1–53.

124. Harris, *On the Plantation*, 3; Twain, *Life on the Mississippi*, 48, 121, 210.

125. Harris, *On the Plantation*, 49.

126. Harris, *On the Plantation*, 226–29.

127. Harris, *On the Plantation*, 232.

128. Harris, "The Comedy of War," 148–183; and "An Ambuscade," 293–344.

129. Harris, "A Story of the War," 175–85.

130. Gordon, "Envion," 1903–06, quotes on 1905, 1906.

131. Edwards, "Captain Isam," 181–92, quotes on 191, 192.

132. Levin, *Searching for Black Confederates*, 29.

133. Morris, *Ambrose Bierce*, 224.

134. Elmer, "American Idiot," 446; Duncan and Klooser, "Introduction," 17, 21.

135. Coleman, *Ambrose Bierce and the Period of Honorable Strife*.

136. Bierce, "Chickamauga," 20–25. For sensory history, especially in regard to the Civil War, see Smith, *The Smell of Battle, the Taste of Siege*.

137. Bierce, "Chickamauga," 22, 23.

138. Bierce, "Jupiter Doke, Brigadier General," 200–08.

139. Bierce, "A Tough Tussle," 136–42, quotes on 136–37, 139, 142.

140. Bierce, "An Occurrence at Owl Creek Bridge," 11–19.

141. Bierce, *The Unabridged Devil's Dictionary*, 110.

142. Bagby, *The Old Virginia Gentleman and Other Stories*. Quote in Page, "Preface," vii–viii, and biographical information from Edward S. Gregory, "George William Bagby," xvii–xxx.

143. Bagby, "The Old Virginia Gentleman," 34; "Bacon and Greens," 45–68.

144. Gregory, "George William Bagby," xxiii–xxv; Bagby, "An Unrenowned Warrior," 135–65, quote on 136.

145. Bagby, "An Unrenowned Warrior," 136, 137.

146. Bagby, "An Unrenowned Warrior," 139, 140, 141.

147. Bagby, "An Unrenowned Warrior," 159, 164.

148. Addums, "Histry uv the Waw," 70–72, 187–90, 312–15, 470–73, 613–16; Rubin, *The History of Southern Literature*, 184.

149. Addums, "Histry uv the Waw," 70.

150. Addums, "Histry uv the Waw," 70, 72.

151. Addums, "Histry uv the Waw," 189, 315.

152. Addums, "Histry uv the Waw," 190; Owsley, *State Rights in the Confederacy*, 1.

153. Bagby, "An Unrenowned Warrior," 136–37; Collins, "The Lost Symphony."

154. Dabney, *The Story of Don Miff*, 4; Collins, "The Lost Symphony."

155. Dabney, *The Story of Don Miff*, 181, 183, 339.

156. Dabney, *The Story of Don Miff*, 183; Collins, "The Lost Symphony."
157. Dabney, *The Story of Don Miff*, 5, 8, 22, 313.
158. Dabney, *The Story of Don Miff*, 33; McWhirter, *Battle Hymns*, 196–97.
159. Dabney, *The Story of Don Miff*, 76, 174, 179, 223.
160. Steinroetter, "Soldiers, Readers, and the Reception of Victor Hugo's *Les Misérables* in Civil War America," 5–28; Moore, "Some Translations of *Les Misérables*," 240–46.
161. Dabney, *The Story of Don Miff*, 170–71.
162. Dabney, *The Story of Don Miff*, 171, 277–78.
163. Dabney, *The Story of Don Miff*, 344.
164. Eggers, "Rediscovering One of the Wittiest Books Ever Written."
165. Dabney, *Gold that Did Not Glitter*.
166. Dabney, *The Story of Don Miff*, 442.
167. Yopp, *A Dual Role*.
168. Yopp, *A Dual Role*, 54.
169. Yopp, *A Dual Role*, 58–59.
170. Yopp, *A Dual Role*, 61.
171. Yopp, *A Dual Role*, 106, 118.
172. Yopp, *A Dual Role*, 136, 145.
173. Yopp, *A Dual Role*, 151–52.
174. Curran, *Women Making War*, 102–21.

Part III

1. Gannon, *Americans Remember Their Civil War*, 1–18, 37–59; Mencken, "The Calamity of Appomattox," 29–31, quote on 31.
2. Gannon, *Americans Remember Their Civil War*, 19–36.
3. Kuiper, "Civil War Films," 82, 83.
4. Stokes, *D.W. Griffith's The Birth of a Nation*; Lehr, *The Birth of a Movement*; Sacco, "Outrageous Inaccuracies."
5. Erickson, *Military Comedy Films*, 314.
6. Kuiper, "Civil War Films," 83; Walker, *Mack Sennett's Fun Factory*, 31–32, 272, 285; Erickson, *Military Comedy Films*, 314–15.
7. Balducci, *Lloyd Hamilton*, 26; *The Daily News* (Nelson, British Columbia), October 21, 1914; Walker, *Mack Sennett's Fun Factory*, 96; Parish and Leonard, *The Funsters*, 647.
8. Kuiper, "Civil War Films," 83; https://en.wikipedia.org/wiki/Grandma%27s_Boy_(1922_film) (accessed August 8, 2020).
9. https://nitratediva.wordpress.com/2014/06/03/hands-up/; http://www.tcm.com/tcmdb/title/498148/Hands-Up/ (both accessed August 8, 2020).
10. Kristin Hunt, "What Drove Buster Keaton to Try Civil War Comedy?"
11. Erickson, *Military Comedy Films*, 322–24; Kuiper, "Civil War Films," 83; http://www.tcm.com/watchtcm/movies/1227/General-Spanky/ (accessed August 9, 2020).
12. http://www.tcm.com/this-month/article/373965%7C133213/The-Littlest-Rebel.html; http://www.tcm.com/tcmdb/title/81513/The-Little-Colonel/articles.html (both accessed August 9, 2020).
13. http://www.tcm.com/tcmdb/title/425/A-Southern-Yankee/ (accessed August 9, 2020); Erickson, *Military Comedy Films*, 326.
14. https://en.wikipedia.org/wiki/Advance_to_the_Rear (accessed August 9, 2020).
15. https://en.wikipedia.org/wiki/The_Fastest_Guitar_Alive (accessed January 8, 2022).
16. Kuiper, "Civil War Films," 81, 85.
17. Thurber, "No More Biographies," 118–20, quotes on 118, 119; Gallagher, "When Did the Confederate States of America Free the Slaves?," 53–61.
18. Waldman, "If Booth Had Missed Lincoln," 473–84; Churchill, "If Lee Had Not Won the Battle of Gettysburg," 587–97.
19. Stevens, *Lincoln's Doctor's Dog and Other Famous Best Sellers*; Morley, "Lincoln's Doctor's Dog," 9–10, 40–42.
20. Long, *Lincoln's Doctor's Dog*.
21. Wharton, *The Spark*, 52, 55.
22. Wharton, *The Spark*, 70, 80, 81, 101, 102.
23. Wharton, *The Spark*, 103, 109.
24. Thompson, "The Civil War in Fiction," 83; https://en.wikipedia.org/wiki/Gone_with_the_Wind_(novel) (accessed June 25, 2020); Gómez-Galisteo, *The Wind Is Never Gone*, 2–3; "The Bible Remains America's Favorite Book."
25. Mitchell, *Gone with the Wind*.
26. Mitchell, *Gone with the Wind*, 6.
27. Mitchell, *Gone with the Wind*, 9, 15, 18.

28. Mitchell, *Gone with the Wind*, 152.
29. Mitchell, *Gone with the Wind*, 178–79; 832.
30. Gómez-Galisteo, *The Wind Is Never Gone*, 80.
31. Kendi, *Stamped from the Beginning*, 344; Hulbert, "Birth of a Genre."
32. "Our Own Previews of Hollywood Attractions: Joan Crawford and Clark Gable in 'Gone With the Birth of a Nation, or The Gold Diggers of 1860,'" 11–12; Schumacher and Kitchen, *Al Capp*, 114–16; Hart and Davis, "Groan With the Wind," 42–47.
33. https://en.wikipedia.org/wiki/Went_with_the_Wind! (accessed June 28, 2020).
34. Randall, *The Wind Done Gone*.
35. Gates, "Declaration of Henry Louis Gates, Jr."
36. Randall, *The Wind Done Gone*, [iv].
37. Sterling, *Laughing on the Outside*, 18; Oster, "Negro Humor" 42–57; Carpio, *Laughing Fit to Kill*; Early, Carpio and Sollors, "Black Humor," 29–47; Gates, "Declaration of Henry Louis Gates, Jr."
38. Dunbar, *The Fanatics*, 27; Hughes, "The Politics of Incongruity in Paul Laurence Dunbar's *The Fanatics*," 295–301, quote on 300.
39. Reed, *Flight to Canada*.
40. "TV's 50 Biggest Bombs and Blunders," 40–41; Hofstede, *What Were They Thinking*, 90–91; Horowitz, *The Dumbest Moments in Business History*, 44–45.
41. Jennifer Schuessler, "The Long Battle over 'Gone With the Wind,'" *New York Times*, June 14, 2020.
42. Kuiper, *Civil War Films*, 83.
43. Schlesinger, *A Thousand Days*, 727.
44. Street, *The Civil War*, 3, 4.
45. Street, *The Civil War*, 8.
46. Street, *The Civil War*, 47, 49, 86.
47. Street, *The Civil War*, 143.
48. https://www.mswritersandmusicians.com/mississippi-writers/james-street; https://www.ncpedia.org/biography/street-james-howell (both accessed February 4, 2022); Street, *The Civil War*, 144.
49. Street, *The Civil War*, 98.
50. Smith, *The Rebel Yell*, 11, 13, 14; "H. Allen Smith, Humorist, Dies," *New York Times*, February 25, 1976.
51. Smith, *The Rebel Yell*, 30, 31.
52. Smith, *The Rebel Yell*, 117, 191.
53. Connelly, *Will Success Spoil Jeff Davis?*, 143; Connelly, "That Was the War that Was," 123–34, quotes on 128, 133, 134.
54. The piece was republished in *The Wisconsin Magazine of History* 45 (Spring 1962): 186–89, quote on 186.
55. Love, *An End to Bugling*, 1–2, 149–50.
56. Hay, *The Mindleberg Papers*, 1, 35–37.
57. Hay, *The Mindleberg Papers*, 122, 146.
58. Hay, *The Mindleberg Papers*, 188.
59. Brautigan, *A Confederate General from Big Sur*.
60. Warner, *Generals in Gray*.
61. Brautigan, *A Confederate General from Big Sur*, 131.
62. https://en.wikipedia.org/wiki/Two_Thousand_Maniacs! (accessed January 8, 2022).
63. Kay, *Zombie Movies*, 176; https://www.allmusic.com/artist/maurice-gibb-mn0000865286/biography (accessed January 8, 2022).
64. Grossman, "Zombies Are the New Vampires," 61.
65. https://en.wikipedia.org/wiki/Abraham_Lincoln_vs._Zombies (accessed January 8, 2022).
66. https://en.wikipedia.org/wiki/Curse of the Cannibal Confederates (accessed January 8, 2022); Russell, *Book of the Dead*, 240.
67. Austin and Grahame-Smith, *Pride and Prejudice and Zombies*.
68. Alcott and Grand, *Little Women and Werewolves*.
69. Thompson, *The Dead Badge of Courage*.
70. Grahame-Smith, *Abraham Lincoln*; Smith and Staskiewicz, "Summer Box Office Winners and Losers," 16.
71. Ireland, *Dread Nation*, 35.
72. Wishnevsky, *Were-Zombies of the Old Dominion*, 60.
73. Miller, *A Zombie History of the United States*.
74. Hely, *How I Became a Famous Novelist*, 22–23, 43.
75. Shaara, *The Killer Angels*; Gorganus, *Oldest Confederate Widow Tells All*; Frazier, *Cold Mountain*; Jiles, *Enemy Women*; Hochbruck, "Mr. Lincoln's Wars."
76. Powell, *Mrs. Hollingworth's Men*.

Notes—Part III

77. Kramer, *The American People, Volume 1*; McCormack, *The Well-Dressed Wound*.
78. Wright, *The Amalgamation Polka*, 12, 91, 286, 295, 296, 300.
79. Saunders, *Lincoln in the Bardo*.
80. McBride, *The Good Lord Bird*.
81. Fraser, *Flashman and the Angel of the Lord*.
82. Fraser, *Flashman*, [6]; *Flashman and the Angel of the Lord*, 103, 104, 391–92n.
83. Tighe, *Sir Thomas "British Tommy" Armstrong and the War Between the States*.
84. Bornstein, "Dixie Belle," 65–84, quote on 68.
85. Kroenung, *Brimstone and Lily*.
86. Lee, *Country in Ruin, 1865*.
87. Lee, *Country in Ruin, 1865*, 7; Magnola, *The Amazing Screw-On Head*; Nelson, *Tucker Teaches the Clockies to Copulate*.
88. Kwapisz, *Rebel Dead Revenge*.
89. Heller, *If the North Had Won the Civil War*.
90. Rodgers, *Close Before Striking*; Hathaway, *Pride, Prejudice and Cheese Grits*.
91. Poe, *Colonel Quicksot*.
92. Anonymous, *Wild Walt and the Rock Greek Gang*.
93. Appel, *Surrendering Appomattox*.

Works Cited

Publications

Addums, Mozis [George W. Bagby]. "Histry uv the Waw." *Southern Magazine* 8 (January–June 1871): 70–72, 187–90, 312–15, 470–73, 613–16.

Alcott, Louisa May, and Porter Grand. *Little Women and Werewolves*. New York: Ballantine, 2010.

Aldrich, Thomas Bailey. *The Story of a Bad Boy*. Boston: Houghton, Mifflin, 1893 [1869].

"The American Civil War Made Easy." *The Wisconsin Magazine of History* 45 (Spring 1962): 186–89.

Appel, Jacob M. *Surrendering Appomattox*. Winston-Salem, NC: C & R Press, 2019.

Armstrong, William H. *Red-Tape and Pigeon-Hole Generals*. New York: Carleton, 1864.

———. *Red-Tape and Pigeon-Hole Generals: Andrew A. Humphrey in the Army of the Potomac*. Edited by Frederick B. Arner. Charlottesville: Rockbridge Publishing, 1999.

"Attention Gynaecologists!—Notes from the Diary of a Field and Hospital Surgeon, C.S.A." *American Medical Weekly* 1 (1874): 233–34.

Austen, Jane, and Seth Grahame-Smith. *Pride and Prejudice and Zombies*. Philadelphia: Quirk Books, 2009.

Bagby, George W. "Bacon and Greens." In *The Old Virginia Gentleman*, 45–68.

———. "My Uncle Flatback's Plantation." In *The Old Virginia Gentleman*, 69–106.

———. *The Old Virginia Gentleman and Other Stories*. New York: Charles Scribner's Sons, 1910 [1884].

———. "The Old Virginia Gentleman." In *The Old Virginia Gentleman*, 1–44.

———. "An Unrenowned Warrior. The Record of a Man Who Shivered through the Manassas Campaign." In *The Old Virginia Gentleman*, 135–65.

Baker, Russell, ed. *Russell Baker's Book of American Humor*. New York: W.W. Norton, 1993.

Balcerski, Thomas J. "'A Work of Friendship': Nathaniel Hawthorne, Franklin Pierce, and the Politics of Enmity in the Civil War Era." *Journal of Social History* 50 (Summer 2017): 655–79.

Balducci, Anthony. *Lloyd Hamilton: Poor Boy Comedian of Silent Cinema*. Jefferson, NC: McFarland, 2009.

Beck, Jerry, and Will Friedwald. *Looney Tunes and Merrie Melodies: A Complete Guide to the Warner Bros. Cartoons*. New York: Henry Holt, 1989.

Bennett, Marek. *The Civil War Diary of Freeman Colby*. Henniker Junction, NH: Comics Workshop, 2016.

———. *The Civil War Diary of Freeman Colby, Volume 2: 1863*. Henniker Junction, NH: Comics Workshop, 2019.

Bense, James. "Nathaniel Hawthorne's Intention in 'Chiefly About War Matters.'" *American Literature* 61 (May 1989): 200–14.

Bierce, Ambrose. "Chickamauga." In Quirk, *Tales of Soldiers and Civilians*, 20–25.

———. "Jupiter Doke, Brigadier General." In Quirk, *Tales of Soldiers and Civilians*, 200–08.

———. "An Occurrence at Owl Creek Bridge." In Quirk, *Tales of Soldiers and Civilians*, 11–19.

———. "A Tough Tussle." In Quirk, *Tales of Soldiers and Civilians*, 136–42.

_____. *The Unabridged Devil's Dictionary.* Athens: University of Georgia Press, 2000.

Blair, Walter. *Native American Humor.* New York: Harper and Row, 1960 [1937].

Blight, David W. *Race and Reunion: The Civil War in American Memory.* Cambridge: Harvard University Press, 2001.

Blount, Roy, Jr. *Robert E. Lee: A Life.* New York: Penguin, 2006 [2005].

Bornstein, Kate. "Dixie Belle: The Further Adventures of Huckleberry Finn." In Cooper and Mansbach, *A Fictional History of the United States,* 65–84.

Brands, H.W. *The Man Who Saved the Union: Ulysses S. Grant in War and Peace.* New York: Anchor Books, 2013 [2012].

Brautigan, Richard. *A Confederate General from Big Sur, Dreaming of Babylon, and The Hawkline Monster: three books in the manner of their original editions.* Boston: Houghton Mifflin/Seymour Lawrence, 1991.

Breeden, James O. "The Case of the Miraculous Bullet." *Military Affairs* 45 (February 1981): 23–26.

Brophy, Alfred L. *Reparations: Pro and Con.* New York: Oxford University Press, 2006.

Brown, John Sullivan. *This War, a Satire for the Times.* New York: S.W. Wood and Co., 1863.

Browne, Charles Farrar. *The Complete Works of Artemus Ward (Charles Farrar Browne.) With a Biographical Sketch (By Melville D. Landon, "Eli Perkins,") and Many Humorous Illustrations. Revised Edition.* New York: G.W. Dillingham, 1898.

Browne, Junius Henri. *Four Years in Secessia: Adventures Within and Beyond Union Lines.* Detroit: W.H. Davis, 1866.

Burlingame, Michael, ed. *"Lincoln's Humor" and Other Essays.* Urbana: University of Illinois Press, 2002.

Butler, Benjamin F. *Butler's Book: Autobiography and Personal Reminiscences of Major General Benj. F. Butler.* Boston: A.M. Thayer and Co., 1892.

Byrne, Frank. "Ralph Orr Bates." In Nevins, Robertson and Wiley, *Civil War Books,* vol. 1: 186.

Camfield, Gregg. *Necessary Madness: The Humor of Domesticity in Nineteenth-Century American Literature.* New York: Oxford University Press, 1997.

Carlisle, Henry C., Jr., ed. *American Satire in Prose and Verse.* New York: Random House, 1962.

Carlson, Peter. *Junius and Albert's Adventures in the Confederacy: A Civil War Odyssey.* New York: Public Affairs, 2013.

Caron, James, and M. Thomas Inge, eds. *Sut Lovingood's Nat'ral Born Yarnspinner: Essays on George Washington Harris.* Tuscaloosa: University of Alabama Press, 1996.

Caron, Timothy P. "'How Changeable Are the Events of War': National Reconciliation in the *Century Magazine*'s 'Battles and Leaders of the Civil War.'" *American Periodicals* 16.2 (2006): 151–71.

Carpio, Glenda. *Laughing Fit to Kill: Black Humor in the Fictions of Slavery.* New York: Oxford University Press, 2008.

Carroll, Bret E. *Spiritualism in Antebellum America.* Bloomington: Indiana University Press, 1997.

Catalogue of Miscellaneous Books of the Pennsylvania State Library, on the First of January, 1878, Being Part II of the General Catalogue. Harrisburg: Lane S. Hart, State Printer, 1878.

Charyn, Jerome. *I Am Abraham.* New York: Liveright, 2014.

Chernow, Ron. *Grant.* New York: Penguin, 2017.

Child, L. Maria, ed. *The Freedmen's Book.* Boston: Ticknor and Fields, 1865.

The Chronology of American Literature: American Literary Achievements from the Colonial Era to Modern Times. New York: Houghton Mifflin, 2004.

Churchill, Winston. "If Lee Had Not Won the Battle of Gettysburg." *Scribner's Magazine* (December 1930): 587–97.

Cloyd, Benjamin G. *Haunted by Atrocity: Civil War Prisons in American Memory.* Baton Rouge: Louisiana State University Press, 2010.

Coleman, Christopher Kiernan. *Ambrose Bierce and the Period of Honorable Strife: The Civil War and the Emergence of an American Writer.* Knoxville: University of Tennessee Press, 2016.

Connelly, T. Lawrence. *Will Success Spoil Jeff Davis? The Last Book about the Civil War.* New York: McGraw-Hill, 1963.

Connelly, Thomas. "That Was the War That Was." *Journal of Mississippi History* 30 (1968): 123–34.

Cooper, T., and Adam Mansbach, eds. *A

Works Cited

Fictional History of the United States (with Huge Chunks Missing). New York: Akashic Books, 2006.

Cronin, Mary M., ed. *High Private: The Trans-Mississippi Correspondence of Humorist R.R. Gilbert, 1862-1865.* Knoxville: University of Tennessee Press, 2018.

Curran, Thomas F. "Quaker Guns." In Heidler and Heidler, *Encyclopedia of the American Civil War*, vol. 3: 1581-582.

———. *Soldiers of Peace: Civil War Pacifism and the Postwar Radical Peace Movement.* New York: Fordham University Press, 2003.

———. *Women Making War: Female Confederate Prisoners and Union Military Justice.* Carbondale: Southern Illinois University Press, 2020.

Dabney, Virginius. *Gold That Did Not Glitter.* Philadelphia: J.B. Lippincott, 1889.

———. *The Story of Don Miff, as Told by His Friend John Bouche Whacker. A Symphony of Life.* Philadelphia: J.B. Lippincott, 1886.

Daniel, Ferdinand Eugene. *Recollections of a Rebel Surgeon.* Monee, IL: Lucy Booker Roper, 2014 [1899].

Davis, Robert Scott. *Ghosts and Shadows of Andersonville: Essays on the Secret Social Histories of America's Deadliest Prison.* Macon: Mercer University Press, 2006.

Davis, Stephen. "'A Matter of Sensational Interest': The *Century* 'Battles and Leaders' Series." *Civil War History* 27 (December 1981): 338-49.

Day, Donald. "The Life of George Washington Harris." In Caron and Inge, *Sut Lovingood's Nat'ral Born Yarnspinner*, 33-68.

De Leon, T.C. *South Songs: From the Lays of Later Days.* New York: Blelock and Co., 1866.

Dictionary of American Biography. 10 vols. New York: Charles Scribner's Sons, 1927-1936.

Diffley, Kathleen, ed. *To Live and Die: Collected Stories of the Civil War, 1861-1876.* Durham: Duke University Press, 2002.

Duberman, Martin B. *In White America: A Documentary Play.* New York: Samuel French, 1964.

Dunbar, Paul Laurence. *The Fanatics.* New York: Dodd, Mead, 1902.

———. *The Heart of Happy Hollow.* New York: Dodd, Mead, 1904.

———. "The Wisdom of Silence." In *The Heart of Happy Hollow*, 191-204.

Duncan, Russell, and David L. Klooser. "Introduction: Fighting and Writing the Civil War." In Duncan and Klooser, *Phantoms of a Blood-Stained Period*, 5-30.

Duncan, Russell, and David L. Klooser, eds. *Phantoms of a Blood-Stained Period: The Complete Civil War Writings of Ambrose Bierce.* Amherst: University of Massachusetts Press, 2002.

Dunne, Michael. *Calvinist Humor in American Literature.* Baton Rouge: Louisiana State University Press, 2007.

Early, Gerald, Glenda Carpio, and Werner Sollors. "Black Humor: Reflections on an American Tradition." *Bulletin of the American Academy of Arts and Sciences* 63 (Summer 2010): 29-47.

Earnest, Matthew. *Dead Letter Office (a prelude to Bartleby the Scrivener).* Huntington, WV: The Lunar Stratagem, 2012.

Eberly, Robert E., Jr. *Bouquets from the Cannon's Mouth: Soldiering with the Eighth Regiment of the Pennsylvania Reserves.* Shippensburg, PA: White Mane Books, 2005.

Edwards, Harry Stillwell. "Captain Isam." In *His Defense and Other Stories*, 181-92.

———. *His Defense and Other Stories.* New York: The Century Co., 1899.

Ellinger, Esther Parker. "The Southern Poetry of the Civil War." Ph.D. dissertation, University of Pennsylvania, 1918.

Ellington, Charles G. *The Trial of U.S. Grant: The Pacific Years, 1852-1854.* Glendale, CA: Arthur H. Clarke, 1987.

Elmer, Jonathan. "American Idiot: Ambrose Bierce's Warrior." *American Literary History* 27 (Fall 2015): 446-60.

Erickson, Hal. *Military Comedy Films: A Critical Survey and Filmography of Hollywood Releases since 1918.* Jefferson, NC: McFarland, 2012.

Eskridge, Sara K. *Rube Tube: CBS and Rural Comedy in the Sixties.* Columbia: University of Missouri Press, 2019.

Fahs, Alice. "The Feminized Civil War: Gender, Northern Popular Literature, and the Memory of the War, 1861-1900." *Journal of American History* 85 (March 1999): 1461-494.

———. *The Imagined Civil War: Popular Literature of the North and South, 1861-*

1865. Chapel Hill: University of North Carolina Press, 2001.

Faust, Drew Gilpin. *This Republic of Suffering: Death and the American Civil War*. New York: Alfred A. Knopf, 2008.

Ferguson, Andrew. *Land of Lincoln: Adventures in Abe Lincoln's America*. New York: Grove Press, 2007.

Fish, Daniel, comp. *Lincoln Literature: A Bibliographic Account of Books and Pamphlets Relating to Abraham Lincoln*. Minneapolis: Public Library Board, 1900.

Fletcher, William A. *Rebel Private: Front and Rear. Memoir of a Confederate Soldier*. New York: Dutton Books, 1995 [1908].

Folsom, Ed. "An Unpublished Whitman Manuscript about Writing the 'History of the Secession War.'" *Walt Whitman Quarterly Review* 23 (Summer 2005): 48–49.

Forehand, Thomas, Jr., ed. *Robert E. Lee's Lighter Side: The Marble Man's Sense of Humor*. Gretna, LA: Pelican, 2006.

Fraser, George MacDonald. *Flashman*. New York: Penguin, 1969.

———. *Flashman and the Angel of the Lord*. New York: Plume, 1996 [1994].

Freemon, Frank R. "The First Neurological Research Center: Turner's Lan Hospital During the American Civil War." *Journal of the History of the Neurosciences* 2 (1993): 135–42.

Fremantle, Arthur. *Three Months in the Southern States: April–June 1863*. Lincoln: University of Nebraska Press, 1991 [1863].

Fremantle, Tom. *The Moonshine Mule: A 2,700-Mile Walk from Mexico to Manhattan*. London: Constable and Robinson, 2003.

Frost, Griffin. *Camp and Prison Journal*. Iowa City: Press of the Camp Pope Bookshop, 1994 [1867].

Fuller, Randall. "Hawthorne and War." *The New England Quarterly* 80 (December 2007): 655–86.

Gallagher, Catharine. "When Did the Confederate States of America Free the Slaves?" *Representations* 98 (Spring 2007): 53–61.

Gallagher, Gary. *The Union War*. Cambridge: Harvard University Press, 2011.

Gallman, J. Matthew. *Defining Duty in the Civil War*. Chapel Hill: University of North Carolina Press, 2015.

Gannon, Barbara. *Americans Remember Their Civil War*. Santa Barbara, CA: Praeger, 2017.

Giesberg, Judith. *Sex and the Civil War: Soldiers, Pornography, and the Making of American Morality*. Chapel Hill: University of North Carolina Press, 2017.

Goler, Robert I. "Loss and the Persistence of Memory: 'The Case of George Dedlow' and Disabled Civil War Veterans." *Literature and Medicine* 23 (Spring 2004): 160–83.

Gómez-Galisteo, M. Carmen. *The Wind Is Never Gone: Sequels, Parodies and Rewriting of Gone with the Wind*. Jefferson, NC: McFarland, 2011.

Gordon, Armistead Churchill. "Envion." *Library of Southern Literature*, vol. 5: 1903–06.

Goss, Warren Lee. *Recollections of a Private. A Story of the Army of the Potomac*. New York: Thomas Y. Crowell, 1890.

Graham, Allison. *Framing the South: Hollywood, Television, and Race during the Civil Rights Struggle*. Baltimore: Johns Hopkins University Press, 2001.

Grahame-Smith, Seth. *Abraham Lincoln: Vampire Hunter*. New York: Grand Central, 2010.

Grant, Ulysses S. *Personal Memoirs of U.S. Grant: Selected Letters, 1839–1865*. New York: Literary Classics of the United States, 1990.

Greenwood, Grace [Sarah Jane Clark Lippincott]. *Records of Five Years*. Boston: Ticknor and Fields, 1867.

Gregory, Edward S. "George William Bagby." In Bagby, *The Old Virginia Gentleman and Other Stories*, xvii–xxx.

Grigsby, Melvin. *The Smoked Yank*, revised edition. N.p.: Sam T. Clover, 1888.

Grimsley, Mark. *The Hard Hand of War: Union Military Policy Toward Southern Civilians*. Cambridge: Cambridge University Press, 1995.

Grinspan, Jon. "'Sorrowfully Amusing': The Popular Comedy of the Civil War." *Journal of the Civil War Era* 1 (September 2011): 313–38.

Grossman, Lev. "Zombies Are the New Vampires." *Time*, April 20, 2009, 61.

Habegger, Alfred. "Nineteenth-Century American Humor: Easygoing Males, Anxious Ladies, and Penelope Lapham." *PMLA* 91 (October 1976): 884–99.

Hajdu, David. *The Ten-Cent Plague: The*

Great Comic Book Scare and How It Changed America. New York: Farrar, Straus, and Giroux, 2008.

Halpine, Charles G. *Baked Meats for the Funeral: Collection of Essays, Poems, Speeches, Histories, and Banquets by Private Miles O'Reilly, late of the 47th Reg't. New York Volunteer Infantry, 10th Army Corps.* New York: Carleton, 1866.

———. *The Life and Adventures, Songs, Services, and Speeches of Private Miles O'Reilly (47th Regiment, New York Volunteers).* New York: Carleton, 1864.

Hanchett, William. *Irish: Charles G. Halpine and the Civil War.* Syracuse: Syracuse University Press, 1970.

Hardeman County, Tennessee, Family History, Vol. II. Paducah, KY: Turner Publishing Company, 2001.

Harris, Joel Chandler. "An Ambuscade." In *Tales of the Home Folks in Peace and War,* 293–344.

———. *On the Plantation: A Story of a Georgia Boy's Adventures During the War.* New York: D. Appleton, 1892.

———. "A Story of the War." In *Uncle Remus,* 175–85.

———. *Tales of the Home Folks in Peace and War.* New York: McKinlay, Stone and MacKenzie, 1898.

———. *Uncle Remus: His Songs and Sayings. The Folk-Lore of the Old Plantation.* New York: D. Appleton, 1880.

Harris, Julia Chandler. *The Life and Letters of Joel Chandler Harris.* Boston: Houghton Mifflin, 1918.

Harrison, Hank, comp. *The Art of Jack Davis!* Lexington, KY: Binary Publications, 2012 [1987].

Hart, Stan, and Jack Davis. "Groan With the Wind." *Mad* 300 (January 1991): 42–47.

Hathaway, Mary Jane. *Pride, Prejudice and Cheese Grits.* New York: Howard Books, 2014 [2013].

Hawthorne, Nathaniel. "Chiefly About War Matters." In George Parsons Lathrop, *The Complete Works of Nathaniel Hawthorne,* vol. 12: 299–345.

———. "Our Whispering Gallery." *The Atlantic* (April 1871): 510–12.

Hay, Jacob. *The Mindleberg Papers.* New York: Macmillan, 1964.

Hayes, Charles H. *Civil War Limericks.* Gretna, LA: Pelican, 2014.

Heller, Andrew J. *If the North Had Won the Civil War.* San Bernardino, CA: Lulu.com, 2015.

Hely, Steve. *How I Became a Famous Novelist.* New York: Black Cat, 2009.

Hesseltine, William B. "The Propaganda Literature of Confederate Prisons." *Journal of Southern History* 1 (February 1935): 56–66.

Hill, A.F. *John Smith's Funny Adventure on a Crutch, or the Remarkable Peregrinations of a One-Legged Soldier after the War.* Philadelphia: John E. Potter, 1869.

———. *Our Boys: The Personal Experiences of a Soldier in the Army of the Potomac.* Philadelphia: John E. Potter, 1864.

———. *The White Rocks, or The Robbers' Den. A Tragedy of the Mountains.* Morgantown, WV: Acme Press, 1900 [1866].

Hill, L.B., ed. *A History of Greater Dallas and Vicinity,* Vol. II. Chicago: The Lewis Publishing Company, 1909.

Hills, Alfred C. *MacPherson, the Great Confederate Philosopher and Southern Blower. A Record of His Philosophy, His Career as a Warrior, Traveller* [sic], *Clergyman, Poet, and Newspaper Publisher. His Death, Resuscitation, and Subsequent Election to the Office of Governor of Louisiana.* New York: James Miller, 1864.

Hinman, Wilbur F. *Corporal Si Klegg and His "Pard."* Lincoln, NE: Bison Books, 2009 [1887].

———. *The Story of the Sherman Brigade.* Alliance, OH: The Author, 1897.

Hofstede, David. *What Were They Thinking: The 100 Dumbest Events in Television History.* New York: Back Stage Books, 2004.

Horowitz, Adam. *The Dumbest Moments in Business History: Useless Products, Ruinous Deals, Clueless Bosses and Other Signs of Unintelligent Life in the Workplace.* New York: Portfolio, 2004.

Horwitz, Tony. *Confederates in the Attic: Dispatches from the Unfinished Civil War.* New York: Vintage, 1998.

Hughes, Jennifer A. "The Politics of Incongruity in Paul Laurence Dunbar's *The Fanatics.*" *African American Review* 41 (Summer 2007): 295–301.

Hunter, Alexander. *Johnny Reb and Billy Yank.* New York: The Neale Publishing Company, 1905.

"In Vinculis." *The Land We Love. A Monthly Magazine Devoted to Literature, Military*

History and Agriculture 2 (March 1867): 387.

Irelan, Scott R. "Goon, Warrior, Communitarian, and Mythos: The Lincoln Legend of Dramatic Literature and Live Performance." *Theater History Studies* 28 (2008): 50–52.

Ireland, Justina. *Dread Nation*. New York: Balzer and Bray, 2018.

Isenberg, Nancy. *White Trash: The 400-Year Untold History of Class in America*. New York: Viking, 2016.

Jack Davis: Drawing American Pop Culture. Seattle: Fantagraphics Books, 2012.

Jackson, Lawrence. *Ralph Ellison: Emergence of Genius*. Athens: University of Georgia Press, 2007 [2002].

Janney, Caroline. *Remembering the Civil War: Reunion and the Limits of Reconciliation*. Chapel Hill: University of North Carolina Press, 2013.

Jimerson, Randall C. *The Private Civil War: Popular Thought During the Sectional Conflict*. Baton Rouge: Louisiana State University Press, 1988.

Jones, Katharine M., ed. *New Confederate Short Stories*. Columbia: University of South Carolina Press, 1945.

Jordan, John W., and James Haddon, eds. *Genealogical and Personal History of Fayette County, Pennsylvania*. 2 vols. New York: Lewis Historical Publishing Company, 1912.

Kadmus, Kristofur [Nathan Brown]. *De Histori ov Magnus Mahárba end de Blak Dragun*. New York: Filolojikad Germána, 1866.

Kaser, James A. *The New Orleans of Fiction: A Research Guide*. Lanham, MD: Rowman & Littlefield, 2014.

Kaufman, Will. "The American Civil War." In McLoughlin, *The Cambridge Companion to War Writing*, 149–58.

Keckley, Elizabeth. *Behind the Scenes, or, Thirty Years a Slave and Four Years in the White House*. New York: Carleton, 1868.

Keiley, Anthony M. *In Vinculis; or The Prisoner of War. Being the Experience of a Rebel in Two Federal Pens, Interspersed with Reminiscences of the Late War; Anecdotes of Southern Generals, etc*. Petersburg, VA: "Daily Index" Office, 1866.

———. *A Rebel in Two Federal Pens*, by A. Rifleman, Esq. N.p.: Big Byte Books, 2014 [1865].

Kelley, Robin D.G. *Freedom Dreams: The Black Radical Imagination*. Boston: Beacon Press, 2002.

Kendi, Ibram X. *Stamped from the Beginning: The Definitive History of Racist Ideas in America*. New York: Bold Type Books, 2016.

Kendrick, James. *She Wouldn't Surrender*. Derby, CT: Monarch Books, 1960.

Kennedy, Dane. "Where's the Humor in History?" *Perspectives on History* 49 (February 2011): 27–28.

Ketcham, Henry. "Biographical Sketch." In Lowell, *The Biglow Papers* [1st Series], xi–xii.

Kidd, Kenneth B. *Making American Boys: Boyology and the Feral Tale*. Minneapolis: University of Minnesota Press, 2004.

Knight, Denise D. *Writers of the American Renaissance: An A-to-Z Guide*. Westport, CT: Greenwood Press, 2003.

Kramer, Larry. *The American People, Volume 1: Search for My Heart*. New York: Farrar, Straus and Giroux, 2015.

Kreger, Erika M. "The Nineteenth-Century Female Humorist as 'Iconoclast in the Temple': Gail Hamilton and the Myth of Reviewers' Disapproval of Women's Comic-Ironic Writings." *Studies in American Humor* New Series 3.11 (2004): 5–38.

Kroenung, Terry. *Brimstone and Lily*. Loveland, CO: Rare Moon Press, 2009.

Kuiper, John B. "Civil War Films: A Quantitative Description of a Genre." *Journal of the Society of Cinematologists* 4/5 (1964–1965): 81–89.

Kutzler, Evan A. *Living by Inches: The Smells, Sounds, Tastes, and Feeling of Captivity in Civil War Prisons*. Chapel Hill: University of North Carolina Press, 2019.

Kwapisz, Gary. *Rebel Dead Revenge: Stonewall's Arm*. N.p.: Dark Legion Comics, 2020.

Lambik, Willie, and Raoul Cauvin. *The Bluecoats, No. 1: Robertsonville Prison*, trans. Erica Jeffrey. Canterbury: Cinebook, 2008.

———. *The Bluecoats, No. 2: The Navy Blues*, trans. Erica Jeffrey. Canterbury: Cinebook, 2008.

———. *The Bluecoats, No. 3: The Skyriders*, trans. Erica Jeffrey. Canterbury: Cinebook, 2009.

———. *Les Tuniques Bleues: Black Face*. Marcinelle, Belgique: Dupuis, 1983.

Landon, Melville D. "A Biographical Sketch." In Browne, *The Complete Works of Artemus Ward*, 13–26.

Lathrop, George Parsons, ed. *The Complete Works of Nathaniel Hawthorne*, Riverside Edition. 13 vols. Boston: Houghton Mifflin, 1883, 1891.

Lee, David. *Country in Ruin, 1865*. Monee, IL: Hatton Cross Steampunk Publishing, 2018 [2013].

Lee, Robert Edward. *Recollections and Letters of Robert Edward Lee*. Mineola, NY: Dover, 2007 [1904].

Lehr, Dick. *The Birth of a Movement: How* The Birth of a Nation *Ignited the Battle for Civil Rights*. New York: Public Affairs, 2014.

"A Letter from a Freedman to His Old Master." *The Negro Quarterly* 1 (Spring 1942): 72–74.

Letters of Major Jack Downing of the Downingville Militia, 3rd edition. New York: Evrie, Horton and Co., 1866.

"Letters of Negroes, Largely Personal and Private [Part 2]." *The Journal of Negro History* 11 (January 1926): 87–112.

Levin, Kevin. *Searching for Black Confederates: The Civil War's Most Persistent Myth*. Chapel Hill: University of North Carolina Press, 2019.

Library of Southern Literature, vol. 5. New Orleans: The Martin and Hoyt Company, 1906.

Linderman, Gerald F. *Embattled Courage: The Experience of Combat in the American Civil War*. New York: The Free Press, 1987.

Litwack, Leon. *Been in the Storm So Long: The Aftermath of Slavery*. New York: Alfred A. Knopf, 1979.

Lloyd, George William. *The Devil in Dixie: A Tale of the Times. Serio-Comical, Semi-Historical, and Quasi-Diabolical*. New York: American News Company, 1865.

Locke, David Ross. *The Nasby Papers. Letters and Sermons Containing the Views on the Topics of the Day, of Petroleum V. Nasby*. Indianapolis: C.O. Perrine and Co., 1864.

Long, James O. *Lincoln's Doctor's Dog*. Boise: Bottlefly Press, 2020.

Love, Edmund G. *An End to Bugling*. New York: Harper and Row, 1963.

Lowell, James Russell. *The Biglow Papers* [1st Series]. New York: A.L. Burt Company, 1900 [1848].

Lowry, Thomas P. *The Stories the Soldiers Wouldn't Tell: Sex in the Civil War*. Mechanicsburg, PA: Stackpole Books, 1994.

Luebke, Peter. "'To Transmit and Perpetuate the Fruits of Victory': Union Regimental Histories, 1865–1866, and the Meaning of the Great Rebellion." Masters thesis, University of Virginia, 2007.

Lynn, Kenneth S., ed. *The Comic Tradition in America: An Anthology*. New York: W.W. Norton, 1958.

Mackowski, Chris, ed. *Entertaining History: The Civil War in Literature, Film, and Song*. Carbondale: Southern Illinois University Press, 2020.

Madden, David. "What Is Civil War Humor?" *Studies in American History* New Series 3:23 (2011): 121–28.

Magnola, Mike. *The Amazing Screw-On Head*. Milwaukee, OR: Dark Horse Comics, 2002.

Martin, Michael J. *A History of the 4th Wisconsin Infantry and Cavalry in the Civil War*. New York: Savas Beatie, 2006.

Martin, Steve. "Introduction to the Modern Library Humor and Wit Series." In Twain, *Mark Twain's Library of Humor*, ix–xi.

Maxwell, Hu. "Sketch of the Author." In Hill, *The White Rocks*, 14–15.

McArthur, Tom. *The Oxford Companion to the English Language*. New York: Oxford University Press, 1992.

McBride, James. *The Good Lord Bird*. New York: Penguin, 2013.

McCall, Laura, and Donald Yacovone, eds. *A Shared Experience: Men, Women, and the History of Gender*. New York: New York University Press, 1998.

McCormack, Derek. *The Well-Dressed Wound*. South Pasadena, CA: Semiotext(e), 2015.

McElroy, John M. *Si Klegg: His Transformation From a Raw Recruit to a Veteran*. Washington, D.C.: The National Tribune Co., 1897.

McLoughlin, Kate, ed. *The Cambridge Companion to War Writing*. New York: Cambridge University Press, 2009.

McPherson, James. *For Cause and Comrades: Why Men Fought in the Civil War*. New York: Oxford University Press, 1997.

McWhirter, Christian. *Battle Hymns: The Power and Popularity of Music in the*

Civil War. Chapel Hill: University of North Carolina Press, 2012.

Mencken, H.L. "The Calamity of Appomattox." *The American Mercury* (September 1930): 29–31.

Miller, Stephen Franks. *Ahab Lincoln: A Tragedy of the Potomac.* Chicago: The Civil War Round Table, 1958 [1861].

Miller, Worm. *A Zombie History of the United States.* Berkeley: Ulysses Press, 2011.

Millett, Allan R. "Introduction." In Hinman, *Corporal Si Klegg and His "Pard,"* vii–xxxiv.

"Miscellaneous." *American Medical Weekly* 1 (1874): 263–64.

"Mr. Bright's Platform." *The Index,* February 24, 1864.

Mitchell, Margaret. *Gone with the Wind.* New York: Warner Books, 1993 [1936].

Mitchell, Reid. *The Vacant Chair: The Northern Soldier Leaves Home.* New York: Oxford University Press, 1993.

Mitchell, S. Weir. *The Autobiography of a Quack and The Case of George Dedlow.* New York: The Century Co., 1900.

———. "Phantom Limbs." *Lippincott's Magazine of Popular Literature and Science* 8 (December 1871), 563–69.

Moody, Minnie Hite. "The Ghost of General Jackson." In Jones, *New Confederate Short Stories,* 146–62.

Moore, Frank, ed. *Rebel Rhymes and Rhapsodies.* New York: George P. Putnam, 1864.

———. *Songs of the Soldiers.* New York: George P. Putnam, 1864.

Moore, Olin H. "Some Translations of *Les Misérables.*" *Modern Language Notes* 74 (March 1959): 240–46.

Morley, Christopher. "Lincoln's Doctor's Dog." *The Saturday Review* (February 12, 1955): 9–10, 40–42.

Morris, Linda. *Women Vernacular Humorists in Nineteenth-Century America.* New York: Garland, 1988.

Morris, Roy, Jr. *Ambrose Bierce: Alone in Bad Company.* New York: Crown, 1995.

Moss, William. *Confederate Broadside Poems: An Annotated Descriptive Bibliography Based on the Collection of the Z. Smith Reynolds Library of Wake Forest University.* Westport, CT: Meckler Corporation, 1988.

National Cyclopaedia of American Biography, 63 vols. New York: James T. White and Co., 1898–1984.

Neary, Janet. *Fugitive Testimony: On the Visual Logic of Slave Narratives.* New York: Oxford University Press, 2016.

Nelson, Anna. "*Behind the Seams*: The 'Colored Historian' of the White House and Her Parodist." *PMLA* 133.3 (2018): 542–58.

Nelson, David Erik. *Tucker Teaches the Clockies to Copulate.* Kindle Edition, 2013.

Nevins, Allan, James I. Robertson, Jr., and Bell I. Wiley, eds. *Civil War Books: A Critical Bibliography.* 2 vols. Baton Rouge: Louisiana State University Press, 1967.

Newell, Robert H. *The Orpheus C. Kerr Papers.* New York: Blakeman and Mason, 1862.

———. *The Orpheus C. Kerr Papers. Second Series.* New York: Carleton, 1863.

Nickels, Cameron C. *Civil War Humor.* Jackson: University Press of Mississippi, 2010.

Northup, Clark Sutherland. "The Novelists." In Stanton, *A Manuel of American Literature,* 115–240.

Odom, John Yancy. *Saving Black America: Economic Civil Rights.* Sauk Village, IL: African American Images, 2001.

O'Grady, Joseph P. "Anthony M. Keiley (1832–1905): Virginia's Catholic Politician. *The Catholic Historical Review* 54 (January 1969): 613–35.

Ohler, Norman. *Blitzed: Drugs in the Third Reich,* trans. Shaun Whiteside. New York: Mariner Books, 2018 [2015].

"Old Woodward": A Memorial Relating to Woodward High School, 1831–1836 and Woodward College, 1836–1851, in the City of Cincinnati. Cincinnati: "Old Woodward" Club, 1884.

"Operation for Club Foot." *The Western Journal of Medicine and Surgery* 5.5 (May 1, 1842): 395.

Oster, Harry. "Negro Humor: John and Old Marster." *Journal of the Folklore Institute* 5 (June 1968): 42–57.

Ottolengui, Daniel. *Behind the Seams.* New York: The National News Company, 1868.

"Our Own Previews of Hollywood Attractions: Joan Crawford and Clark Gable in 'Gone With the Birth of a Nation, or The Gold Diggers of 1860.'" *New Yorker,* February 20, 1937, 11–12.

Owsley, Frank L. *State Rights in the Confederacy*. Chicago: University of Chicago Press, 1925.

Page, Thomas Nelson. "Preface: A Virginia Realist." In Bagby, *The Old Virginia Gentleman and Other Stories*, v–xiii.

Parish, James Robert, and William Leonard. *The Funsters*. New Rochelle, NY: Arlington House, 1979.

Peck, George W. *How Private Geo. W. Peck Put Down the Rebellion, or the Funny Experiences of a Raw Recruit*. Chicago: Belford, Clarke and Co., 1887.

Perry, Lewis. *Radical Abolitionism: Anarchy and the Government of God in Antislavery Thought*. Ithaca: Cornell University Press, 1973.

Perry, Mark. *Grant and Twain: The Story of an American Friendship*. New York: Random House, 2004.

Pickett, LaSalle Corbell. *What Happened to Me*. New York: Brentano's, 1917.

Pierson, William Whatley, Jr., ed. *Whipt 'em Everytime: The Diary or Bartlett Yancy Malone*. Wilmington, NC: Broadfoot, 1991.

Poe, Heironymus. *Colonel Quicksot*. Charleston, SC: Quixotic, 2019.

Powell, Padgett. *Mrs. Hollingworth's Men*. Boston: Houghton Mifflin, 2000.

Prokopowicz, Gerald J. *Did Lincoln Own Slaves? And Other Frequently Asked Questions about Abraham Lincoln*. New York: Vintage, 2008.

Quirk, Tom, ed. *Tales of Soldiers and Civilians and Other Stories*. New York: Penguin, 2000 [1891].

Rachels, David, ed. *Mark Twain's Civil War*. Lexington: University Press of Kentucky, 2007.

Randall, Alice. *The Wind Done Gone*. New York: Houghton Mifflin, 2001.

Rebelle, A. Young. *Abram, A Military Poem*. Richmond, VA: Macfarlane and Ferguson, 1863.

Redding, Saunders. "Escape into Pride and Dignity." In Sterling, *Laughing on the Outside*, 17–19.

Reed, Ishmael. *Flight to Canada*. New York: Simon & Schuster, 1976.

Revelations: A Companion to the "New Gospel of Peace." According to Abraham. New York: M. Doolady, Agent, 1863.

Richardson, Albert D. *The Secret Service, the Field, the Dungeon, and the Escape*. Hartford, CT: American Publishing Company, 1865.

Robertson, James I., Jr. "Morford, Henry 1823–1881." In Nevins, Robertson and Wiley, *Civil War Books*, vol. 1: 133.

Robson, John S. *How a One-Legged Rebel Lives. Reminiscences of the Civil War. The Story of the Campaigns of Stonewall Jackson, as told by a High Private in the "Foot Cavalry."* Durham: The Educator Co. Printers and Binder, 1898.

Rodgers, J. Clayton. *Close Before Striking*. Kindle Edition, 2005.

Roosevelt, Theodore. "Expansion and Peace." In *The Strenuous Life* (West Valley City, UT: Waking Lion Press, 2007), 21–33.

Rubin, Louis D., et al., eds. *The History of Southern Literature*. Baton Rouge: Louisiana State University Press, 1985.

Russell, Jamie. *Book of the Dead: A Complete History of Zombie Cinema*. London: Titan Books, 2014.

Sacco, Nick. "Interpreting the Man: General Ulysses S. Grant and His *Personal Memoirs*." In Mackowski, *Entertaining History*, 29–37.

Sanborn, Kate. *Memories and Anecdotes*. New York: G.P. Putnam's Sons, 1915.

Sanders, Mark. *Ambiguities of Witnessing: Law and Literature in the Time of a Truth Commission*. Palo Alto: Stanford University Press, 2007.

Saunders, George. *Lincoln in the Bardo*. New York: Random House, 2017.

Scharnhorst, Gary, ed. *Mark Twain: The Complete Interviews*. Tuscaloosa: University of Alabama Press, 2006.

Schlesinger, Arthur M., Jr. *A Thousand Days: John F. Kennedy in the White House*. Boston: Houghton Mifflin, 2002 [1965].

Schumacher, Michael, and Denis Kitchen. *Al Capp: A Life to the Contrary*. New York: Bloomsburg, 2013.

Shaara, Michael. *The Killer Angels*. New York: David McKay Company, 1974.

Sharp, Rayburn. *From the Case Files of Abraham Lincoln's Penis, Private Eye, Part 1, Gettysburg Address 150th Anniversary Edition*. Kindle Edition, 2013.

Silsbee, Samuel. *D.D.D.: Or Death, the Devil, and the Doctor, on the War*. Cincinnati: Moore, Wilstach, Keys and Co., 1862.

Simms, William Gilmore. *A City Laid*

Waste: The Capture, Sack, and Destruction of the City of Columbia. Columbia: University of South Carolina Press, 2005 [1865].

_____. *The Sword and the Distaff: Or, "Fair, Fat and Forty." A Story of the South, At the Close of the Revolution.* Philadelphia: Lippincott, Grambo, and Co., 1852.

_____. *War Poetry of the South.* New York: Richardson and Company, 1866.

Smith, Charles Henry. *Bill Arp, So Called. A Side Show of the Southern Side of the War.* New York: Metropolitan Record Office, 1866.

_____. *Bill Arp's Peace Papers.* Columbia: University of South Carolina Press, 2009 [1873].

Smith, Grady, and Keith Staskiewicz. "Summer Box Office Winners and Losers." *Entertainment Weekly,* September 7, 2012, 16.

Smith, H. Allen. *The Rebel Yell: Being a Carpetbagger's Attempt to Establish the Truth Concerning the Screech of the Confederate Soldiers Plus Lesser Matters Appertaining to the Peculiar Habits of the South.* Garden City, NY: Doubleday, 1954.

Smith, Mark M. *The Smell of Battle, the Taste of Siege: A Sensory History of the Civil War.* New York: Oxford University Press, 2015.

Smith, William Russell. *The Royal Ape: A Dramatic Poem.* Richmond: West and Johnston, 1863.

Solomon, Jon. *The Complete Three Stooges: The Official Filmography and Three Stooges Companion.* Glendale, CA: Comedy III Productions, 2001.

Southwood, Marion. *Beauty and Booty: The Watchword of New Orleans.* New York: M. Doolady, 1867.

Stanton, Theodore, ed. *A Manuel of American Literature.* New York: G.P. Putnam's Sons, 1909.

Starkeeper, Sage. *The Un-Promised Generation.* Lexington, KY: BookSurge, 2006.

Starr, Stephen Z. "The Grand Old Regiment." *Wisconsin Magazine of History* 48 (Autumn 1964): 21–31.

"Statement of Policy." *The Negro Quarterly* 1 (Spring 1942): 3–4.

Steiner, Bernard C. *Descriptions of Maryland.* Johns Hopkins University Studies in History and Political Science. Baltimore: Johns Hopkins University Press, 1904.

Steinroetter, Vanessa. "Soldiers, Readers, and the Reception of Victor Hugo's *Les Misérables* in Civil War America." *Reception* 8 (2016): 5–28.

Sterling, Philip. *Laughing on the Outside: The Intelligent White Reader's Guide to Negro Tales and Humor.* New York: Grosset and Dunlap, 1965.

Stevens, George. *Lincoln's Doctor's Dog and Other Famous Best Sellers.* Philadelphia: J.B. Lippincott, 1938.

Steward, Barbara, and Dwight Steward. *The Lincoln Diddle.* New York: William Morrow, 1979.

Stewart, Randall. "Hawthorne and the Civil War." *Studies in Philology* 34 (January 1937), 91, 96–98.

Stokes, Melvyn. *D.W. Griffith's* The Birth of a Nation: *A History of "The Most Controversial Motion Picture of All Time."* New York: Oxford University Press, 2007.

Stokes, Sally. "Elements of Bile: Placing Daniel Ottolengui (1836–1918) in the Heritage of Hate." *Journal of Hate Studies* 13 (2015–16): 115–49.

Stowe, Christopher S. "Humphreys, Andrew Atkinson (1810–1883)." In Heidler and Heidler, *Encyclopedia of the American Civil War,* vol. 2: 1016–017.

Street, James. *The Civil War: An Unvarnished Account of the Late but Still Lively Hostilities.* New York: Dial Press, 1953.

Swiggett, S.A. *The Bright Side of Prison Life: Experiences in Prison and Out, of an Involuntary Sojourner in Rebeldom.* Baltimore: Fleet McGinley and Co., 1897.

Tandy, Jennette. *Crackerbox Philosophers in American Humor and Satire.* New York: Columbia University, 1925.

Thomas, Benjamin P. "Lincoln's Humor: An Analysis." In Burlingame, *"Lincoln's Humor" and Other Essays,* 3–22.

Thompson, Lawrence S. "The Civil War in Fiction." *Civil War History* 2 (March 1956): 84–85.

Thompson, Steven A. *The Dead Badge of Courage.* Kindle Edition, 2012.

Thurber, James. *Collecting Himself: James Thurber on Writing and Writers, Humor and Himself.* New York: Harper and Row, 1989.

_____. "If Grant Had Been Drinking at Appomattox." In *The Thurber Carnival*, 140–42.
_____. "No More Biographies." In *Collecting Himself*, 118–20.
_____. *The Thurber Carnival*. New York: Harper and Brothers, 1945.
Tighe, Barry. *Sir Thomas "British Tommy" Armstrong and the War Between the States*. Wanstead: Can Write Will Write, 2013.
"To My Old Master." *Negro History Bulletin* 32 (January 1, 1969), 15.
["To My Old Master"]. *The New Crisis: A Magazine of Opportunities and Ideas* (January/February 1999), 2.
"Topics of the Time." *Century Magazine* 28 (October 1884), 943.
Trapp, Marjorie. "Sentimental Poetry of the American Civil War." PhD dissertation, University of California, Berkeley, 2010.
"TV's 50 Biggest Bombs and Blunders." *Entertainment Weekly*, January 29, 2010, 40–41.
Twain, Mark. "A Curious Experience." *The Century Magazine* 23 (November 1881): 35–46.
_____. *Following the Equator: A Journey Around the World*. Hartford, CT: The American Publishing Company, 1897.
_____. *Huck Finn and Tom Sawyer among the Indians and Other Unfinished Stories*. Berkeley: University of California Press, 1989.
_____. *Life on the Mississippi*. Mineola, NY: Dover, 2000 [1883].
_____. "Lucretia Smith's Soldier." In *Mark Twain: Collected Tales, Sketches, Speeches & Essays, 1852–1890*, 108–12.
_____. *Mark Twain: Collected Tales, Sketches, Speeches & Essays, 1852–1890*. New York: The Library of America, 1992.
_____. *Mark Twain's Library of Humor*. New York: The Modern Library, 2000 [1888].
_____. "The Private History of a Campaign that Failed." *The Century Magazine* 31 (December 1885): 193–204.
_____. "Tom Sawyer's Conspiracy." In *Huck Finn and Tom Sawyer among the Indians and Other Unfinished Stories*, 136–38.
_____. "A True Story, Repeated Word for Word as I heard It." *The Atlantic Monthly* (November 1874): 578–82.

Vowell, Sarah. *Assassination Vacation*. New York: Simon & Schuster, 2005.
Waldman, Milton. "If Booth Had Missed Lincoln." *Scribner's Magazine* (November 1930): 473–84.
Walker, Brent. *Mack Sennett's Fun Factory: A History and Filmography of Studio and His Keystone and His Mack Sennett Comedies with Biographies of Players and Personnel*. Jefferson, NC: McFarland, 2010.
Walker, Nancy, and Zita Dresner, eds. *Redressing the Balance: American Women's Literary Humor from Colonial Times to the 1980s*. Jackson: University Press of Mississippi, 1988.
Walsh, Chris. "'Cowardice Weakness or Infirmity, Whichever It May Be Termed': A Shadow History of the Civil War." *Civil War History* 59 (December 2013): 492–526.
War of the Rebellion: A Compilation of the Official Records of the Union and Confederate Armies. 70 vols. in 128 books. Washington, D.C.: Government Printing Office, 1880–1901.
Warner, Ezra J. *Generals in Gray: Lives of the Confederate Commanders*. Baton Rouge: Louisiana State University Press, 1959.
Watkins, Sam. *Company Aytch: Or, a Side Show of the Big Show and Other Sketches*. New York: Plume Books, 1999 [1882].
Waugh, Avery. *Abraham Lincoln Spanked Me: Punished by the President*. Kindle Edition, 2017.
Waugh, Joan. *U.S. Grant: American Hero, American Myth*. Chapel Hill: University of North Carolina Press, 2009.
Waugh, John C. *Reelecting Lincoln: The Battle for the 1864 Presidency*. New York: Crown, 1997.
Webster, H.T. "Wilbur F. Hinman's *Corporal Si Klegg* and Stephen Crane's *The Red Badge of Courage*." *American Literature* 11 (November 1939): 285–93.
Wertheim, Stanley. "*The Red Badge of Courage* and Personal Narratives of the Civil War." *American Literary Realism* 6 (Winter 1973): 61–65.
Wharton, Edith. *The Spark*. New York: D. Appleton, 1924.
Whitcher, Frances M. *The Widow Bedott Papers*. New York: J.C. Derby, 1856.
White, E.B., and Katherine S. White, eds. *A Subtreasury of American Humor*. New York: Coward-McCann, 1941.

White, Richard Grant. *The New Gospel of Peace: According to St. Benjamin*. New York: The American News Company, 1866.

———. *Poetry: Lyrical, Narrative and Satirical of the Civil War*. New York: The American News Company, 1866.

White, Ronald C. *American Ulysses: A Life of Ulysses S. Grant*. New York: Random House, 2016.

Whitney, Blair. "Lincoln's Life as Dramatic Art." *Journal of the Illinois State Historical Society* 61 (Autumn 1968): 333–49.

Wild Walt and the Rock Greek Gang. N.p.: Oakwood Terrace Publishing, 2019.

Wiley, Bell Irvin. "A Time of Greatness." *Journal of Southern History* 22 (February 1956): 3–35.

Wilkeson, Frank. *Turned Inside Out: Recollections of a Private Soldier in the Army of the Potomac*. Lincoln: University of Nebraska Press, 1997 [1886].

Wilson, Edmund. *Patriotic Gore: Studies in the Literature of the American Civil War*. Boston: Northeastern University Press, 1984 [1962].

Wishnevsky, St. *Were-Zombies of the Old Dominion*. Lexington, KY: The author, 2018.

Wood, Forrest G. *Black Scare: The Racist Response to Emancipation and Reconstruction*. Berkeley: University of California Press, 1970.

Woodson, Carter G., ed. *The Mind of the Negro: As Reflected in Letters During the Crisis 1800–1860*. Mineola, NY: Dover, 2013 [1926].

Wright, Steven. *The Amalgamation Polka*. New York: Alfred A. Knopf, 2006.

Yacovone, Donald. "'Surpassing the Love of Women': Victorian Manhood and the Language of Fraternal Love." In McCall and Yacovone. *A Shared Experience: Men, Women, and the History of Gender*, 195–221.

Yopp, William Isaac. *A Dual Role: A Romance of the Civil War*. Dallas: John F. Worley, 1902.

Young, Elizabeth. *Disarming the Nation: Women's Writing and the American Civil War*. Chicago: University of Chicago Press, 1999.

Zinsser, Hans. *Rats, Lice and History*. Boston: Little, Brown, 1935.

Web Sites and Webinars

"Abraham Lincoln vs. Zombies." https://en.wikipedia.org/wiki/Abraham_Lincoln_vs._Zombies.

"Advance to the Rear." http://www.tcm.com/tcmdb/title/856/Advance-to-the-Rear/.

"Advance to the Rear." https://en.wikipedia.org/wiki/Advance_to_the_Rear.

"The Bible Remains America's Favorite Book." https://theharrispoll.com/new-york-n-y-april-29-2014-theres-always-one-it-might-be-something-you-remember-fondly-from-when-you-were-a-child-or-it-could-be-one-that-just-resonated-with-you-years-after-your-first-expe-2/.

Breed, Allen G., and Hillel Italie. "How did ex-slave's letter to master come to be?" http://www.boston.com/news/education/articles/2012/07/14/how_did_ex_slaves_letter_to_master_come_to_be/.

"Check Out Rejected Comic Strip by Jack Davis." The Cartoon Daily, August 23, 2011. http://www.dailycartoonist.com/index.php/2011/08/25/check-out-rejected-comic-strip-by-jack-davis/.

Collins, Paul. "The Lost Symphony." *Believer* (November 2004). https://believermag.com/the-lost-symphony/.

Dalton, Curt. "The Life of Jourdon Anderson." https://web.archive.org/web/20160303234714/http:/www.daytonhistorybooks.com/jourdon_anderson.html.

Eggers, Dave. "Rediscovering One of the Wittiest Books Ever Written." https://www.newyorker.com/books/second-read/rediscovering-one-of-the-wittiest-books-ever-written.

"The Fastest Guitar Alive." https://en.wikipedia.org/wiki/The_Fastest_Guitar_Alive.

"50th Anniversary Production of IN WHITE AMERICA to Play New Federal Theater, 10/15–11/15." https://www.broadwayworld.com/article/50th-Anniversary-Production-of-IN-WHITE-AMERICA-to-Play-New-Federal-Theatre-1015-1115-20150918.

"Frank Moore (journalist)." https://en.wikipedia.org/wiki/Frank_Moore_(journalist).

"Frank Wilkeson." https://en.wikipedia.org/wiki/Frank_Wilkeson.

Works Cited

Gates, Henry Louis, Jr. "Declaration of Henry Louis Gates, Jr." In Information about *SunTrust Bank v. Houghton Mifflin Company*." http://www.houghtonmifflinbooks.com/features/randall_url/pdf/Declaration_Henry_Louis_Gates.pdf.

"*General Spanky.*" http://www.tcm.com/watchtcm/movies/1227/General-Spanky/.

"George William Lloyd." http://hymntime.com/tch/bio/l/l/o/y/lloyd_gw.htm.

"*Gone with the Wind* (novel)." https://en.wikipedia.org/wiki/Gone_with_the_Wind_(novel).

"*Grandma's Boy* (1922 film)." https://en.wikipedia.org/wiki/Grandma%27s_Boy_(1922_film).

"*Hands Up.*" http://www.tcm.com/tcmdb/title/498148/Hands-Up.

"*Hands-Up!* (1926): Top Secret." https://nitratediva.wordpress.com/2014/06/03/hands-up/.

Hindley, Meredith. "What Drove Ulysses Grant to Write about the Civil War: On the Motives of a Reluctant Memoirist." *Humanities* 39 (Winter 2018). https://www.neh.gov/humanities/2018/winter/feature/what-drove-ulysses-grant-write-about-the-civil-war.

Hochbruck, Wolfgang. "Mr. Lincoln's Wars: A Novel in Thirteen Stories." *Civil War Book Review* 5:2. https://digitalcommons.lsu.edu/cwrb/vol5/iss2/11.

Hulbert, Matthew Christopher. "Birth of a Genre: 100 Years of Slavery on the Solver Screen." New Perspectives in the Civil War Series (webinar), Virginia Center for Civil War Studies, February 8, 2021.

Hunt, Kristin. "What Drove Buster Keaton to Try Civil War Comedy?" https://daily.jstor.org/what-drove-buster-keaton-to-try-a-civil-war-comedy/?utm_term=What%20Drove%20Buster%20Keaton%20to%20Try%20a%20Civil%20War%20Comedy&utm_campaign=jstordaily_07022020&utm_content=email&utm_source=Act-On+Software&utm_medium=email.

"Jack Davis's 'Beauregard.'" http://potrzebie.blogspot.com/2008/02/jack-davis-beauregard.html.

"James Street." https://www.ncpedia.org/biography/street-james-howell.

"Jordan Anderson Writes a Letter." https://www.detroitperforms.org/2013/03/jordan-anderson-writes-a-letter/.

Lee, Trymaine. "In Rediscovered Letter from 1865, Former Slave Tells his Master to Shove It (Update)." https://www.huffpost.com/entry/in-recently-discovered-le_n_1247288.

"*Les Tuniques Bleues.*" https://en.wikipedia.org/wiki/Les_Tuniques_Bleues.

"*The Littlest Colonel.*" http://www.tcm.com/tcmdb/title/81513/The-Little-Colonel/articles.html.

"*The Littlest Rebel.*" http://www.tcm.com/this-month/article/373965%7C133213/The-Littlest-Rebel.html.

"Maurice Gibbs." https://www.allmusic.com/artist/maurice-gibb-mn0000865286/biography.

"*Peck's Bad Boy.*" https://en.wikipedia.org/wiki/Peck%27s_Bad_Boy.

Robin, Corey. "A Most Delightful Fuck You." https://coreyrobin.com/tag/jourdan-anderson/.

Sacco, Nick. "Outrageous Inaccuracies: The Grand Army of the Republic Protests *Birth of a Nation*." https://www.journalofthecivilwarera.org/2017/11/outrageous-inaccuracies-grand-army-republic-protests-birth-nation/.

"Samuel Wilkeson." https://en.wikipedia.org/wiki/Samuel_Wilkeson.

"*A Southern Yankee.*" http://www.tcm.com/tcmdb/title/425/A-Southern-Yankee/.

"Street, James Howell." https://www.ncpedia.org/biography/street-james-howell.

"Thomas Cooper De Leon." http://en.wikipedia.org/wiki/Thomas_Cooper_de_Leon.

"Timothy Dexter." http://en.wikipedia.org/wiki/Timothy_Dexter.

"*Two Thousand Maniacs!*" https://en.wikipedia.org/wiki/Two_Thousand_Maniacs!

"Went with the Wind!" https://en.wikipedia.org/wiki/Went_with_the_Wind!

Index

abolitionists 8–9, 14, 176
Abraham Lincoln (comic book) 96
Abraham Lincoln Spanked Me 36
Abraham Lincoln: Vampire Hunter (book) 172–73
Abraham Lincoln: Vampire Hunter (film) 171, 173
Abraham Lincoln vs. Zombies 170–71
Abram, a Military Poem 36–38
Addams, Mozis *see* Bagby, George W.
Advance to the Rear 144–45
The Adventures of Huckleberry Finn 80
African Americans 3, 12, 68–69, 81, 93, 97–98, 102–9, 118–22, 126, 151–57, 165, 167, 172–73, 180–81
Ah! Zombies!! 169
Ahab Lincoln 36
Aladdin 179
alcohol 16, 58, 85, 86, 88, 111–12, 131, 150, 180
Alcott, Louisa May: *Little Women and Werewolves* 172
Aldrich, Thomas Bailey: *The Story of a Bad Boy* 77
"All Quiet Along the Potomac, Tonight" *see* "The Picket Guard"
The Amalgamation Polka 176
The Amazing Screw-On Head (animated film) 180
The Amazing Screw-On Head (graphic novel) 180
"An Ambuscade" 120
Amelia Bedelia 162
"The American Civil War Made Easy" 162
The American People, Volume 1 175–76
amputation 23, 37, 38, 52, 53, 56, 57–59, 82
Anderson, Jordan 104–9, 155
Anderson, P.H. 104, 107, 109
Anderson, Valentine Winters 107
The Andy Griffith Show 15–16
Anna and the Apocalypse 169

Antietam 37, 52, 53, 56, 61
Appel, Jacob M.: *Surrendering Appomattox* 183
Appomattox 111, 129
Armstrong, William H: *Red Tape and Pigeon Hole Generals* 59–65, 69, 85, 88
Arner, Frederick 61, 62, 65
Arp, Bill 2, 13–14, 128; *see also* Smith, Charles Henry
Assassination Vacation 48
Asylum film company 171
Austen, Jane: *Pride and Prejudice* 182; *Pride and Prejudice and Zombies* 169, 171–72
Austin Powers 164

"Bacon and Greens" 126
Badeau, Adam 110
Bagby, George W. 29, 125–28, 129, 149; *see also* "Bacon and Greens"; "Histry uv the Waw"; "The Old Virginia Gentleman"; "An Unrenowned Warrior"
Baker, Joe Don 168
Baker, Russell 16
The Ballad of Virgil Cane see *The Shadow of Chikara*
Barnum, P.T. 19
Bart Simpson 77
Bates, Ralph O.: *Billy and Dick from Andersonville Prison to the White House* 93–94
"Battle Hymn of the Republic" 29, 39
The Battle of Pussy Willow Creek 181
Battle of the Wilderness 165
Battle of Who Run 210
"Battles and Leaders" series 72–73, 77, 110
Baxter, William J.: *Today's Revolution in Weather* 160
bayonets 84, 115
Beau Geste 65
Beauregard! 96–97, 153

213

214 Index

Beauregard, Pierre Gustave Tutant 44, 111, 126, 127
Beauty and Booty 35
Beauty and the Beast 179
Beers, Arthur J.: *Jordan Anderson Writes a Letter* 107
Behind the Seams 103–4
Behind the Scenes 102–3, 155
Benjamin, Judah P. 163
Bennett, Marek: *The Civil War Diary of Freeman Colby* 84, 85, 88, 90, 95–96; *The Civil War Diary of Freeman Colby, Volume 2, 1863* 96
Bernsen, Corbin 168
Berry, Thomas: *Four Years with Morgan and Forrest* 94
Best, Willie 144
The Beverly Hillbillies 15–16
Biblical Satire 19–22
Bierce, Ambrose 122–25, 172; *see also* "Chickamauga"; *The Devils Dictionary*; "Jupiter Doke, Brigadier General"; "An Occurrence at Owl Creek Bridge"; "A Tough Tussle"
Biglow, Hosea 9; *see also* Lowell, James Russell
Billings, Josh 16, 188n30
Billy and Dick from Andersonville Prison to the White House 93–94
The Birds 179
Birth of a Nation 140, 152
Black Face (comic book) 97–98
Black Panther 96
Blight, David 66, 71–72
Blount, Roy, Jr. 112, 113
The Bluecoats 97–98
Bohemian Brigade 98–99
Book of the Prophet Stephen 21
Booth, John Wilkes 146, 156, 171, 175–76
Bornstein, Kate: "Dixie Bell" 178–79
Boyd, Belle 35
boyology 77
Bradford, William 23
Bragg, Braxton 44
Brautigan, Richard: *A Confederate General from Big Sur* 165, 183
The Bright Side of Prison Life 82, 90
Brimstone and Lilly 179, 180
Brooks, Max 169
Brophy, Alfred L.: *Reparations: Pro and Con* 107
Brown, John 38–39, 41, 131, 132, 162, 177–78
Brown, John Sullivan: *This War, a Satire for the Times* 29–31
Brown, Joseph 14, 89

Brown, Nathan: *De Histori ov Magnus Mahárba* 22
Browne, Charles Farrar 6–7
Browne, Junius Henri: *Four Years in Secessia* 98–102
Bull Run 13, 25, 34, 37, 40, 41, 53, 82–83, 126–27, 141, 148
Bull Run, Second Battle 53–54
Burnett, Carol 153
Burns, Ken 49, 181
Burton, Levar 168
Burton, Tim 173
Butler, Benjamin 18–19, 66–67, 174; *see also* "Woman Order"

Calhoun, John C. 174
"Call All! Call All!" 41
Calvinist humor 22–23, 24
camaraderie 86–88
Camp and Prison Journal 91–92
Capers, Le Grand 50–51
Capp, Al 227
"Captain Issam" 177–78
Carlin, George 51
Carlisle, Henry C., Jr. 16
The Carol Burnett Show 153
"The Case of George Dedlow" 57–59
Castle Thunder Prison 101
Catch 22 52, 65, 88, 145
Catton, Bruce 109
Cauvin, Raoul 97
centennial 157–58
Century Magazine 72–73, 74, 110; *see also* "Battles and Leaders" series
Cervantes, Miguel de 182
Chamberlain, William 145
Chancellorsville 171
Charyn, Jerome: *I Am Abraham* 35–36
Chase, Salmon P. 9
Chernow, Ron 112
Chickamauga 57, 94, 121
"Chickamauga" 123–24
"Chiefly About War Matters" 23–28
Child, Lydia Maria 154
Chinese immigration, Chinese Exclusion Act 131
Churchill, Winston (American author): *The Crisis* (comic book) 96
Churchill, Winston (British statesman): 96; "If Lee Had Not Won the Battle of Gettysburg" 146–47
Civil Rights movement 104, 107–8, 145, 155, 166, 167
The Civil War 158–59, 169
The Civil War Hoax 183
Civil War Limericks 42–43

Index

Civil Wargasm 49
The Clansman 140
Classic Illustrated collection 96
Clemens, Samuel *see* Twain, Mark
Close Before Striking 181–82
closet drama 33
Cockneys vs. Zombies 169
Cohan Saves the Flag 141
Cohen, Wendy Jo 181
Colby, Freeman 84, 85, 88. 95–96, 98; *see also* Bennett, Marek
Collins, Paul 129
Colonel Quicksot 182
"The Comedy of War" 119–20
Company Aytch 81–82, 83, 89
Company of Cowards 145
Company Q 114, 117, 144–45
Comstock, Anthony 35, 135
Confederacy, Confederate States of America 13–15, 33–35, 43–46, 56, 78, 119, 133, 158–59, 160, 174, 180–81
A Confederate General from Big Sur 165, 183
Confederate Honey 32
Confederate Zombie Massacre! 169–71
Confederates in the Attic 48–51
Connelly, T. Lawrence *see* Connelly, Thomas
Connelly, Thomas: "That Was the War that Was" 162; *Will Success Spoil Jeff Davis?* 161–62
Conway, Tim 153
Copperheads 7–9, 17–18, 19–22, 23–24, 28, 30
Corporal Si Klegg and His "Pard" 113–18
Country in Ruin, 1865 179–18
crackerbox philosophers 5–16, 147, 158
Crane, Stephen: *The Dead Badge of Courage* 172; *The Red Badge of Courage* (comic book) 96; *The Red Badge of Courage* (novel) 114, 122
The Crisis (comic book) 96
C.S.A.: The Confederate States of America 181
Cullen, Charles E. 170
"A Curious Experience" 81
Curran, Thomas F. 26
The Curse of Demon Mountain see *The Shadow of Chikara*
Curse of the Cannibal Confederates 171
Curse of the Screaming Dead see *Curse of the Cannibal Confederates*

Dabney, Virginius 128–34; *The Story of Don Miff* 129–34; *Gold That Did Not Glitter* 133

Dahlgren, John 11
Daniel, Ferdinand Eugene: *Recollections of a Rebel Surgeon* 83–84, 87, 115
Davis, Jack: *Beauregard!* 96–97, 153; "Groan with the Wind" 153, 155
Davis, Jefferson 6, 20, 37, 39, 44, 102, 163, 174
Davis, Robert Scott 93–94
Day, Doris 164
D.D.D. 33
De Histori ov Magnus Mahárba 22
The Dead Badge of Courage 172
The Dead Don't Die 169
Dead Letter Office 107
Dead of Night see *The Shadow of Chikara*
The Deadly Battle of Hicksville 141
De Leon, Thomas C.: *South Songs* 42
Democratic Party, Democrats 7–9, 19–22, 23, 28, 32, 38, 53, 55, 56; *see also* Copperheads
Demon Mountain see *The Shadow of Chikara*
Dennis the Menace 77
The Devil in Dixie 31–32
The Devil's Disctionary 125
Dexter, Timothy: *A Pickle for the Knowing Ones* 52
Dickinson, Emily 29, 38
Divine 137
"Dixie Bell" 178–79
Dixon, Thomas: *The Clansman* 140
Dr. Seuss 19, 141
Downing, Maj. Jack 8–9; *see also* Smith, Seba
Dread Nation 96–99
Droopy the Dog 67
A Dual Role 134–36, 177
Duberman, Martin B.: *In White America* 107
DuBois, W.E.B. 108
Duck Soup 10
Dunbar, Paul Laurence: *The Fanatics* 155–56; "The Wisdom of Silence" 106–7
Duncan, Russell 122
Dunne, Michael 22–23
DuPont, Samuel 11
dystopian stories 173–74, 179–80

E.C. Comics 96–97
Earnest, Matthew: *Dead Letter Office* 107
Edwards, Jonathan 23
Edwards, Harry Stillwell: "Captain Issam" 121
Eggers, David 133
Election of 1864 55, 56–57, 69
Elliott, Joseph 91–92

Index

Ellison, Ralph 104, 106
Elmer, Jonathan 122, 125
emancipation 8–9, 13, 17, 32, 65, 128
An End to Bugling 162–63
Englund, Robert 167
enlisting 71, 73–74, 77–78, 114, 115–16
"Envion" 120–21, 122
Erickson, Hal 141
Exit Humanity 171
eye dialect 6, 15, 19

The Fanatics 155–56
farbs 49–114
The Fastest Guitar in the West 145
Feldman, Marty 141
Feminine Joe *see* Elliott, Joseph
Ferguson, Andrew: *Land of Lincoln* 48
Fields, James T. 28
Fish, Daniel 33
Flashman 178
Flashman and the Angel of the Lord 177–78
Flashman and the War Between the States 179
Fletcher, William A.: *Rebel Private: Front and Rear* 35, 83, 84, 87, 89, 92, 114, 117
Flight to Canada 156
Floyd, George 151, 157
foraging 85–86, 87
Ford, Glen 144–45
Forehand, Thomas, Jr. 112
Forrest, Nathan Bedford 134, 137–38, 174, 175
Fort Pillow 99, 137
Fort Sumter 5, 11, 13, 37, 44
Fort Warren 23–24
Four Years in Secessia 98–102
Four Years with Morgan and Forrest 94
Foxworthy, Jeff 75–6
Fraser, George McDonald: *Flashman* 178; *Flashman and the Angel of the Lord* 177–78
Fredericksburg 49
Freedom Dreams 107
Freeman, Douglas Southall 160
Fremantle, Arthur: *Three Months in the Southern States* 43–46, 50
Fremantle, Tom: *The Moonshine Mule* 46–48, 50
Frémont, John C. 33
From the Case Files of Abraham Lincoln's Penis, Private Eye 36
Frontline Combat series 96
Frost, Griffin: *Camp and Prison Journal* 91–92

Gable, Clark 162
Garland, Judy 137
Garrison, William Lloyd 105
Gartner, Joseph 183
Gates, Henry Louis, Jr. 154
gender 91–92, 131, 132–33, 134–38, 153–54, 161, 171–72
The General 142–43
General Spanky 143–44
Generals in Gray 165
Gettysburg 28, 37, 44, 45–46, 49–50, 141, 145, 147, 169, 162–63, 165, 170, 173, 180, 181, 182
Gettysburg (film) 46, 47, 49
"The Ghost of General Jackson" 59
Giamatti, Paul 180
Gibb, Maurice 168
Gilbert, Rensalear Reed 14–15, 99
Gilbertson publishers 96
Glory 49
Gold That Did Not Glitter 133
Gomer Pyle, U.S.M.C. 15–16, 114
Gone with the Wind (book) 149–55
Gone with the Wind (film) 10, 32, 125, 149, 152, 157
The Good Lord Bird 177, 178
Gordon, Armistead Churchill: "Envion" 120–21, 122
Gordon, John B. 129
Goss, Warren Lee: *Recollections of a Private* 84, 115
"Grafted into the Army" 40
Grahame-Smith, Seth: *Abraham Lincoln: Vampire Hunter* (book) 172–73; *Pride and Prejudice and Zombies* 169, 171, 172
Grand, Porter: *Little Women and Werewolves* 172
Grand Army of the Republic 117, 140, 141
Grandma's Boy 142
Grant, Cary 243
Grant, Ulysses S. 35, 43, 79, 80, 85, 95, 109–12, 113, 146, 162, 165, 175; *Personal Memoirs of U.S. Grant* 109–12, 113
Green Acres 15
Greenwood, Grace 18–19; *see also* Lippincott, Sarah Jane
Grey Knight 168
Griffith, D.W. 140
Grigsby, Melvin: *The Smoked Yank* 86, 93
Grimes, Charity 16–18, 38; "The 'Peace Democracy'" 38
Grimsley, Mark 191n168
Grinspan, Jon 69, 191n168
"Groan with the Wind" 152–53, 155
Groening, Matt 95
Grossman, Lev 169

Index

Habegger, Alfred 16
Halpine, Charles Graham 11–13, 39; *see also* O'Reilly, Miles; "Sambo's Right to Be Kilt"
Hancock, Winfield Scott 85
Hands Up! 142, 145
hard war humor 69
Hardee, William J. 45
Harlem Renaissance 106
Harris, George Washington 15
Harris, Joel Chandler 2, 15, 118–120, 125, 149; *see also* "An Ambuscade"; "The Comedy of War"; *On the Plantation*; "A Story of the War"
Harry Potter series 179
Hart, Stan 153
Hathaway, Mary Jane: *Pride and Prejudice and Cheese Grits* 182
Hawthorne, Nathaniel 23–28, 55, 71, 182; *see also* "Chiefly About War Matters"
Hay, Jacob: *The Mindleberg Papers* 242–44
Hayes, Charles H.: *Civil War Limericks* 42–43
Hayes, Mollie *see* Pitman, Mary Ann
Hee Haw 15
Heller, Andrew J.: *If the North Had Won the Civil War* 180–81
Heller, Joseph: *Catch 22* 52, 65, 88, 145
Hely, Steve: *How I Became a Famous Novelist* 175
Henniker (N.H.) Historical Society 94, 95
Herndon, Angelo 106
Hesseltine, William 94
Hill, Ashbel Fairchild 51–57, 60, 61, 68–69, 84, 88; *see also John Smith's Funny Adventures on a Crutch*; *Our Boys*
Hills, Alfred C.: *MacPherson, the Great Confederate Philosopher and Southern Blower* 13
Hinman, Wilber F. 166–73, 180; *see also Corporal Si Klegg and His "Pard"*; *The Story of the Sherman Brigade*
"Histry uv the Waw" 127–28
Hitchhiker's Guide to the Galaxy 29, 179
Hochbruck, Wolfgang 175
Hogan's Heroes 65
Holmes, Oliver Wendell, Sr. 29
homosexuality 91–92, 167, 175–76
Hood, John Bell 36
Hooker, Richard: *MASH* (book) 52
Horwitz, Tony: *Confederates in the Attic* 48–51
Houston, Sam 43
How a One-Legged Rebel Lives 82–83
How I Became a Famous Novelist 175

How Private Geo. W. Peck Put Down the Rebellion 73–77
Howe, Julia Ward 29, 39; *see also* "Battle Hymn of the Republic"
Hughes, Jennifer A. 156
Hughes, Roger 47
Hugo, Victor 192, 193; *see also Les Misérables*
Hulbert, Matthew Christopher 152
Humphreys, Andrew A. 62–65, 85
The Hunger Games 173
Hunter, Alexander: *Johnny Reb and Billy Yank* 82
Hunter, David 11, 12

I Am Abraham 35–65
"If Booth Had Missed Lincoln" 146
"If Grant Had Been Drinking at Appomattox" 10–12, 147
"If Lee Had Not Won the Battle of Gettysburg" 146–47
If the North Had Won the Civil War 180–81
illness 63, 87, 95
In Vinculis 65–69, 90
In White America 107
Ireland, Justina: *Dread Nation* 173
It's a Mad, Mad, Mad, Mad World 164

Jackson, Lawrence 104
Jackson, Thomas "Stonewall" 37, 59, 146, 171, 180
Jim Crow 155, 159, 161, 181
"John Brown's Song" 38–39
John Smith's Funny Adventures on a Crutch 55–56, 57
Johnny Reb and Billy Yank 82
Johnston, Albert Sydney 111
Johnston, Joseph 14, 44
Jordan Anderson Letter 104–9, 155
Jordan Anderson Writes a Letter 107
Joyce, Charles T. 60
Juan of the Dead 169
"Jupiter Doke, Brigadier General" 124

Kadmus, Kristofur *see* Brown, Nathan
Kansas-Nebraska Act 28
Kaufman, Lloyd 171
Kaufman, Will 5, 59
Keaton, Buster 142–43, 144, 162
Keckley, Elizabeth: *Behind the Scenes* 102–3, 155
Keiley, Anthony M. 29, 65–69, 90; *see also In Vinculis*; *A Rebel in Two Federal Pens*
Kelley, Robin D.G.: *Freedom Dreams* 107
Kendi, Ibram X. 152

Index

Kendrick, James: *She Wouldn't Surrender* 35
Kennedy, Dane 1
Kennedy, John F. 166
Kennedy, Robert F. 166
Kerr, Orpheus C. 9–11; *see also* Newell, Robert H.
Kidd, Kenneth B. 77
The Killer Angels 46
King, Martin Luther, Jr. 166
King of the Hill 114
"Kingdom Coming" 39
Klooser, David L. 122
Korean War 158
Korman, Harvey 153
Kramer, Larry: *The American People, Volume 1* 175–76
Krapp, George P. 6
Kroenung, Terry: *Brimstone and Lilly* 179, 180
Ku Klux Klan 49, 139, 140, 152
Kutzler, Evan A. 99
Kwapisz, Gary: *Rebel Dead Revenge* 180

Lambillotte, Willy 97
Land of Lincoln 48
Laughing on the Outside 108, 155
Lawrence, Vicky 153
Lee, Annie 113
Lee, David: *Country in Ruin, 1865* 179–80
Lee, Robert E. 20, 32, 37, 44, 47–48, 93, 102, 112–13, 142, 151, 162, 163, 165, 181
Lee, Robert E., Jr. 112–13
Lee's Miserables see Hugo, Victor
Levin, Kevin M.: *Searching for Black Confederates* 122
Libby Prison 99, 101
lice 41, 89–90, 99, 100
Life on the Mississippi 79, 118
Li'l Abner 15, 152–53
Lincoln, Abraham 2, 8–9, 10–11, 12, 13–14, 15, 18–19, 19–20, 24–25, 26, 32, 33, 34, 35–36, 41, 48, 55, 56, 61, 94, 96, 102, 142, 144, 146, 147, 156, 157, 159, 162, 170–71, 172–73, 174, 175–76, 176–77, 179–80, 181, 185
Lincoln, Mary Todd 35, 102–3, 146, 172
Lincoln, Robert 34
Lincoln, Willie 176
The Lincoln Diddle 36
Lincoln in the Bardo 176–77
"Lincoln's Doctor's Dog" (article) 147, 152
Lincoln's Doctor's Dog (book, 1938) 147
Lincoln's Doctor's Dog (book, 2020) 147
Linderman, Gerald 51
Lippincott, Sarah Jane 18; *see also* Greenwood, Grace

The Little Colonel 144
Little Women and Werewolves 172
The Littlest Rebel 144, 152
Litwack, Leon 104
Lloyd, George William: *The Devil in Dixie* 31–32
Lloyd, Harold 142
Locke, Alain 106
Locke, David Ross 6, 7–8, 16, 17; *see also* Nasby, Petroleum V.
Locke, Sondra 168
Long, James O.: *Lincoln's Doctor's Dog* (book, 2020) 147
Longstreet, James 44, 45, 47
Lost Cause myth 42–43, 80, 81–82, 108, 129–30, 139, 141, 150–51, 157, 158, 164–65, 167, 174, 182
Love, Edmund G.: *An End to Bugling* 162–63
Lovingood, Sut *see* Harris, George Washington
Lowell, James Russell 9; *see also* Biglow, Hosea
"Lucretia Smith's Soldier" 81
Lynn, Kenneth S. 16

MacPherson, James B. *see* Hills, Alfred C.
MacPherson, the Great Confederate Philosopher and Southern Blower 13
Mad magazine 96, 153, 155
Mad Men 164
Magnola, Mike: *The Amazing Screw-On Head* (graphic novel) 180
Malanowski, Tony 171
Malcolm X 166
Malone, Bartlett Yancy: *Whipt 'em Everytime* 94
Manassas *see* Bull Run
Manuel-Miranda, Lin 112
"Marching Through Georgia" 40
Martin, Steve 3
Marx, Groucho 10
Marx Brothers 10
MASH (book) 52
*M*A*S*H* (film) 52, 145
*M*A*S*H* (television) 52, 65
McBride, James: *The Good Lord Bird* 177, 178
McCarthyism 158
McClellan, George 10–11, 25–27, 32, 52–55, 56–57, 61–62, 69, 84, 88
McCormack, Derek: *The Well-Dressed Wound* 176
McDaniel, Hattie 144
McElroy, John: *Si Klegg* 117–18

Index

McFarland, George "Spanky" 143
McFeely, William 109
McPherson, James 109
Meade, George 85
Meigs, Montgomery 11
Melville, Herman 29, 38
memoirs 43–44, 51–57, 65–69, 71–96, 98–104, 109–12
Mencken, H.L. 139–40, 147
mental illness 64–65, 88
Miller, Stephen Franks: *Ahab Lincoln: A Tragedy of the Potomac* 36
Miller, Worm: *A Zombie History of the United States* 174
Millett, Allan R. 114, 117
The Mind of the Negro 106
The Mindleberg Papers 163–64
Les Misérables 132
Mitchell, Margaret 149–52; *see also Gone with the Wind* (book)
Mitchell, Silas Weir: "The Case of George Dedlow" 57–59, 69
Moby Dick 179
Monty Python and the Holy Grail 38, 179
Mooching Through Georgia 143
Moody, Minnie Hite: "The Ghost of General Jackson" 59
Moore, Frank: *Rebel Rhymes and Rhapsodies* 42; *Songs of the Soldiers* 42
Morford, Henry 59–60, 65
Morley, Christopher: "Lincoln's Doctor's Dog" (article) 147
Mrs. Hollingsworth's Men 175
Murray, Bill 168

NAACP 106, 140
Nasby, Petroleum V. 2, 6, 7–8, 16, 17; *see also* Locke, David Ross
Native Americans 131, 142, 145
Neely, Ted 168
Nelson, David Erik: *Tucker Teaches the Clockies to Copulate* 180
Nevins, Allen 94
New Christy Minstrels 145
The New Gospel of Peace 19–22, 188n44, 190n97
New York City draft riots 20, 32, 44
Newell, Robert H. 9–11; *see also* Kerr, Orpheus C.
Nichols, Nichelle 168
Nickels, Cameron C. 2, 3, 5
Nicolay, John 11
"The Night They Drove Old Dixie Down" 168
Nixon, Richard 158
"No More Biographies" 145–46

Normand, Mabel 141
The North, Northerners 23–24, 40, 71–72, 139–40, 150, 158–59, 159, 60, 161, 178

"An Occurrence at Owl Creek Bridge" 124–25
Odom, John Yancy 104
officers 37, 52–55, 62–65, 71, 72–73, 81–82, 84–85, 88, 89, 110, 124
On the Plantation 118–19
Orbison, Roy 145
O'Reilly, Miles 11–13; *see also* Halpine, Charles Graham
Oswald, Patton 180
Ottolengui, Daniel: *Behind the Seams* 103–4
Our Boys 51–55, 56–57, 68–69, 84
Our Gang 143
Owsley, Frank Lawrence 14, 128

pacifism 20, 23
Page, Thomas Nelson 125, 149
Parker, David B. 14
"The 'Peace Democracy'" 38
Peace Democrats *see* Copperheads
Peck, George 72–77, 81, 114; *see also How Private Geo. W. Peck Put Down the Rebellion*; "Peck's Bad Boy"
"Peck's Bad Boy" 113, 114
Peninsula Campaign 25, 54
Personal Memoirs of U.S. Grant 109–12, 113
Petticoat Junction 15
"The Picket Guard" 131
Pickett, George 93
Pickett, LaSalle Corbell: *What Happened to Me* 93
Pickett's Charge 45–46, 47, 49–50
Pickens, Slim 168
A Pickle for the Knowing Ones 37
Pierce, David Hyde 180
Pierce, Franklin 28
Pitman, Mary Ann 137–38
Poe, Edgar Allan 125, 156
Poe, Heironymus: *Colonel Quicksot* 182
poetry 3, 12, 29–43, 93, 148, 159
Poetry: Lyrical, Narrative, and Satirical of the Civil War 38–41
Pogo 15
Pope, John 54
Powell, Padgett: *Mrs. Hollingsworth's Men* 175
Pride and Prejudice 182
Pride and Prejudice and Cheese Grits 182
Pride and Prejudice and Zombies 169, 171, 172

Index

The Princess Bride 179
prisoners of war 66, 67–68, 75, 90–92
"A Private History of a Campaign That Failed" 77–79

Quaker guns 26

race, racism 4, 78, 12, 52, 55–56, 65, 68–69, 81, 97–98, 103–4, 104–9, 116, 119, 119–122, 126, 144, 151–52, 152–57, 161
Rachels, David 79
Ramis, Harold 168
Randall, Alice: *The Wind Done Gone* 153–55
Rats, Lice and History 100
The Real McCoys 15
Rebel Dead Revenge 180
A Rebel in Two Federal Pens 65–69, 90
Rebel Private: Front and Rear 35, 83, 84, 87, 89, 92, 114, 117
Rebel Rhymes and Rhapsodies 42
Rebel Without Claws 33
The Rebel Yell (book) 159–61
rebel yell (yell) 115, 159
Rebelle, A. Young: *Abram, A Military Poem* 36–38
Recollections of a Private 84
Recollections of a Rebel Surgeon 83–84, 87, 115
reconciliation 72, 73, 74, 75, 116, 119–20, 158
The Red Badge of Courage (comic book) 96
The Red Badge of Courage (novel) 114, 179
Red Tape and Pigeon Hole Generals 59–65
Reddick, L.D. 106
Redding, Saunders 108
Reed, Ishmael 2, 156; *see also Flight to Canada*
Reparations: Pro and Con 107
Republican Party 9, 15, 29, 33, 60
Revelations: A Companion to the "New Gospel of Peace" 21
Revenge of the Nerds 92
Richardson, Albert D. 101, 102
Richmond 32, 44, 47, 54, 83, 99, 101, 127, 129, 130, 132, 173
Roach, Hal 143
Robertson, James I. 60
Robin, Corey 109
Robinson, Bill "Bojangles" 144
Robson, John A.: *How a One-Legged Rebel Lives* 82–83, 114
Rodgers, J. Clayton: *Close Before Striking* 181–82
Rooney, Mickey 107

Roosevelt, Theodore 21–22, 171
Rowlandson, Mary 23
Rowling, J.K. 182
The Royal Ape 33–35, 36
"The Run from Manassas Junction" 40
Russell, Jamie 171
Rutledge, Ann 35

Sacco, Nick 111
Salisbury Prison 101
Salome vs. Shenandoah 141
"Sambo's Right to Be Kilt" 12, 39
Sanborn, Kate 16, 18
Saturday Night Live 176
Saunders, George: *Lincoln in the Bardo* 176–77
Schlesinger, Arthur M., Jr. 157
Searching for Black Confederates 122
secession 6–7, 20, 23, 24, 68, 73–74
The Secret Diary of Desmond Pfeiffer 157
Sennett, Mack 141
Shaara, Michael: *The Killer Angels* 46
The Shadow of Chikara 168
Shaefer, Jack: *Company of Cowards* 216
Shannon, Molly 266
Sharp, Rayburn: *From the Case Files of Abraham Lincoln's Penis, Private Eye* 36
Sharpsburg *see* Antietam
Shaun of the Dead 169
She Wouldn't Surrender 35
Sheen, Martin 168
Sherman, William Tecumseh 14, 40, 83, 89, 118, 119, 159, 162, 182
Shiloh 111
"Shoddy" 38
Shore, Dinah 153
Si Klegg 117–18
Silsbee, Samuel: *D.D.D.* 33
Silver, Jon 183
Simms, William Gilmore: *War Poetry of the South* 41–42, 190n97
Sir Thomas "British Tommy" Armstrong and the War Between the States see Tighe, Barry
Sitting Bull 142
Skelton, Red 144
Skinflint, Obadiah *see* Chandler, Harris Joel
slavery 4, 8–9, 28, 31, 33, 39–40, 45, 47, 102, 103, 104–9, 116, 118–22, 129–30, 139, 143–44, 150, 151, 152, 153, 153–54, 158, 173–74, 178, 181
Smith, Charles Henry 13–14, 128; *see also* Arp, Bill
Smith, H. Allen: *The Rebel Yell* 159–61

Index

Smith, Seba 8-9; *see also* Downing, Major Jack
Smith, William Russell: *The Royal Ape* 33-35
The Smoked Yank 86, 93
Snively, Devi 169
Snuffy Smith 15
Social Darwinism 131
Song of the South 152
Songs of the Soldiers 42
Sons of the Confederate Veterans 49
The South, Southerners 13-15, 27-28, 29-33, 34, 25, 36-38, 40-42, 43-46, 59, 65-69, 72, 77-80, 81-86, 87, 89-92, 97, 100-1, 112-23, 116, 118-22, 125-38, 139-40, 142-45, 149-52, 153-56, 158-61, 162-65, 166-67, 167-70, 174, 175, 180-82
South Park 95
South Songs 42
The South Will Rise Again 170
Southern Fried Rabbit 32-33
A Southern Yankee 144, 157
Soward, Joseph 91-92
The Spark 148
Speed, Joshua 172, 176
spiritualism 57-59
Stanton, Edwin 11
Stanton, Elizabeth Cady 89
Star Trek 168
Star Trek: The Next Generation 168
Star Wars 179
Starkeeper, Sage: *The Un-Promised Generation* 107-8
Steampunk fiction 179-80
Stein, Gertrude 109
Steiner, Bernard C. 60
Stephens, Alexander 14, 89
Sterling, Philip: *Laughing on the Outside* 108, 155
Stevens, George: *Lincoln's Doctor's Dog* (book, 1938) 147
Stevens, Stella 144
Stolen Glory 141
The Story of a Bad Boy 77
The Story of Don Miff 129-34
"A Story of the War" 176-77
Stowe, Harriett Beecher 58, 141, 232; *see also Uncle Tom's Cabin* (book); *Uncle Tom's Cabin* (comic book)
Street, James: *The Civil War* 158-59, 160
Stripes 168
Stuart, Jeb 146, 162-63
Sumner, Charles 20
supernatural 167-74, 176-77, 179-81
The Supernaturals 168
Surrendering Appomattox 183

Swiggett, Samuel A.: *The Bright Side of Prison Life* 82, 90
Switzer, Carl "Alfalfa" 143

Tandy, Jennette 6, 29
Tarantino, Quintin 85
Temple, Shirley 144
This War, a Satire for the Times 29-31
Thomas, Billie "Buckwheat" 143
Thompson, Lawrence S. 94, 149
Thompson, Steven A.: *The Dead Badge of Courage* 172
Thornton, Billy Bob 168
Three Months in the Southern States 43-46
The Three Stooges 10
Three's Company 92
Thumb, Lavinia 18-19
Thumb, Tom 18-19
Thunder Mountain see *The Shadow of Chikara*
Thurber, James 3, 163-64, 217-19; *see also* "If Grant Had Been Drinking at Appomattox"; "No More Biographies"
Tighe, Barry: *Flashman and the War Between the States* 179
Till, Emmitt 151
Today's Revolution in Weather 160
"Tom Sawyer's Conspiracy" 80-81
"A Tough Tussle" 124
Troma Entertainment 171
"A True Story, Repeated Word for Word as I Heard It" 81
Tubman, Harriet 172
Les Tuniques Bleues see *The Bluecoats*
Turned Inside Out 85, 87-89
Turpin, Ben 141
Twain, Mark 3, 114-19, 120, 160, 161, 163, 173, 174, 264, 269; *see also The Adventures of Huckleberry Finn*; "A Curious Experience"; *Life on the Mississippi*; "Lucretia Smith's Soldier"; "A Private History of a Campaign that Failed"; "Tom Sawyer's Conspiracy"; "A True Story, Repeated Word for Word as I Heard It"
The Twilight Zone 58, 59, 124-25
2001 Maniacs! 167
Two Thousand Maniacs! 166-67

Uncivil War Birds 10
Uncivil Warriors 10
Uncle Remus 118, 120, 122, 152, 170
Uncle Tom's Cabin (book) 41
Uncle Tom's Cabin (comic book) 96

United Daughters of the Confederacy 49, 59, 158, 162, 164
The Un-Promised Generation 107–8
"An Unrenowned Warrior" 126–27, 129

Velazquez, Loreta Janeta 44
Vallandigham, Clement 7, 44
vampires 169, 172–73, 174
Vicksburg 37, 43–44, 50–51, 101
Vietnam 143, 166
Village of the Damned 179
Vogon poetry 29
Vowell, Sarah: *Assassination Vacation* 48

Waldman, Milton: "If Booth Had Missed Lincoln" 146
The Walking Dead 89, 169
Walters, Barbara 156
The War Between the States (comic book) 96
War Poetry of the South 41–42, 190n97
Ward, Artemus 2, 6–7; *see also* Browne, Charles Farrar
Warner, Ezra J.: *Generals in Gray* 165
Warner Brothers cartoons 32–33, 67
Watergate 166
Watkins, Sam: *Company Aytch* 81–82, 83, 89, 114, 115
Waters, John 137
Waugh, Joan 112
The Well-Dressed Wound 176
Wells, Gideon 11
"Went with the Wind" 153
Were-Zombies of the Old Dominion 173–74
Wharton, Edith 3, 148; *see also The Spark*
Whipt 'Em Everytime 94
Whitcher, Frances M.: *The Widow Bedott Papers* 16–17
White, E.B. 3, 16
White, Richard Grant 19–22, 38–41; *see also The New Gospel of Peace*; *Poetry: Lyrical, Narrative, and Satirical of the Civil War*
Whitman, Walt 1, 29, 38, 51, 69, 96, 97, 148, 156, 162, 165, 176, 181, 182, 185

Wild Walt and the Rock Creek Gang 182–83
Wiley, Bell Irvin 72
Wilkeson, Frank: *Turned Inside Out* 85, 87–89
Wilmott, Kevin 181
Wilson, Edmund 2, 29, 109, 110
Wilson, Woodrow 26, 140
"The Wisdom of Silence" 106–7
Wishbone Cutter see *The Shadow of Chikara*
Wishnevsky, St.: *Were-Zombies of the Old Dominion* 173–74
Wister, Owen 109
"Woman Order" 66
women 3, 16–19, 34–36, 37, 44–45, 50–51, 66, 76–77, 81, 92–93, 100–1, 102–4, 130–31, 132–33, 134–38, 149–50, 152, 153–54, 161, 169–70, 172, 173–74
Wood, Fernando 20
Wood, Forrest G. 21
Woodson, Carter G.: *The Mind of the Negro* 106
Work, Henry Clay: "Grafted into the Army" 40; "Kingdom Coming" 39–40; "Marching Through Georgia" 40
World War Z 169
Wright, Stephen: *The Amalgamation Polka* 176, 178

"Yakety Sax" 145
Yeadon, Richard 18
"The Year of Jubilee" see "Kingdom Coming"
Yopp, William Isaac: *A Dual Role* 134–37; *Yopp's Cypher Code* 137
Yopp's Cypher Code 137
Young, Brigham 142

Zinsser, Hans: *Rats, Lice and History* 100
zom coms 168–71
A Zombie History of the United States 174
Zombieland 169
Zombieland: Double Tap 169
zombies 3, 169–74

www.ingramcontent.com/pod-product-compliance
Lightning Source LLC
Chambersburg PA
CBHW032040300426
44117CB00009B/1137